# Russian Economic Reform

Attempts to portray the reform of the Russian economy as a disaster are misleading because they fail to take account of the complexities of the transition from socialism to capitalism. *Russian Economic Reform* brings a coherent view to the Russian transition, by focusing on the actual pre-reform conditions including the widespread private, informal economic activity. The framework that emerges highlights the similarities among many seemingly disparate aspects of the reforming Russian economy – from inflation to organized crime, from barter to military conversion. Throughout the emphasis is on real economic activity, rather than on formal plans for economic reform and the individuals behind them.

Perceptions of the pre-reform Russian economy are often inaccurate, primarily because the logic of a centrally planned economy is so different from a capitalist one that familiar economic phenomena, such as unemployment and inflation, take unfamiliar forms. Likewise, conventional statistics such as Gross National Product measured different things in socialist economies than they did in capitalist ones. Staggering amounts of black market and hidden private economic activity contribute to the difficulties in gauging the pre-reform state of affairs. The misconceptions about the starting point for Russian economic reform that result lead to an exaggeration of the costs of transition. Many of the costs associated with the transition process are not new, though during the reform process they may be borne in different forms and by different people. Meanwhile some of the costs which are new are the result of either partial reform measures or new problems caused by regional political upheavals. The short-term benefits of reform also tend to be exaggerated, however, due to an insufficient accounting of the pre-reform market economy.

Written in an accessible and lively style throughout, *Russian Economic Reform* sheds much new light both on changes within Russia and on the transition process in general. It will be essential reading for social scientists, college students and others interested in the economic transitions of the formerly-socialist world.

**Jim Leitzel** is Associate Professor of Public Policy Studies and Economics at Duke University.

# Acknowledgements

Chapter 6, 'Monopoly', closely follows my article, 'A Note on Monopoly and Russian Economic Reform', that appeared in *Communist Economies and Economic Transformation* 6: 45–53, 1994. It is republished here with the permission of the Carfax Publishing Company, 875–81 Massachusetts Avenue, Cambridge, MA. An earlier version of the sidebar 'Parking and Perestroika' served as the first draft of an op-ed article that I wrote with Michael Alexeev and Clifford Gaddy, published in the *Journal of Commerce*, April 14, 1992, under the title, 'When Parking Meets Perestroika'. *The Brookings Review*, a quarterly publication of The Brookings Institution, published two short articles, that I co-authored with Michael Alexeev and Clifford Gaddy, 'Getting the Picture Right: Soviet Collapse, Transition Troubles, and Western Aid' (Winter 1992, pp. 14–17), and 'Mafiosi and Matrioshki, Organized Crime and Russian Reform' (Winter 1995, pp. 26–29). Early drafts of some of the material in this book served as a basis for those articles. Other material is drawn from 'Russian Economic Reform: Is Economics Helpful?', *Eastern Economic Journal*, 10, Summer 1993.

This book was begun when I was a National Fellow at the Hoover Institution on War, Revolution, and Peace, Stanford, California, during 1991–92. Many thanks to the Hoover Institution, and in particular Tom Henriksen and Wendy Minkin, for their support. Financial assistance from the National Council for Soviet and East European Research, for which I am grateful, contributed to this research. Comments on draft material were supplied by many individuals, including Michael Alexeev, Charles Clotfelter, Lydia Faulkner, Clifford Gaddy, Craufurd Goodwin, Simon Johnson, LynnErin McNeil, Kimberly Neuhauser, Will Pyle, Gertrude Schroeder, the late Jill Stuart, Vladimir Treml, and Erik Weisman. My deepest appreciation to them all.

This book is dedicated to my parents.

# Russian Economic Reform

Jim Leitzel

London and New York

First published 1995
by Routledge
11 New Fetter Lane, London EC4P 4EE

Simultaneously published in the USA and Canada
by Routledge
29 West 35th Street, New York, NY 10001

© 1995 Jim Leitzel

Typeset in Garamond by LaserScript, Mitcham, Surrey
Printed and bound in Great Britain by
Mackays of Chatham PLC, Chatham, Kent

*British Library Cataloguing in Publication Data*
A catalogue record for this book is available from the British Library.

*Library of Congress Cataloging in Publication Data*
Leitzel, Jim.
  Russian economic reform/Jim Leitzel.
  p. cm.
  Includes bibliographical references (p. ) and index.
  ISBN 0–415–12510–3. – ISBN 0–415–12511–1
  1. Russia (Federation) – Economic policy – 1991– . 2. Soviet Union
Economic conditions. 3. Post-communism – Economic aspects –
Russia (Federation). I. Title.
HC340.12.L45  1994
338.947 – dc20                                              94-24768
                                                            CIP

ISBN 0–415–12510–3
ISBN 0–415–12511–1 (pbk)

# Contents

# Preface

## AN ECONOMIC EXCURSION

A quaint Russian tradition governs the preparation for a journey. Immediately prior to embarking, travellers sit down to observe a brief moment of silence. The enforced calm provides a gentle counterpoint to the coming commotion and locomotion of travel.

Russia has now embarked on a monumental collective journey, that between socialism and capitalism. Perhaps the 'period of stagnation', as the late 1970s and early 1980s came to be known in Russia, represented the quiet moment that signalled the initiation of economic relocation. Imagine all of Russia sitting in silence in a huge living room, or more appropriately, around a large-scale kitchen table, scene of so many conversations with friends and family. What would be going through the minds of the apprentice travellers?

Hospitality is another cherished Russian tradition. At such a large table they would surely make room for unexpected visitors. This book represents my thoughts on the journey that the Russians are undertaking. I reflect on the starting point, the final destination, and potential transitional paths between today's and tomorrow's Russian economies. In the process, I hope to demonstrate that not all transitional paths are 'just as fair', and to illuminate desirable properties of reform programmes.

The stakes involved in choosing the best reform path are immense, with the lives and livelihoods of 150 million Russian citizens riding in the balance. Nor is the Russian journey a matter of indifference for those beyond Russian borders. There are humanitarian concerns. There is also self-interest, as the potential instability of a military superpower lends global significance to Russian economic reform. The humility requisite for entering the debate on Russian reforms brings to mind the words of Alexander Pope, 'in tasks so bold, can little men engage . . .?'. But it is to little men and women that the task of Russian economic reform has fallen.

The abrupt changes in Eastern Europe and the former Soviet Union caught economists in both the East and West unprepared for their new task. Most economists trained in the Soviet Union had little notion of the workings of market economies, or even how Western economists approached questions concerning markets. Simultaneously, the great majority of Western economists were similarly untutored in the ways of the centrally-planned economies of Eastern Europe and the Soviet Union. Those who were knowledgeable concerning socialist economies were inexperienced in analysing transitions from socialism to capitalism. Perhaps the closest parallel in Western experience is the return to peacetime economies from more centrally-controlled systems after the Second World War, but that analogy is far from unequivocal, and often misleading. The extent of central planning in Western war-time economies was never as large as in the socialist countries, and the return to the more decentralized world of consumer sovereignty occurred after an interregnum of just a few years. More than 60 years of extensive central planning in Russia have left generations of Russians unfamiliar with the workings of a widespread and legal market economy.

Furthermore, the economics discipline is limited in the insights it can bring to the analysis of economic transition. Western economic theory, which has found much success in analysing the properties of various equilibrium states, admittedly has very little to say about the paths between equilibria. Economic theory is also more developed with respect to efficiency concerns – the size of the economic pie – than with considerations about the distribution among individuals and groups of the shares of the pie. To the extent that successful reform depends on the actual or feared distributional effects of transition, economic analysis may be less useful than political or ethical analysis. Even many economists question the ability of their discipline to add constructively to the reform debate. One leading Western expert on the economic system of the former Soviet Union, Dr Ed Hewett, sounded this theme:

> Economists, Eastern and Western, excel in analyses and criticism of existing centrally planned economic systems, and in extolling the virtues of a decentralized system relying heavily on markets. But they are almost no help in devising a strategy for the transition from the old to the new system.'[1]

I contend that, even in its infancy, transitional economics is vital to successful Russian market reform. The complicated mathematical models that mark the pages of the leading economics journals are generally not the stuff of transitional economics, though some useful lessons can be taken from formal models. Rather, the core of transitional economics consists of the application of basic economic reasoning (some might call it common sense) to the situation faced by the transforming economies.[2] The trick, if there is one, lies in understanding the real initial situation – the main theme developed in the pages that follow.

One implication of the novelty of transitional economics is that the pedigree of an extensive economics education is neither necessary nor sufficient for contributing to the debate on Russian economic reform. There is room at the imaginary kitchen table for business people, lawyers, labour union officials, social scientists, politicians: fellow travellers are welcomed, not blacklisted. Wide-ranging input is necessary to avoid the pitfall identified by Pope: 'a little learning is a dang'rous thing'. Reform is too important to be left to the economists.

The discussion in the pages that follow presents an analysis that is far from definitive in formulating the best policies for a successful transition. Not all significant aspects of economic transformation, particularly those concerned with the politics of reform, receive the warranted attention. Nevertheless, the analysis is ambitious in another respect. The framework presented here, with its emphasis on private, often informal economic activity and the hidden aspects of the pre-reform situation, is designed to lend structure to the reform conversation. In adopting the perspective employed below, reform issues that usually appear to be unconnected are shown to have important similarities: similarities that can be exploited in the formulation and analysis of reform policies.

In attempting to help organize the reform conversation, this book, while written by an economist and adopting a distinctly 'economic' view of reform issues, is intended to be useful for non-economists interested in Russian reform. Economist Donald McCloskey notes that the 'opportunity cost of enchanting one's fellow economists is alienating non-economists. There is no such thing as a free argument.'[3] I have chosen to speak (not argue!) with non-economists, at the risk of (further) alienating my fellow economists. Nor is the discussion here aimed at specialists on the Russian economy, though perhaps they too may find some value in the framework that is offered. Indeed, while Russia serves as the case study, the approach to reform adopted in this book applies more generally to transitions from socialism, and even perhaps (though much less directly) to reforms within Western economies, such as corporate restructurings or defence industry conversion. For the ideas presented in this book, I share the hope that Russians have for their traditionally state-owned enterprises, namely, that they remain valuable long beyond the time frame of the current reform debates. Hope is not completely triumphant over experience; it must be recognized (and even welcomed) that the brisk pace of change in Russia guarantees the rapid obsolescence of many details in the exposition.

The nature of transition economics gives much of the discussion that follows the air of an introductory economics book. An unintended side effect of examining the reforming Russian economy is, for me at least, a better understanding of Western economic phenomena, and I hope that this side benefit will apply more generally. In the analysis that follows, the problems of Western market economies are often ignored, while the problems of central planning are closely examined. This omission is not a wholesale endorsement of market economies; rather, it simply reflects the fact that the discussion here pertains to the journey the Russians are committed, or appear to be committed, to undertaking, now that their silent interlude has passed.

# Introduction

## THE DESTINATION OF RUSSIAN ECONOMIC REFORM

Russia, where are you flying to? Answer!

Nikolai Gogol, *Dead Souls*, 1842[4]

An old saying has it that if you don't know where you want to go, any road will take you there. This saying could serve as the slogan for the first six years of perestroika, the restructuring that then General Secretary Mikhail Gorbachev announced for the Soviet economy in 1985. These years were marked by abrupt changes in the course of economic policy: from an acceleration in investment to an acceleration in consumer goods production; from a campaign to reduce the consumption of alcohol to efforts to sell more alcohol for increased tax revenue; from intensified legal restrictions on private economic activity to legal equality between private and state businesses.[5]

After these six years of confusion came three days that shook the world. The dramatic 72 hours of August 1991 that witnessed the victory of democratic forces in the Soviet Union also provided the future direction for the Soviet economy. Few voices were left calling for the reform of socialism: even the coup plotters made no appeal to Marxism–Leninism. Within the political mainstream, a Western-style market economy became the only goal in town, in St Petersburg, Russia, as in St Petersburg, Florida.

Since the failed coup attempt, a normal, Western-style capitalist country has remained the desired destination of the Russian economic transition, despite a steady diet of political twists, turns, and occasional upheavals. But there are several versions of 'normal' Western capitalism, including those of Sweden, Great Britain, Japan, and St. Petersburg, Florida. Which of these is the model that the Russians have, or should have, in mind? For the purpose of examining the journey between Russian socialism and Western capitalism, the precise Western model is irrelevant. Each of the Western models are sufficiently similar, and the current Russian economy is sufficiently dissimilar from all of them, that the transitional path can largely be plotted without exact knowledge of the destination. In driving from New York to Los Angeles, 99 per cent of the route can be determined without knowing whether the precise destination is Anaheim or Malibu. Similarly, the Russian economy must head West, and only upon arrival in the general vicinity of Tomorrowland need it concern itself with the local geography.

At this stage of the Russian transition, the precise destination is as unknowable as it is irrelevant. Countries are unique, and while we can be confident that a greater reliance on legal markets will be good for Russia, we cannot know what the best mix of market institutions will be. Many aspects of the final destination will only be learned through an evolutionary process. Given the unavoidable uncertainties, pre-commitment to a comprehensive map during the early phases of a transition to capitalism is unwise. (And of course, there is no 'final' destination. Institutions are continually evolving in Western market economies, too.) This reasoning, common enough in the West, is less familiar in a society where the primary organizing feature has long been, at least officially, the government's central plan – though the results of central planning may lend credence to the preceding argument. Western economist Richard Ericson notes that

> a final lesson for successful reform taught by the nature of the traditional Soviet-style system is to abandon the Faustian urge to control, to know in advance, and thus to allow economic outcomes to arise naturally as the unpredictable consequences of market interaction.[6]

There are some features of the destination that the travellers should understand before they embark, lest they be disappointed upon arrival – or even choose to turn back. First, as all Westerners know from an experience that Russians have not shared, Western capitalism is not without its own difficulties. Becoming a Western-style capitalist economy will not solve all of Russia's problems, and will even generate some new ones, such as open unemployment. Second, arrival at capitalism will not, at least in the near term, change the fact that Russia is a poor country relative to the United States, Japan, and most nations in Western Europe. Living standards in Russia are about one-fourth the level of the United States. (The 'precise' relationship between Russian and US living standards, obviously a chimera, is a matter of great controversy.[7]) If tomorrow Russia successfully completes the transition to capitalism, Russian living standards will still be about one-fourth of those in the United States. Capitalism holds the promise for faster growth rates, implying that Russians should live better than they would have had the economy remained centrally-planned, though they will not immediately achieve the economic levels of mature Western capitalist economies. This dose of pragmatism is not intended to be a counsel of despair. The rapid growth of West Germany and Japan after the Second World War, and of China in recent years, indicates that economic reform can yield tremendous achievements in relatively short periods of time. But these short periods of time are measured in years, not days.

## THE THEME

> What we have to deal with here is a communist society, not as it has *developed* on its own foundations, but, on the contrary, just as it *emerges* from capitalist society, which is thus in every respect, economically, morally, and intellectually, still stamped with the birthmarks of the old society from whose womb it emerges.
>
> Karl Marx[8]

With a Western-style capitalist economy providing the destination, the starting point and the transitional path are the other elements of the journey that must be specified. The interaction between these two basic components of reform provides the theme for the analysis that follows. The theme begins with the contention that the pre-reform Russian economy is generally mis-perceived, both in the West and in Russia. The misperception arises for many reasons, most particularly because the logic of a centrally-planned economy is so different from a capitalist economy that familiar Western economic phenomena such as unemployment and inflation take on unfamiliar forms. Likewise, common statistics such as Gross National Product measure different properties in socialist economies than in capitalist economies. Significant (even staggering) amounts of black market and hidden private economic activity contribute to the difficulties in gauging the pre-reform state of affairs.

The common misperception of the starting point for Russian economic reform leads to an exaggeration of the costs of transition. Many, if not most, of the identified costs and difficulties that accompany a transition from socialism to capitalism are not new costs at all. The same or even greater costs were being borne in the unreformed Russian economy – though in a different form, and by different people, and somewhat less visibly. Meanwhile, some costs attributed to reform are indeed new costs, but are the result either of bad reform policies – more on this below – or of basically unrelated problems such as trade disruptions arising from regional political disputes. As Marx noted for transitions in the other direction, what the Russians have to deal with now is a capitalist society, not as it has developed on its own foundations, but rather, stamped with the birthmarks and even the deformities of the old socialist society from whose womb it emerges.

Correcting misperceptions of the pre-reform Russian economy does not imply that the transition path is free of thorns, or that all transition paths are equally efficient. It does suggest that a well-designed transition from socialism to capitalism can be accomplished without a precipitous short-term fall in living standards, while providing some guidelines for the properties that a 'well-designed transition' should possess.

## IMPLICIT VERSUS EXPLICIT

Looking for a job, particularly if you are already out of work, is one of the more stressful, frustrating, and potentially demeaning tasks that accompanies life in a Western market economy. After repeated failures at finding a job, some people simply give up the search. Such people are called 'discouraged workers' in economics jargon, and there were an estimated one million discouraged workers in the United States in 1992.[9] Perhaps surprisingly, discouraged workers are *not* defined as unemployed, at least by the official compilers of economic statistics – even though discouraged workers would like to work and do not have jobs. The reason for this omission lies in the definition of 'unemployment' that is used by the US Department of Labour. To be officially unemployed (and, perhaps not incidentally, to collect unemployment benefits), a person has to be out of work *and* actively searching for employment. Since discouraged workers have given up the search for jobs, they are not officially unemployed.

Consider what would happen if the Department of Labour were to change its definition of unemployment to include any out-of-work person who would prefer to have a job, whether or not the person was actively searching for employment. Overnight, the number of 'unemployed' people would increase by one million.[10] Such an instantaneous jump in unemployment would be quite unprecedented, and to those who did not know that the definition of 'unemployed' had been altered, this increase in unemployment would be a signal of dramatically declining economic conditions. The signal would be misleading, though, because no real change in unemployment took place, despite the phenomenal change in measured unemployment, as implicitly unemployed workers are newly counted among the explicitly and officially unemployed.

In the current US economy, whether discouraged workers can be characterized as 'implicitly unemployed' may be largely a matter of semantics. Discouraged workers obviously share many important characteristics with officially unemployed workers. These shared circumstances are less conspicuous in the case of discouraged workers than they are for the explicitly unemployed, since discouraged workers are not getting turned down for jobs or collecting unemployment benefits. It therefore does no injustice, and perhaps is even illuminating, to signal the similarities between discouraged workers and explicitly unemployed workers by applying the term 'implicit unemployment' to discouraged workers. Likewise, in the Russian economy there are many phenomena that bear significant, though somewhat hidden, similarities with other, more widely recognized phenomena. The adjective 'implicit' (or 'repressed') will be used below to describe these aspects of the pre-reform Russian economy, in order to highlight the similarities with their more familiar, explicit (or 'open') siblings, which will emerge during transition to a market economy.

Inflation, private property rights, and monopoly power – like various non-economic features such as the degree of nationalist or religious sentiment – are phenomena that were previously present in Russia largely in a repressed or hidden form. For such phenomena, referring to the pre-reform situation as 'implicit' and the post-reform situation as 'explicit' seems natural. For other pre-reform conditions the appropriateness of the adjective 'implicit' is perhaps less apparent: many of the Russians whom I describe as 'implicitly unemployed' actually have jobs. The usage of the terms 'implicit' or 'repressed' may then grate some sensibilities. But these terms are only shorthand for the notion that, in judging the effects of reform, knowledge of the actual pre-reform conditions is indispensable. And the key to understanding the pre-reform Russian economic system, and hence the characteristics of a successful reform, lies in exposing disguised, 'implicit' elements.

During Russia's transition to a market economy, some implicit economic phenomena such as inflation or unemployment will automatically become explicit – indeed, the process is already well underway. In many cases, as in the parable of the discouraged worker, the transition from an implicit to an explicit form does not significantly alter reality, even as the economic statistics change precipitously.

## PARTIAL REFORM

Semi-effective, semi-actions push the half people back to the half rear
From 'Half Measures', by Russian poet Yevgeny Yevtushenko[11]

There are still other economic phenomena in Russia that existed in implicit form under central planning, but that do not automatically metamorphose into an explicit form during the transition to a market economy. The old, implicit form of the phenomenon disappears and a new, explicit counterpart must be established. Two such phenomena are the methods of taxation and the social welfare system. Market-oriented reform undermines the implicit versions of these structures. Explicit systems of taxation and social welfare (unemployment benefits, etc.) then have to be specifically created during the transition. Economic reform runs into difficulties when the explicit forms of these systems fail to be created – when reform stops halfway.

Other varieties of partial reform measures also generate problems during a transition to a market economy.[12] Consider, for example, the impact of one type of 'halfway' reform, a selective price liberalization. If the price of milk is controlled by the government and kept low while the price of sour cream is freed, there is likely to be too much sour cream relative to milk. Producers of dairy products who are free to choose their product mix will find that they can do better by producing sour cream, because the high prices make sour cream production more profitable than milk production. Unless dairies are somehow forced to produce milk, shortages of milk may well increase during the partial reform period. Such partial controls can also be counter-productive if the remaining price controls are aimed at reducing inflationary pressure. Not having to spend much money on milk (because it is either unavailable or, if available, sold at a low fixed price), consumers will have more cash available to spend on other goods, causing the price of sour cream to be higher than it would be if all price controls were removed.[13] The milk–sour cream example is not merely a hypothetical scenario; the problems associated with this incomplete reform actually arose in Russia following a partial price liberalization on 2 January, 1992.[14]

Partial reforms create a second barrier to successful transition beyond the additional costs imposed on the reforming economy. This barrier to transition lies in the tendency for the controls on the economy that remain after partial reform to snowball into more and more controls. For example, increasing shortages of price-controlled milk and relatively high prices for sour cream following a partial price liberalization will lead to calls for either price controls on sour cream, or for commands to be given to dairies to increase their production of milk. With low fixed prices on their outputs, dairies become unprofitable. The likely next step is to regulate the prices of inputs used by dairies. But then the producers of the inputs will have to be commanded to sell at the low fixed prices, and the snowballing of controls continues.

Such a cascade of controls helped create Russia's centrally-planned economy in the first place.[15] During the New Economic Policy instituted under Lenin in 1921, most large industries were state-owned and their output prices were fixed, while small-scale economic activity soon became pre-dominately private and was conducted via free markets. With high, free market prices for their inputs but low fixed prices for their outputs, state enterprises were unprofitable. In an attempt to make state enterprises more profitable, the Soviet government extended price controls to the inputs used by these enterprises. A private supplier of inputs then faced the choice of selling the inputs to the state at low prices or selling the inputs on free markets at high prices. Not surprisingly, the sellers preferred to transact on the free markets, leaving state enterprises without adequate supplies. The government then set voluntary quotas on the amount of supplies that private firms were to sell to the state; when there were insufficient volunteers, the quotas were made mandatory. The final result, unforeseen in the early years of the New Economic Policy, was a centrally-planned regime by 1930.

The snowballing of controls is not inevitable. Many other factors led to the Soviet centrally-planned economy. In particular, a single-party monopoly on political power played an important role, as the concerns of those who would be hurt by further economic restrictions were not well represented. Nevertheless, the tendency for price controls to propagate, and then lead to quantity controls, is unmistakable.

Related to the propagation of controls is the notion that, for all of its difficulties, the centrally-planned economic system in the former Soviet

Union was 'internally consistent'. Given that output prices were fixed, it was nearly a requirement that input prices be fixed; otherwise, firms would be unprofitable. But in order to induce sales of inputs at fixed prices, most economic activity had to be state-controlled. A state monopoly on foreign trade (an official Soviet policy) was also necessary. Consider what would have occurred had individuals been allowed to export. Entrepreneurs would have bought up goods that were relatively underpriced (at the fixed prices) in the USSR, and sold them abroad at world prices. While such entrepreneurs would have done well by this trade, the government would have found that the subsidies inherent in its fixed prices were benefiting only such entrepreneurs and the foreign buyers. In essence, it would have amounted to a large wealth giveaway by the government.

The internal consistency of the planning system and the tendency of controls to snowball into more and more controls, together imply that partial reforms can be particularly dangerous. Taking away one element of the old economic structure, such as the state foreign trade monopoly, can create large losses if not accompanied by other reforms, such as price liberalization. Despite an apparently strong desire in Russia for a fully-fledged market economy, the dynamics of partial reforms could lead to a gradual re-institution of controls. For this reason, and because of the considerable costs generated by incomplete reforms, care must be given to the choice of the transition path, even if the initial conditions are accurately perceived.

## PRE-REFORM STATISTICS

Economic statistics can be useful guideposts in locating the starting point for Russian reforms. Appropriately interpreting measures of economic activity is not always straightforward, though, and sometimes it is even difficult to collect accurate measures at the outset. Statistics can be misleading or perverse under any setting: recall the exclusion of discouraged workers from US unemployment statistics. But the difficulties in interpreting statistics tend to be appreciably greater in planned economies with large fixed-price state sectors.

One reason we cannot rely on pre-reform Russian economic statistics is that a large amount of private economic activity took place outside the official sector and was consequently not counted. The parallel in Western economies is traffic in illicit commodities such as narcotics, and transactions conducted surreptitiously for reasons of tax evasion. In Russia, though, such exclusion from official statistics arose to some degree for virtually all private activity.

Furthermore, pre-reform Russian statistics that were dependent on prices (i.e., statistics in value terms) generally used the official fixed state prices, which rendered them largely arbitrary. One hundred roubles worth of steel could just as easily be 200 or 50 roubles worth, if the government chose to double or halve the fixed price of steel. While free prices considerably reduce the scope of this problem in Western market economies, there are some analogues. Consider, for instance, tickets to popular Broadway shows or sporting events. The tickets have an official price, but are often purchased from scalpers at much higher prices. The original sale to the scalper at the official price is captured in Western economic statistics, but the next transaction, from the scalper to the Broadway or sports enthusiast, is not counted, even though the price of that transaction is a better measure of the value of the ticket than the official price. In pre-reform Russia, most consumer goods that were supplied via the official state sector were like scarce tickets in the West, in that their official prices were lower than their actual value on free markets. (Incidentally, this was true of tickets to productions at popular Russian theatres, where the majority of tickets were not sold through the normal box office channels, but rather distributed informally in exchange for scarce goods or services or at higher, black market prices.[16])

Economic statistics that did not incorporate prices, however, were immune to the arbitrariness of the centrally-determined pricing system. Accordingly, official Soviet statistics in terms of physical units, say tons of steel, traditionally were accepted in the West as fairly reliable, even as some problems with the statistics were acknowledged.[17] For example, there were obvious incentives for enterprises to exaggerate their production, because higher production meant higher bonuses for workers and managers. There were gaps in the availability of statistics: a dearth of information on the extensive defence sector comprised the most blatant omission. Nor were the statistics that were provided always easy to interpret. At one point, for example, Soviet statisticians began including sales of used cars in their figures for car sales, without documenting the methodological change.[18] Nevertheless, there was confidence in the general integrity of Soviet physical-unit statistics.

Recently, however, this confidence has been called into question. It now appears that the 'free invention' of statistics was perhaps quite considerable.[19] In fact, it is hard to escape the conclusion that output was grossly exaggerated, given Russian living standards in comparison with the claimed output growth over the years.

One story of falsified production figures demonstrates the scope of the potential distortions in official statistics. In a Soviet scandal of almost breathtaking proportions, the cotton output of the central Asian republic of Uzbekistan was systematically overestimated by hundreds of thousands of tons annually. Payments based on the non-existent output then flowed to Uzbekistan, providing the incentive to engage in such blatant misrepresentation. Official estimates indicate that between 1978 and 1983, the fictitious output came to 4.5 million tons of cotton, or more than twelve per cent of total state cotton purchases.[20] The overlord of the operation, which involved 'practically the whole population of the republic',[21] was the top Communist Party official in Uzbekistan. Soviet journalist Arkady Vaksberg, in relating the story of the scandal, notes that:

a commodity is not a thing, an object, something real, visible and tangible. It is a figure printed on paper, kept in an office in a statistical record. Since one eats bread not numbers, wears clothes not figures, it is possible and logical for the people to be destitute whilst the statistics demonstrate a country of riches and abundance.[22]

Compare this description, drawn from the real-life Soviet Union, with George Orwell's presentation of the fictional country of Oceania in *Nineteen Eighty Four*, where Winston Smith was called on to change, after the fact, the number of boots that had been planned to be produced:[23]

Statistics were just as much a fantasy in their original version as in their rectified version. A great deal of the time you were expected to make them up out of your head. For example, the Ministry of Plenty's forecast had estimated the output of boots for the quarter at a hundred and forty-five million pairs. The actual output was given as sixty-two millions. Winston, however, in rewriting the forecast, marked the figure down to fifty-seven millions, so as to allow for the usual claim that the quota had been overfilled. In any case, sixty-two millions was no nearer the truth than fifty-seven millions, or than a hundred and forty-five millions. Very likely no boots had been produced at all. Likelier still, nobody knew how many had been produced, much less cared. All one knew was that every quarter astronomical numbers of boots were produced on paper, while perhaps half the population of Oceania went barefoot.

The extent to which official Soviet statistics generally masked the truth was boldly investigated by two Soviet citizens, the journalist Vasiliy Selyunin and the economist Grigoriy Khanin. In their 1987 article (appropriately titled 'The Cunning Figure') in the influential Soviet journal *Novy Mir*, Selyunin and Khanin provided alternative estimates of the growth of national income in the USSR.[24] Official statistics state that Soviet national income increased by a factor of 89 during the 1928–1985 period, while Selyunin and Khanin estimated that income increased by a factor of 6.6. The incredible difference between the estimates arose from a combination of different statistical techniques and 'corrections' made by Khanin to the official statistics. (It is perhaps even more surprising given that exaggerating growth rates requires an increased exaggeration of output *levels* over time, i.e., a constant 20 per cent exaggeration of output would have no effect on calculations of growth rates.[25]) While the analysis of Khanin and Selyunin may have painted too dire a picture – by taking insufficient notice of underground economic activity, for instance – the extent to which official statistics exaggerated Russian achievements was clearly extraordinary.

Even those at the highest levels did not have access to accurate information. Former Soviet leader Nikita Khrushchev noted in his memoirs his own distrust of Soviet statistics:

Having lived under Stalin, I tend to think that the figures for average yield which you read in the press these days reflect wishful thinking rather than reality. . . . In other words, Stalin arbitrarily dictated the average yield. Nowadays [Khrushchev tape-recorded his memoirs between 1966 and 1971] it isn't that bad, but I still don't trust our bureau of statistics. I think there remains a tendency among our statisticians to conceal setbacks and tell the leadership what it wants to hear. . . . They're clever at hiding the truth.[26]

Mikhail Gorbachev, likewise, had trouble getting reliable economic information, both as a Politburo member and later as General Secretary.[27] The Soviet penchant for secrecy combined with data distortions and limitations to provide a misleading economic view from the political summit. Such a situation would be troubling for economic policy-makers anywhere. But in a centrally-planned system, where all important economic decision making is concentrated at the highest political level, unreliable statistics represent a major disability.[28]

Completely reliable output statistics would not solve the task of correctly gauging the pre-reform Russian economy. The correlation between official economic activity and human welfare was less pronounced in Russia than in Western market economies. For example, if a Western company makes a product that few people want to purchase, the company will go out of business, and the resources used in making the product can then move to more highly-valued tasks. But if a state-owned enterprise in a fixed-price socialist state makes a product with little value, the enterprise need not go out of business. Indeed, increases in the enterprise's output will lead to increases in measured GNP, even if the output is not valuable relative to the inputs used in producing it.

## STATISTICS AND REFORM

The catalogue of biases and mis-representations in pre-reform Russian statistics might suggest that economic transition would offer a more accurate statistical picture of the Russian economy. Unfortunately, in many instances the process of economic reform tends to add to the distortion of the statistical image.

The implicit-to-explicit conversion of economic phenomena that accompanies reform is one source of new difficulties in the interpretation of statistics. Inflation, for example, in the pre-reform era, took on its repressed or implicit form, and generally was not captured in official price statistics. With market-oriented reform, inflation becomes explicit, and price level changes are reflected in statistical measures of the price level. The post-reform price indices therefore are more accurate measures of inflation than they were pre-reform. During the transition itself, however, inflation statistics will be particularly misleading. The transformation during economic reform from implicit to explicit inflation will be recorded in statistics as a substantial increase in the price level, even if there is actually no new inflation during reform. More generally, changes in statistical measures during reform may not reflect real changes in conditions, as in the discouraged workers story; rather, the changes simply reflect the shift from implicit to explicit forms of previously-existing economic phenomena.

Reform also relaxes the legal constraints on private economic activity, which therefore blossoms. Nevertheless, such activity often remains undetected by the statistical authorities. Partly this under-counting of private economic activity results from the statistics-gathering resources inherited from the planning era. Under Soviet central planning, Goskomstat, the state statistical agency, was devoted to the collection of statistics on economic activity that was in accordance with the plan. Russian statistical practices are therefore not geared towards counting private economic activity. To effectively collect information in the emerging market environment will require a time-consuming restructuring within Goskomstat – its own mini-perestroika.[29] The transition period may be particularly hard on Russian statistics, as new opportunities in the private sector have drawn leading Russian statisticians away from Goskomstat.

Private activity is also under-counted because individuals and enterprises often prefer to conceal it. (This was true under central planning as well, but the amount of private activity has skyrocketed during reform.) Many conditions give rise to an incentive to hide private economic activity. First, much of it remains, to some extent, illegal. Second, taxes can be evaded by concealing private economic activity. Third, open activity might come to the attention of racketeers or simply envious neighbours.

The use of economic statistics as propaganda has become more complicated during the reform era. Under the Soviet regime, statistical methodology served political tasks.[30] The bias was clearly to paint a pretty picture, and information that reflected badly on the government was suppressed. In some instances this may still be the case, as Western and, in particular, International Monetary Fund support for Russia is conditional on certain economic criteria being met. The chairman of the Russian Central Bank has accused the government of deliberately understating the size of its budget deficit in order to mislead foreign lending institutions, and other accusations of 'two sets of books' have been raised.[31] On the other hand, two deputy prime ministers apparently exaggerated the inflation rate in order to convince the prime minister of the risk of hyperinflation, and the total amount of foreign aid is likely to be an increasing function of the amount of unfavourable economic dispatches from Russia.[32] There are now constituencies for both good and bad economic news.

Discrepancies between economic statistics and economic reality are not limited to centrally-planned economies. Former Prime Minister Andreas Papandreou of Greece once remarked that 'the figures prosper while the people suffer'.[33] This aphorism was generally applicable to pre-reform

Russia: the Uzbekistan cotton statistics being a particularly egregious example. Reform turns this message on its head, however, as statistics begin to capture changes from implicit to explicit forms of economic difficulties, but fail to capture much of the growth of private economic activity.

## LIMITS TO UNDERSTANDING

Statistics concerning the Russian economy are often misleading, but this is just one aspect of a more general phenomenon. To an extent well beyond that of Western market economies, the Russian economy is, well, unknowable. First there is the obvious point that the term 'Russian economy' is itself ambiguous. Economic conditions vary widely across Russia, among individuals, enterprises, industries, and regions. While this has always been the case to some extent, the reform process has often multiplied the disparities. State-owned enterprises and localities that have enthusiastically embraced reform are in many instances doing better than their counterparts that have been slower to change. As is common in macroeconomics, a wealth of diversity is lost when speaking of 'the' Russian economy.

But the difficulty with understanding the Russian economy goes beyond the variance that is hidden in aggregate statistics. Almost any sort of information, statistical or otherwise, involves generalizing from individual, anecdotal accounts, as noted by economist Ed Hewett:

> The problem is one of weighting the various anecdotes, and there is no easy solution. Drawing inferences from a mass of anecdotes is a highly subjective enterprise and is not amenable to replication by others. The best one can do is to make prior assumptions (or biases) clear.[34]

My bias, as is probably already clear, is to focus on the informal, unofficial activity in the Russian economy, particularly during the years when the formal activity was prescribed in a central plan.

One reason that the process of aggregating individual bits of information seems more arduous for the Russian economy than elsewhere lies in the unofficial activity itself. Most Russians have developed informal methods for procuring goods or just generally 'beating the system'. Russians are naturally reluctant to discuss their own informal machinations; again, illegality, racketeers, and envy-avoidance all play a role in keeping the unofficial economy under wraps. Another important factor is that informal connections are often valuable only to the extent to which they are not widespread. If I have a good friend who occasionally can secure tickets to the Bolshoi for me, I do not particularly want all my acquaintances to also befriend this person, since then my access will be lessened. Publicity of informal economic relationships may create undesired competition.

For these reasons, Russians themselves may know little about the informal economic behaviour of other Russians. Susan Richards, a Western historian of the USSR, travelled to the Soviet Union four times between 1988 and 1990 and wrote a book about the lives of 'everyday' Russians.[35] Here is her description of this phenomenon:

> The economy that worked was subterranean, amenable neither to description nor, therefore, to reform. It consisted of a series of microscopic cells which, in a parody of revolutionary political tactics, were safe from control or infiltration because each cell knew nothing of the others. Beyond their own lives, or those of their friends, people knew little about how 'the system' worked. It was absurd not because it did not make sense, but because it was unknowable.[36]

The reluctance of Russians to disclose information concerning the reality of their economic lives, combined with the relative isolation of the Soviet period, implied that Western scholars of the Soviet economy faced a daunting task, which they not infrequently compared to archaeology.[37] How could one appraise the economic situation in the Soviet Union given such fragmentary information? One tendency in Western social science was to rely, perhaps too heavily, on almost the only source of information that appeared to be scientific, namely, the official statistics.[38] 'Anecdotal' or 'literary' evidence, such as the thousands of published letters in Soviet newspapers that exposed true local conditions, descriptions in Soviet novels, or firsthand accounts from émigrés, was discounted.[39] The basis for even the CIA's estimates of Soviet GNP was official Soviet statistics.[40]

(I am painting with too broad strokes myself here, in that there was a good deal of Western detective work that scrutinized Soviet statistics carefully, and took account of other sources of information. For many researchers, the Khanin–Selyunin recalculations of Soviet growth were newsworthy only in that they had been published in the Soviet press – similar, and perhaps methodologically superior, statistical work had long been accomplished in the West. My view of the Western consensus on the Soviet economy, however, to the extent a consensus existed, is that it took too little account of informal economic activity and relied too heavily on official statistics. A similar point probably applies to the consensus view of the US economy, but on a reduced scale.)

While the amount of subterranean economic activity remains substantial, the increased openness in Russia is allowing better pictures of 'the' Russian economy to emerge. But the ongoing reform generates many changes that require a continual updating of the picture. And with the pre-reform situation not well understood, the effects of reform are hard to discern, even as the current Russian economy becomes better known.

## THE PATH AHEAD

The discussion in this introduction highlights three considerations that are helpful to keep in mind when attempting to understand Russian reform.

First, great care (and numerous grains of salt) should be directed at the interpretation of economic statistics during transition. Second, the interconnections between reform measures and the internal consistency of the pre-reform system render it unwise – even if, to a degree, unavoidable – to assess elements of reform on a piecemeal basis. Third, Russian conditions are so far removed from those in normal market economics that typical Western standards cannot be applied to the impact of reform; thus a fall in industrial production is not necessarily bad, nor is a large increase in measured GNP necessarily good, even though they generally would merit such interpretations in market economies.

Expediting a trip to the market requires (or at least is simplified by) knowing both where you are starting from and where the market is. Surprisingly, the quality of information in Russia on the location of the market is relatively better than the information on the starting point. Implicit economic phenomena and unreliable statistics combine to make delineation of the pre-reform Russian economy quite imprecise. Much of the remainder of this book is devoted to triangulating on the location of the pre-reform Russian economy, and the lessons for reform that can be drawn from an improved understanding of initial conditions in Russia. The next step on this journey is to review market and centrally-planned economies, in theory and practice.

# Chapter 1

# Markets and plans

The empirical evidence seems to be in: market economies generally out-perform centrally-planned economies in terms of living standards. But why? Could it not just as easily have worked out the other way around? This chapter provides a brief theoretical guide to market and centrally-planned economies which suggests that the answer is 'no': market economies have inherent advantages over centrally-planned economies.

Incidentally, looking at market and centrally-planned economies side by side generates a certain complementarity. Though there is some irony in the proposition, nevertheless it seems to be the case that a good way to understand free markets is to study societies where markets are suppressed – and vice versa. One final note before the tour of the wisdom of Adam Smith and his intellectual descendants begins: the relatively simplistic overview below will tax the patience of the economically sophisticated.

## ECON 101

Economics 101 typically starts with a gloomy characterization of a post-Eden world of scarcity. Resources such as land, labour, buildings, and machines, that together can be used to produce goods, are limited. Meanwhile, human desires, if not infinite, at least exceed the current capacity for goods' production. Scarcity of resources implies that more of one good means less of some other good, so it is important to produce those goods that best satisfy human wants. An increase in the production of buggy whips is probably not going to do much to raise US living standards (unless the buggy whips can then be traded to foreign countries in exchange for goods more highly desired by US citizens.) What should be produced?

A question that should be answered along with the 'what to produce' question is 'how should it be produced?'. Various combinations of labour and capital (non-human goods such as machines that are used to produce other goods and are not immediately used up in the process) can be employed in the production of goods. An example familiar to paper pushers concerns copies of documents. Suppose you need thirty copies of a ten-page document. One way to get the thirty copies is the medieval method: put some monks to work with parchment, pens, and ink, and have them transcribe thirty copies. Alternatively, a typewriter and carbon paper (capital goods) can be substituted for some human labour. A photocopier substitutes for even more labour. And photocopiers themselves range in the amount of labour required to produce copies; some (the ones I like) will automatically collate and staple the copies.

In free enterprise market economies, the questions concerning what goods to produce and how to produce them are answered by individuals who respond to the prices in the marketplace. If the price of a good is high, and I can produce it cheaply, I will try to produce it in quantity. If lemonade were to sell for $1 million a cup (while the costs of producing it stay about what they are now, say 50 cents a cup), I would stop writing this chapter and be out on the street selling lemonade. So would you, though, and our competition to attract the occasional thirsty customer would eventually drop the price down to something close to the 50 cents a cup that it costs to make. As for how we would make the lemonade, well, we could probably buy some lemon soda at the grocery store, distil the lemon juice out of the soda, and then combine it with sugar to get lemonade; but, it is probably cheapest (based on those market prices) to procure lemons (from people who are growing them because it is worth it to them given the price of lemons and the alternative uses of their land, labour, and capital) and combine them directly with sugar, water, and cups.

An attractive feature of free prices is that people have incentives to provide what other people are willing to pay a high price for, i.e., what people value highly. There are also good incentives for producing goods in the least costly way. Entrepreneurs have inducement to develop new products that consumers will value, and to find innovative methods to lower production costs. Simultaneously, consumers are motivated to consume less of those goods that require relatively scarce resources to provide, since the prices of those goods will be high.

Another assumption has slipped into the discussion; namely, that people are free to respond to price signals and personally profit or lose by doing so. This 'private enterprise' part of the story is inextricably intertwined with free prices. The social value of goods generally gets reflected in free prices. Private ownership ties individual self-interest – making money – to social benefit, by inducing people to make decisions based on those social values of goods. There is little use, and maybe even disutility, in having either free prices or private enterprise in isolation, without its companion. For this reason, fixed-price regimes commonly find it prudent to restrict private enterprise. As we have already noted, the regulations within centrally-planned economies display a sort of internal consistency.

Two well-known examples help to illustrate the potential incompatibilities of free enterprise with fixed-prices. First, consider the situation of private agriculture in pre-reform Russia. While farming was collectivized into large state-owned farms in the Soviet Union in the 1930s, farmers were still permitted a small individual private plot and the right to own some livestock. These private plots, therefore, presented the possibility for free enterprise. Fixed prices created incentives for farmers to make perverse decisions in feeding their livestock. Price controls on bread meant that it was cheaper than the grain used to make it. Peasants chose to fatten pigs with bread rather than feed grain. Soviet statistics indicated that 10–13 per cent of bread sold in retail trade was fed to livestock. Despite legal penalties, the state could not eliminate such privately profitable activity.

A second example of incompatibility between fixed prices and free enterprise is drawn from the case of partial reform that recently existed in Poland. After private enterprise was allowed to develop, Poland maintained an extremely low price for coal. Despite Poland's cold climate, cheap energy led entrepreneurs to grow tropical flowers in Poland and export them.[41] The chief input into raising tropical flowers is heat, and since heat provided by coal was so inexpensive, growing tropical flowers was profitable for private producers. Simultaneously, the actual costs to society from this activity were quite large. Every tropical flower that Poland produced made Poland a poorer country relative to the situation that would have arisen if the price of coal reflected its actual scarcity. It would have been better for Poland to import tropical flowers than to grow them internally, and to put the coal saved in this fashion to some higher-valued use, such as home heating. Russia did not heed the Polish lesson and kept energy prices highly subsidized while most other prices, and foreign trade, moved towards liberalization in January 1992.[42] One Russian commentator noted in mid-1993 that 'Today a ton of coal is cheaper than an imported Snickers bar.'[43]

Returning to the Econ 101 lecture: By responding to the signals provided by free prices, the Adam Smith effect kicks in. One is 'led by an invisible hand to promote an end which was no part of his intention'.[44] That 'end' is benefit for society. Anarchic, individual action in a competitive market setting generally leads to good social outcomes – the miracle of the market.

This free price paradise is lost in some circumstances, however. There are some situations where decision makers don't face the full benefits or costs of their actions, even when prices are not fixed by the state (i.e., unlike the Polish tropical flowers story). Economists call these situations 'externalities'. One example is the air pollution that often accompanies industrial production. A more mundane example concerns talking in a movie theatre. While those conversing enjoy the benefit of their discussion, the costs – here, noise during the feature film – are borne by those around them. If, fully informed of the costs and benefits of various outcomes, the parties had bargained ahead of time and talkers paid the other theatre-goers a freely negotiated fee for the right to talk (or the others paid the talkers for silence), then the invisible hand argument applies.[45] Otherwise, talkers (or the others) are just being rude. They are imposing costs on other people without the consent of the others. But aside from those externalities that private bargaining is insufficient to control, free prices in competitive markets generally deliver the goods – the right goods, and made the right way.

## SOVIET ECON 101

The statesman who should attempt to direct private people in what manner they ought to employ their capitals would not only load himself with a most unnecessary attention, but assume an authority which could safely be trusted, not only to no single person, but to no council or senate whatever, and which would nowhere be so dangerous as in the hands of a man who had folly and presumption enough to fancy himself fit to exercise it.

Adam Smith[46]

In a free market, private enterprise economy, the what to produce and how to produce questions are answered by individual initiative responding to price signals. What about in a Soviet-type, centrally-planned economy?

Before examining how these questions have been answered in the Soviet case, consider a thought experiment. You are the dictator of the world. No other countries or worlds exist that can serve as your guide. Command your people – what should they produce, and how should they produce it? Think hard, for the welfare of all the inhabitants on your world depends upon your answers.

The task is impenetrable. How can any one person, or any committee, or any Gosplan organization, know what goods should be produced and how they should be produced? At least with current technology, the answer seems to be that they can not. In theory, though certainly not in practice, there might be methods whereby central planners can mimic market pricing to make these decisions.[47] But then they might as well rely on markets, and put the central planners' time to more productive pursuits.

The Soviet Union was fortunate, though, because it did not have to answer the what and how questions de novo. It inherited a certain productive legacy from czarist times. More importantly, it was surrounded by a world that did rely on markets: the hostile capitalist encirclement. Because they continued to measure themselves against the West, Soviet planners could look to Western nations in order to determine what goods to produce and how to produce them. If personal computers were made in the West, then the Soviets would consider making them. If buggy whips were no longer being made in the West, maybe they should be discontinued in the Soviet Union too. But it was tougher to phase-out industries in a society where all industries were state-owned, just as it is hard to close government enterprises in the West.

So the Soviets looked to the West to help them answer the what and how questions of production. One difference between the Soviet Union and the West, however, is that the West is continually re-answering these questions. The Soviets found it much more difficult to innovate, to change the answers to the what and how questions.[48] That is why visitors to Soviet state industrial enterprises might be forgiven for thinking that they have been transported into the past. In a sense, they have been. For many Soviet enterprises, the what and how questions were answered during the industrialization drive in the 1930s, and only marginal changes have taken place since. Even official Soviet sources suggested that 48 per cent of the fixed capital in industrial production in 1989 was obsolete.[49] Two American researchers spent two months at a Moscow rubber goods production enterprise, Rezina, in early 1991, and wrote of their impressions:[50]

> To walk around these production departments is to be transported back to the last century. They are dark and dingy and the noise from the antiquated machinery can be deafening. The technology is so old – some of it harkens back to pre-World War II days – that many of its own employees liken it to an industrial museum.

The reluctance to innovate is partly a result of planning necessity. The overwhelming task of planning almost all of the production of a large country is made easier (or even made possible) by specifying only incremental changes. A declaration that 'This year's plan is last year's output, plus 3%', while rudimentary, is a feasible planning exercise. Reconsidering the what and how to produce questions from scratch, every plan period, is infeasible.

Incremental changes were also in the best interests of managers and workers. Enterprise managers lacked strong incentives to radically upgrade their existing facilities, because the short-term drop in output that such restructuring would entail would mean a loss of bonuses for workers and management, and the future benefits from the upgrading would largely accrue to the state, not the managers.

For these reasons, central planning tends to lock in an existing structure of production. This problem is less acute when the main task facing an economy is to recover production that has been temporarily lost, because of a war, say. But when the task is to increase productive capacity in unknown directions, as opposed to more fully utilize the existing capacity, planning is less successful.[51] While new investment is the area of economic activity over which central planners can exercise the highest degree of control, it is also an area in which planners are particularly poorly situated to make good decisions.

Dictating part of his memoirs in 1969, former Soviet leader Nikita Khrushchev favourably compared Japanese and West German science and technology with that of the Soviet Union:

technological knowledge is so advanced in Japan. Some say West Germany gives them competition. There's another country that was utterly destroyed in the war! These facts force us to look at the way we're organized and to think about the work our scientific research institutes do.

There is apparently some great defect in our system, for we have no fewer engineers, scientists, or mathematicians than West Germany or Japan. Statistics show that the number of scientists and technicians we produce is constantly increasing. How many master's degrees and doctorates do we have? Yet we still need to buy the best things overseas. It makes you think.[52]

The difficulty that central planners have in answering the what to produce question means that in the Russian official economy there are large discrepancies between what people want and what is produced. Also, there are large discrepancies between how a good gets produced and the least-cost method of producing it. A third problem is that citizens' demand for goods does not take into consideration the true costs of supplying those goods – witness the use of bread as animal feed.

Making and consuming the wrong goods in the wrong way – what economists term 'resource misallocations' – are at the heart of the economic difficulties in centrally-planned economies. Resource misallocations caused by fixed prices and state ownership of production have been a leading factor behind the difference in living standards between the economies of the two Germanys, Koreas, and Chinas, and are the main reason for Russia's relatively poor economic performance.

This description of the perils of central planning differs somewhat from conventional wisdom. When Westerners think about the problems of the Russian economy, they typically think of shortages, limited work incentives, wasteful production, and low-quality goods. But probably the main cost engendered by central planning is that the wrong goods are produced.[53] For example, beyond raw materials and (to a degree) military equipment, Soviet goods had trouble finding export markets. Many of the 'goods' found in Soviet state stores were barely recognizable to Westerners, and were often not strongly sought out by Soviet citizens, either. The peculiarities of goods from the former USSR, particularly their tendency to be too large and too heavy, are legion. 'We make the largest portable computers in the world!' brags a Soviet official in one version of a familiar joke.

That the major problem under fixed prices lies in deciding what to produce, as opposed to motivating people to produce efficiently and with high quality standards, was noted by Nobel prize-winning economist Friedrich Hayek in his classic 1944 critique of central planning, *The Road to Serfdom*. In the context of a worker choosing the right occupation, Hayek states:

The problem of adequate incentives which arises here is commonly discussed as if it were a problem mainly of the willingness of people to do their best. But this, although important, is not the whole, nor even the most important, aspect of the problem. It is not merely that if we want people to give their best we must make it worth while for them. What is more important is that if we want to leave them the choice, if they are to be able to judge what they ought to do, they must be given some readily intelligible yardstick by which to measure the social importance of the different occupations. Even with the best will in the world it would be impossible for anyone intelligently to choose between various alternatives if the advantages they offered him stood in no relation to their usefulness to society. To know whether as the result of a change a man ought to leave a trade and an environment which he has come to like, and exchange it for another, it is necessary that the changed relative value of these occupations to society should find expressions in the remunerations they offer.[54]

Central planners in a fixed-price regime face the same difficulties in determining what and how to produce, lacking any 'readily intelligible yardstick' with which to gauge their decisions.

Fortunately, there has always been a free market, a second economy, ready to step in where the resource misallocations in the first economy were most severe. As we will see, Soviet free markets were not the most efficient free markets in the world, but they nevertheless helped to overcome some of the more glaring central-planning mistakes. If Soviet consumers valued very highly a good that the Soviet official economy did not produce, entrepreneurs were there to supplement official activity. Second economy operators could either produce the good themselves, or, despite the official state monopoly on foreign trade, import the good from the West. If a Soviet factory produced a good in a high-cost way, the managers and workers had incentives to informally use a lower-cost production method, sell or trade the unnecessary inputs, and pocket the proceeds.

This discussion indicates the inherent difficulty that central planners have in answering the what to produce and how to produce questions for literally millions of goods. But what did Soviet planners do?

## THE MYTH OF THE PLAN[55]

All this makes it perfectly clear that Soviet plans bear not the least resemblance to planning as we generally conceive it. Those plans are not prompted by the slightest intention of establishing a conscious, lucid management of economic life and thus eliminating the elements of anarchy and chaos.

Paul Barton, 'The Myth of Planning in the U.S.S.R.', 1957[56]

Not uncommonly, the Western image of the Soviet centrally-planned economy, at least until recently, was that of a workable, if not exactly a finely-tuned, machine. Economists at Gosplan, the State Planning Committee, trained in the latest mathematical, statistical, and computational techniques, sent orders out of Moscow, resulting in the systematic production and distribution of literally millions of goods. If a steel-making enterprise in Magnitogorsk needed more coal for its coke production, the planners would send the appropriate message to a coal mine in the Donbass, and soon the requisite coal would roll into the Magnitogorsk factory gates. Problems that arose in the system, such as a prevalence of low quality output, could be corrected (or at least improved) through minor administrative changes, such as adding quality control inspectors to state-owned enterprises, and giving the inspectors the power to reject low quality goods – to take just one example of an early Gorbachev-era reform.[57]

The reality of centrally-planned systems tells a markedly different story, however. Planning in practice was about as far removed from machine-like, high-tech precision as could be imagined. As Ed Hewett has written, 'The fact that plans are made and that economic activity then occurs need not mean that the two are closely linked in all, or even many, ways.'[58]

First, machine-like precision in central planning is simply not feasible. Central planners do not have the information to be continually re-assessing what goods would best satisfy consumers, or even what combinations of goods could be produced with the available resources, or even what the available resources are. The result, as noted in the previous section, is that instructions given to enterprises tend to be along the lines of 'produce the same things that you produced last year, only 3% (or 5% or 8%) more'.[59] The production profile within enterprises then tends to get locked in, and over time centrally-planned economies are inclined to fall further and further behind market economies in providing the mix of goods most desired by consumers. Second, even planning in growth rates does not work very well. Some enterprises fail to meet their plan, despite their managers' attempts to ply the underground economy for the needed inputs. But the plan must be fulfilled, and so it generally was in the Soviet Union, often by reducing, after the fact, the enterprise's target – another harkening of *Nineteen Eighty Four*.[60] Together, these two conditions indicate the extent that planning followed production, rather than the other way around.

The planners' relative lack of information regarding productive capabilities implied that plan formation, that three or five or eight per cent growth in output targets, became the object of an intense bargaining game between planners and firms and ministries, what Ed Hewett characterized as 'a ritualized battle for real resources'.[61] Writing in 1952 (based on information concerning the high-Stalin years of 1938–1941), Western economist Joseph Berliner noted that

> The firm's output plan depends to a large extent upon what the plant officials have been able to bargain out of 'Moscow', the supply plan hinges upon

how much can be haggled out of the functionary in the State Planning Commission, and the financial plan is based upon currying the favour of a minor official in the Commissariat of Finance [endnote omitted].'[62]

The endnote omitted from the previous quote discusses the convergence of senior enterprise officials from all over the USSR on Moscow in the months when a new plan was being finalized, in order to conduct the last round of bargaining. That such officials would not typically arrive in Moscow empty-handed goes without saying.

While existing production tended to become locked in, the central planners had considerable leeway in determining in what areas new investment would occur. Western researcher John Howard Wilhelm suggests that 'affecting the configuration of productivity capacity as it develops over time . . . [is] . . . the only meaningful type of planning' that the Soviets could carry out.[63] Thus the considerable resources devoted to the defence sector and heavy industry in the Soviet Union resulted from continued large investments mandated over the years by state and Communist Party officials.

The major day-to-day activity of Soviet planners was to ensure that the supply of inputs to state-owned enterprises more-or-less balanced the enterprises' demands, consistent with the output plans – a process known as 'material balancing'.[64] Most 'planning,' had little to do with 'what we in the West usually understand by this term, namely, the delineation of economic goals and the selection of strategies and instruments for their realization'.[65] The planners' necessity to ensure an adequate match of resources with plan requirements in turn required a focus on gross output such as tons of steel, while other objectives such as the quality or value of output became marginalized. When shortages developed, planners intervened in order to increase the supply or ration the demand. And since shortages were endemic to the system,[66] material balancing itself was an incredibly complex task. The planners alone could not ensure an equilibrium in the supply and demand for the myriad goods in the economy. Material balancing was only sustainable through the widespread resort to informal and illegal activity on the part of enterprise managers, their ministerial overseers, and local party officials.[67]

The dysfunctions of the planning system were legion. One of the most destructive and pervasive was 'storming', in which an enterprise would produce the bulk of its monthly output in the final few days of the month, in order to fulfil the plan – at least on paper – and thereby earn bonuses for the managers and workers.[68] The workers would then relax at the beginning of the next month – or work at their unofficial, private activities – only to repeat the supercharged production at the end of the month. Enterprises could hardly avoid such behaviour because often they did not receive their inputs until the end of the month, from suppliers that were likewise storming. The system of storming was not only disliked by workers, it also resulted in lower quality output produced at the end of planning periods. Soviet citizens were well aware of the problem, and tried to avoid purchasing major items that were produced at the end of the month or year.[69]

Problems that were identified in the planning system were addressed by marginal changes in the planning mechanism. Nevertheless, the problems remained. Minor adjustments were followed by further adjustments in a seemingly endless series of tinkerings, while the systemic problems such as low quality and waste continued unabated. This process was well described in a 1979 article by Professor Gertrude Schroeder, appropriately entitled 'The Soviet Economy on a Treadmill of "Reforms"'.[70]

Central planning has, since Marx (and earlier), been promoted as a rational alternative to the 'anarchy of the market'. But for sheer anarchy, planning in practice has few peers. As the director of a pharmaceutical enterprise in Chelyabinsk, Russia, told my colleagues and me in 1993, after the collapse of the planned system and the end of storming in his enterprise, 'It is only now that there is no plan that we can actually plan production.'

One of the most instructive lessons concerning the difficulties of central planning is provided by Russian economist S. A. Belanovskii, in an article entitled 'The Army As It Is'.[71] If any part of the Soviet system worked as a well-oiled machine, surely it was the Soviet army, the height of regimentation in a highly regimented society. But the army that Belanovskii describes is harrowing in its lack of formal discipline, particularly in those units that did not serve a high military purpose. The formal system of regulations was augmented, challenged, and in many cases surpassed by an informal caste system, which involved ritualized hazing that in some instances could only be termed torture. (Indeed, rape was a standard part of the hazing for those soldiers – 'snitchers' – who complained to the formal authorities about bad treatment in the informal system.) The weakness in the formal Army regulations that led to this state of affairs, was, according to Belanovskii, an inadequate system of incentives in the formal system – an almost exact (though unstated) parallel with the weakness in the formal economic system. The second factor that contributed to the elevation of the informal incentive system over the formal one in the Soviet military is also familiar in the economic sphere: the lack of a 'useful occupation'. Many soldiers had no important military duties, and were therefore assigned to civilian projects such as building construction. A final parallel between the informal incentive system in the Army and in the economy is the extent to which the official goals of the formal system were, in some circumstances, furthered by the informal system. Thus informal, underground dealing allowed enterprises to obtain the supplies necessary to fulfil their formal plan, and the caste system in the army helped to keep the equipment in militarily-important units in good repair.

Now that centrally-planned economies are largely a thing of the past, the gulf between central planning theory and practice might seem to be mainly of historical interest. But there are compelling contemporary reasons for understanding planning in practice. First, and most obvious, there remain important economies, China in particular, that still rely significantly on central planning. Second, the dynamics of intervention, the snowballing of controls, could bring other economies to widespread central planning, despite no prior intention to embrace this form of organization. Third, the starting point for Russian reforms is determined by the outcome of the planning system and its unofficial, parallel economy. Gauging the effects of reform requires knowledge of the actual pre-reform conditions.

Perhaps most important, though, the lessons that history takes from the experience of Soviet-type economies hinge on understanding the workings of planning in practice. One popular explanation for the collapse of the Soviet Union, for example, is that central planners put a high priority on military production, which therefore received a large share of economic resources. This priority of the armed forces eventually undermined civilian living standards. In some versions of this reasoning, it was the Reagan-era US arms build-up that was the final straw for central planning, since the additional costs needed for the Soviets to keep up were too much for the civilian economy to bear. In a sense, this argument holds that it was the effectiveness of central planning at mobilizing resources in the sectors favoured by the planners that led to its own demise: a Marxian-style contradiction of socialism. The difficulty of this explanation is that it seems to take central planning at face value, and implicitly suggests that a relatively minor adjustment, a diminution in the size of the defence complex, could have prevented the system from failing.[72]

The over-militarization of the Soviet economy may have played a role in the exact timing of the demise of the centrally planned system. Nevertheless, as the root cause of the systemic failure, a more compelling explanation would focus on the resource misallocations that arise in a fixed-price system, and on the extent to which planning in practice diverged, of necessity, from an idealized version of central planning.

## SUFFICIENT REFORMS?

> O, reform it altogether.
> > William Shakespeare, *Hamlet*

Now that market and planned economics have been discussed in more detail, it might make sense to revisit the issue of partial reforms in the transition from plan to market. I have claimed that partial reforms are dangerous, because of the possibility of backsliding towards central planning and the imposition of new costs during transition. But almost all elements of Russian society require substantial change during the transition to a market economy. Not everything can change at once, so reforms cannot help but be both partial and gradual. From this perspective, an argument against partial reform is an argument against any reform.

But all hope is not lost, because not all partial reforms are dangerous. In order to give meaning to the notion of a partial reform, I need to outline what I would view as a sufficiently full reform, one that is capable of avoiding the problems of 'partial' reforms that have already been described. I believe, for reasons discussed throughout this book, that a full reform requires at least four elements, implemented quickly and more-or-less simultaneously: (1) near complete price liberalization; (2) a liberal environment for private economic activity; (3) an explicit social safety net; and (4) an explicit taxation system. Free prices (1) and free enterprise (2) are the cornerstones of any market economy. Explicit social welfare (3) and tax (4) systems must be established in Russia, because the reform process automatically undermines the pre-reform, implicit versions of these institutions. The traditional social safety net consisted in part of low-fixed prices for basic consumer goods in the state sector and full employment policies, both of which are doomed by reform. Taxes were raised in large measure through the administered price system and the claims of the government on the 'profits' of state-owned enterprises. Again, reform severely restricts the functioning of this implicit taxation system.

Of course, there are a host of other reform measures that would be beneficial to the Russian economy. The aim here, however, is to put forth the minimal set of reforms that is required for a fighting chance at a successful transition. Without these four measures, other reforms tend to be much more likely to fail, or to make matters worse: those dangerous partial reforms warned about earlier!

## MORE ON THE PATH AHEAD

This chapter has provided a rough picture of market and planned economies. In trying to fix the starting point for Russian reforms, and some mileposts along the way, the next chapter will examine those numerous elements of the Russian economy that have already arrived at the market. For these portions of the Russian economy, the relevant reform question is not 'how to get to the market?', but rather, 'how can the market be made most effective?'.

# Chapter 2

# Russian market activity

## SOVIET-ERA MARKET BEHAVIOUR

> An international committee of experts charged with compiling a list of
> conditions that maximize the potential for a large underground economy
> would invent the Soviet Union.
>
> Western economists Gregory Grossman and Vladimir G. Treml, 1987.[73]

Russia has a market economy. It has had a market economy for decades. All
told, private, capitalist-style behaviour accounted for perhaps as much as 25
per cent of all economic activity in the pre-reform USSR.[74] Some of it was
even legal.

The legal part of the Soviet market economy was dominated by collective
farm (kolkhoz) markets. Farmers who worked on the large state and cooperative farms also were permitted small private plots for growing produce
and raising a limited amount of livestock. The output from these private plots
provided the legal source for private sales of food on 'collective farm'
markets in Soviet cities. Unlike the official state markets, the prices of goods
at collective farm markets were more-or-less unregulated. In addition to
private farming, some 100,000 Soviet citizens were legally involved in small-
scale crafts and trades.[75]

The remainder of the Soviet market economy was technically illegal, and
therefore to some degree hidden; hence, the 'underground economy'. Other
terms used to describe this activity include 'second economy', 'parallel
economy', and 'black markets'.[76] Ignored in official Soviet research or
statistics, the second economy was nevertheless a pervasive element of
Soviet life. Indeed, it is impossible to precisely delineate the second
economy from the official planned economy, so intertwined were they.

In order to fulfil the plan, for example, managers of state-owned enterprises employed *tolkachi* (expediters or 'pushers') who would scour the
country in search of needed inputs. Engaged to a large extent in technically
illegal activity, Soviet tolkachi were nevertheless tolerated by the regime.
The bribing and bartering that formed their stock in trade were required to
keep the official economy running. But the market activity went beyond the

acquisition of material inputs. It applied as well to labour, and to the disposition of output. Soviet second economy experts Gregory Grossman and Vladimir Treml noted that a 'very common practice, often on the scale of even a whole factory, is the use of a socialist facility by insiders as a facade for a private business'.[77] Private repair of automobiles in ostensibly state-owned garages was a recurrent example within the service sector.

The day-to-day activity within the Soviet official economy was therefore flush with private economic endeavours. Consider the case of a state-owned restaurant. The official version of how the restaurant operated is as follows. The restaurant would receive its inputs (food, equipment) from the state, and hire employees at wages that were state-controlled. It would then sell meals to customers, also at state-controlled prices. If it happened to make a profit (measured in terms of the fixed prices), then, for the most part, it would have to return the profit to the state. To encourage output, however, employees would generally receive a bonus if they served more than the number of meals called for in the restaurant's plan.

In practice, this ideal form of central planning worked much differently, as the earlier section on 'The myth of the plan' might suggest. As noted, the restaurant manager may have had to provide gifts or bribes to ensure that his or her restaurant actually received its needed supplies. Many of the food (and other) inputs were diverted into employees', or their friends', kitchens. There was little incentive to provide high quality meals or good service, and these dimensions of dining out suffered. A well-placed bribe could go a long way towards improving the availability and quality of a diner's meal, however.

The effect of all this informal activity was to turn the official command economy into a quasi-market economy. Bribes, whether paid in cash or given in the form of a favour or a non-monetary gift, lent flexibility to the fixed prices, and helped to equate supply and demand, just as free prices do in market economies. The theft of goods and time from work played a similar role, by adding flexibility to centrally-mandated wage scales.[78]

Market activity likewise thrived more far removed from the official economy. Individual artisans of all sorts operated illegally, either because their activity was prohibited or because they failed to procure the required licence (perhaps to evade taxes). Private seamstresses, handymen, middle-men, professionals such as doctors and teachers: all proliferated in the underground economy, though many of their inputs were obtained, legally or illegally, from the state-owned sector. Moonlighting outside of one's main job was engaged in by more than twenty million Soviet citizens.[79] Private production and sale of alcoholic beverages formed a useful supplement to the pension of many a babushka. Groups of cooperating individuals, from moonlighting private construction crews to full-scale underground factories, also dotted the Soviet economic landscape. The existence of the legal collective farm markets provided a handy outlet for agricultural goods illegally diverted from the state sector.

Any sort of visible, illegal activity that was not aimed at plan fulfilment was likely to require bribes to one or more patrons who could provide protection. Berkeley Professor Gregory Grossman, a pioneer in the study of the Soviet second economy, describes Soviet-era bribery:

> The patron, often some official, grants his permission, or at least his forbearance, and extends some measure of conditional protection. The client pays in cash or kind, and not infrequently buys his way into the particular niche. Indeed, second economy operations of even modest size require multiple and periodic payoffs – to administrative superiors, party functionaries or secretaries, law-enforcement personnel, innumerable inspectors and auditors, and diverse actual or potential blackmailers.[80]

The market economy of the Soviet era was an indispensable part of the overall economy. Consider once again the private agricultural plots. Despite accounting for only three per cent of the cultivated land, it is estimated that private plots traditionally contributed nearly one-third of Soviet agricultural output.[81] Much of this enormous productivity can be attributed to the improved incentives to work hard on private plots as opposed to state farms. Private plot output is magnified, however, by the diversion of state-owned inputs (fodder, fertilizer, tractors) to use on private plots, and by sale of illegally obtained state output on the private markets.

## MARKET BEHAVIOUR DURING REFORM

The reform years have brought with them a partial surfacing of pre-existing economic activity, as well as a spurt in new private enterprise, both legal and illegal. Countless individual decisions to conduct private business have expanded enormously the Russian market economy. But the burst in private activity in the late 1980s did not occur simply because Russians suddenly developed a taste for entrepreneurship. Indeed, the extent of pre-reform private economic activity indicated that business acumen was long prevalent. The environment for private enterprise, as opposed to the nature of the Russian people, was what changed. Government economic reform policies since 1987 have played a major role in promoting Russian marketization, by increasing the scope of legal private economic activities and by simultaneously providing a cover for quasi-legal undertakings. Top-down pressure gave a further boost to free enterprise through the official privatization programme begun in 1992.

Mikhail Gorbachev succeeded Konstantin Chernenko as General Secretary of the Communist Party of the Soviet Union in 1985 and initiated a series of economic reforms that came to be known as *perestroika* (restructuring). The promotion of private economic activity was an important aspect of the *perestroika* reforms. In May, 1987, the Law on Individual Labour Activity took effect. This measure greatly enhanced legal private economic opportunities, permitting individuals to work alone or to unite into small groups called 'cooperatives'. Many restrictions remained in place following the Law on Individual Labour Activity, though. First, an individual or co-operative could not hire workers, reflecting the traditional Marxian prohibition against treating labour as a commodity. This meant that all individuals in a cooperative had to be 'owners', and not simply employees. Second, workers were not allowed to leave their state-sector employment in order to join a cooperative. The law was aimed at providing opportunities only for those who were not already in the labour force, such as housewives, pensioners, and students, and for moonlighters.

Restrictions on private activity were further eased in 1988, particularly by the Law on Cooperatives. Hired labour, generally illegal in the pre-perestroika Soviet Union, was permitted, and state enterprise employees could leave their jobs to work in cooperatives. State enterprises (or parts of state enterprises) could themselves become cooperatives, leasing the assets of the pre-existing enterprise. Joint ventures with foreign partners received government imprimatur, and cooperatives were given the right to sell their output at market-determined prices. In essence, cooperatives could operate like capitalist firms. The single remaining legal concession to the 'socialist' nature of cooperatives was a continued prohibition on outside investors. The only people who were supposed to receive income from a cooperative were those who actually worked there.

The cooperative sector mushroomed quickly following the liberalizing legislation. Starting from scratch in mid-1987, by June 1990 some five million Soviet citizens were working in cooperatives.[82] All indications pointed to a tremendous increase in unregistered private economic activity as well.

Following the abortive coup of August 1991, a further liberalization of economic activity took place. Land ownership, stock markets, commodity exchanges, free prices, and many other fixtures of normal market economies became commonplace. The liberalization thus far remains incomplete, and many steps backwards, including onerous licensing requirements and other central and local government restrictions on competitive markets, have been taken.[83] Nevertheless, the scope of the open Russian market economy of 1994 would have amazed a Russian transported forward in time from 1985. One rough estimate indicated that by mid-1994, half of Russian output and employment was in the private sector.[82*]

## SPONTANEOUS PRIVATIZATION

The intensified market activity of the Gorbachev–Yeltsin years, like the extent of the pre-reform market economy, has probably received insufficient attention in the West. The reason for this situation is not solely the unavailability of information, though much private activity does evade official statistics. I believe that the main cause, rather, lies in the nature of the change that has led to *de facto* marketization of the Russian economy. It was a change that was not heralded in any government decree, not announced in any Kremlin press conference. Instead, it was brought about by widespread, 'grassroots' activity, whereby people took advantage of a few reform measures to further wrest control of the economy out of the state's hands and into their own pockets. 'Spontaneous privatization' is the name given to this change, and it gave many, if not most, Russian workers a chance to work for quasi-profit-maximizing, quasi-free-enterprise firms, even prior to the official privatization programme. In fact, as noted earlier in this chapter, much of the quasi-market economy was well-established long before the Gorbachev era.

Perhaps the simplest form of spontaneous privatization, common in the late 1980s and early 1990s, is known as the 'privatization of profits'. Under this process, the informal activity that constituted much of the actual working of state-owned enterprises moved completely to the forefront. Consider once again the example of a state-owned restaurant. With the privatization of profits, the restaurant managers and employees began to charge whatever prices the market would bear. The official menu and prices slipped further into meaninglessness. Diners negotiated over the constitution of the meal and the price. The restaurant accepted any inputs that it could acquire through official state channels, because those inputs remained low-priced. But since the suppliers of inputs also spontaneously privatized their enterprises, the restaurant probably had to pay quasi-market prices as well. In short, the restaurant began to operate like any restaurant in capitalist countries, except that the remains of the old state sector had not entirely disintegrated.

The process of spontaneous privatization has been pervasive in Russia. The 'liberal' Russian economist Vitaliy Nayshul' described the result in 1991, prior to official privatization: 'State property de facto is nearly non-existent. Somebody has made a common law claim to every piece of public property, and it would be impossible to take them away without force.'[84]

How were the managers and employees of the restaurant able to assert their common law claim, or to convert their enterprise from the state sector to the free market sector? They may have simply escalated the same illegal behaviour that they informally employed to some degree before. Alternatively, they may have tried to more-or-less legally commandeer the restaurant's assets for their own personal gain.

The more formal route to spontaneous privatization relied upon taking advantage of the legal possibilities that arose through Gorbachev-era reforms. The possibility of starting a cooperative enterprise and the possibility of leasing capital goods from the state provided the main sources of opportunities to spontaneously privatizing establishments.

One quasi-legal route to privatization worked something like this. A state-owned enterprise's employees and managers formed several overlapping cooperatives. Various stages of the state enterprise's production process were then controlled by the members of the cooperative that was established in the corresponding part of the plant. To acquire the legal right to use the state's productive assets, the cooperatives leased the productive equipment from the enterprise. This was far from an 'arm's-length' transaction, however; the people who determined the cost of leasing the equipment were generally the same people doing the leasing.[85] To the extent that higher-ups in the government apparatus who formally oversaw the state-owned enterprise could control the leasing, they were brought into the cooperative as well. Eventually, there existed a crypto-private enterprise, otherwise little different from the state enterprise that preceded it. The incentives to efficiently produce goods consumers actually valued highly were much greater, however, once the enterprise moved into private hands, since the new 'owners" well-being was tied closely to the enterprise's profits.

The account of spontaneous privatization presented above is much over-simplified. There were many other devices for shifting state assets into private hands, beyond the official privatization plan.[86] Some of these involved setting up a private bank and selling newly-created ownership shares of the enterprise to the bank. The owners of the bank, who thereby became de facto stockholders of the enterprise, were typically the managers, employees, and possibly higher level officials of the enterprise.

The details of how spontaneous privatization has been carried out remain obscure, and for good reason. Since the usual routes to spontaneous privatization were at best semi-legal, the participants had an incentive to muddy the waters as much as possible. Consequently, outsiders have frequently been at a loss to discover how privatization took place, and how co-operatives interacted within privatized firms. Recall the American researchers who spent two months at the Moscow rubber goods producer, Rezina, in early 1991. Despite their extraordinary access to the inner sanctum of a Russian state-owned enterprise, the machinations underlying the spontaneous privatization eluded them:

> Try as we might to disentangle the details of this network, we could not. Some cooperatives were empty shells or accounting devices, some were mainly connected to ventures outside Rezina, others were merely fronts for dispensing overtime. Different people gave us different accounts of the system as a whole, and the accounts from the same person might vary from conversation to conversation or even within the same conversation. It seemed that the network was designed, on the one hand, to make it impossible for outsiders to distinguish real from nominal transactions and, on the other hand, to create opportunities for flexible response to the barrage of decrees regulating the operation of cooperatives. The system was meant to remain a mystery.[87]

Glasnost' has not diminished the relevance of Winston Churchill's dictum concerning Russia, at least in the economic sphere: 'a riddle wrapped in a mystery inside an enigma'.

Whether a state-owned firm in Russia was spontaneously or officially privatized during the Gorbachev–Yeltsin years, or whether it remained in state hands, it very likely changed its behaviour in response to market conditions. New products, increased geographical distribution of output, and an unprecedented concern with costs and marketing, have all been among the strategies that enterprises have had to adopt – sometimes quite unwillingly – as market pressures, still limited, have developed. One survey indicated that between mid-1991 and mid-1993, '80% of enterprises had changed their circle of suppliers and customers to some degree or other'.[88]

## MORE PRIVATE ACTIVITY

The conversion of existing state enterprises is only one route to privatization. A second route is the development of a private business de novo. Small-scale enterprises have been blooming throughout the former Soviet Union; by mid-1993, prior to most official privatization, some 40 per cent of the Russian non-agricultural work force was employed in the private sector.[89] Cooperative restaurants are one area of private activity. Private construction firms are widespread – they always were, but legality has made them more so.[90] Trade and services in general, undersupplied during the planning regime – in 1988, the USA had 61 retail shops per 10,000 residents, while Russia had only 20 – have been popular sectors for new private activity.[90a] In the industrial city of Perm', with a total workforce of slightly more than 600,000 people, as many as 100–125,000 had become involved in private street vending by mid-1992.[91] Some cooperatives have entered joint ventures with Western companies. Alas, even selling protection services to other private businesses appears to be an expanding industry. In short, there are many free market opportunities being seized upon by Russian entrepreneurs.

In agriculture, the average size of a Russian private plot increased by 80 per cent between 1991 and 1993, to nearly nine-tenths of an acre.[92] Small private agricultural plots farmed by town dwellers ('garden plots') are also common, and have enjoyed enormous recent growth: the amount of land devoted to the private plots of city dwellers doubled in 1991.[93] Official statistics indicate that in 1992, 54 per cent of vegetables and 78 per cent of potatoes were grown on private plots, while the corresponding figures for meat, milk, and eggs were near 40 per cent.[94] Private land 'ownership' is surprisingly common in Russia. In the late 1980s more than half of all Soviet families had access to a parcel of land.[95] This figure increased to nearly 90 per cent of households by mid-1993, when there were 41 million small plots of land in Russia alone (including those for summer cottages – dachas).[96] Included in this figure are more than 250,000 full-sized private farms (as of mid-1993); there were no such farms in the pre-reform period.[97]

## COSTS OF DOING BUSINESS

Whether in small business, industry, or agriculture, many Russians are already active in the private sector, and often have been for years. It bears repeating – Russia has a market economy. But not all market economies are created equal, and the Russian version is substantially less efficient than its Western counterparts, even as it is considerably more efficient than the moribund state sector. The reason lies in what economists refer to as 'transactions costs'. The costs of conducting business are high in Russia, primarily because of difficulties with – another favourite phrase for economists – 'property rights'. The major stumbling blocks are uncertainty as to who are the actual owners of property, uncertainty as to what transactions are legal, a wide variety of restrictions that render much private activity clearly illegal, and little hope of state enforcement of private contracts. Together, these obstacles make it very difficult to enter enforceable, legally-binding business agreements.

Imagine that you are a Russian entrepreneur and you wish to start a construction business. You would like to enter an agreement with a timber supplier. If you deal with a state timber enterprise, precisely with whom do you transact? the managers of the enterprise? the Ministry in charge of timber? local government authorities, or the republic government, or (until the demise of the USSR in late 1991) the All-Union government? What happens if you pay a deposit for the timber, and then the enterprise fails to deliver? Is there any legal mechanism whereby you can recover your deposit and other damages arising from the breach? If instead you deal with a private timber producer, can you be sure that it is operating legally? Again, where do you turn in case of a dispute? Furthermore, government regulations concerning private economic activity are changing at a dizzying pace.[98] Today's legal agreement may be illegal or heavily taxed tomorrow, though it is probably impossible to discern even today's laws, regulations, and taxes, which themselves may be contradictory.[99]

All of this uncertainty over who owns what and what transactions are legal exacts a heavy toll on the Russian economy. Consider the ownership uncertainty. A Western analogy may be useful here. Say that you wanted to build a home. What would you do if the only land that was available could be leased for at most one year? It is unlikely under these circumstances that you would build any appreciable home, since after a year the landowner could greatly increase the rent or simply kick you off the land. To be willing to build the house, you would need either to own the land yourself, or to have a very secure long-term lease. But in Russia, the existing 'ownership' of many (if not most) assets amounts to a short-term lease.[100] The government or perhaps some other firm or individual could step in and challenge your ownership claim. Even if the ownership claims were undisputed, though, transactions would still be difficult, since the rights of owners remain unclear. For land, for example, owners generally cannot sell their claim to any prospective buyer at full market value, at least through the end of 1993.

Uncertain property rights and continuing state controls lead to massive corruption, perhaps exceeding that of the pre-reform era, since there is more private activity and even more state officials who might be able to stake a claim. The effect of this widespread corruption on foreign investment in Russia is described by two Western economists, Andrei Shleifer and Robert W. Vishny:

> To invest in a Russian company, a foreigner must bribe every agency involved in foreign investment, including the foreign investment office, the relevant industrial ministry, the finance ministry, the executive branch of the local government, the legislative branch, the central bank, the state property bureau, and so on. The obvious result is that foreigners do not invest in Russia.[101]

With unclear ownership claims, a restricted set of rights accruing to legiti mate owners, and little protection offered by contract law, the incentives for even local owners to invest have been relatively paltry.[102] Credit is difficult to come by, since without clear ownership, assets cannot be utilized as collateral. Add to this the complication of trying to contract securely with a legitimate business such as a home builder, and the scope of the difficulties facing potential investors becomes almost overwhelming. Nevertheless, this state of affairs represents a considerable liberalization relative to the pre-reform situation. Then, the impediments to market activity were generally even higher, because most such activity was explicitly illegal.

## CONDUCTING BUSINESS IN TRANSITIONAL RUSSIA

The barriers to doing business in Russia are therefore substantial. In most cases they go well beyond the market restrictions and imperfections in developed Western market economies. Nevertheless, the barriers to Russian private enterprise are not insuperable. A lack of legal safeguards does not preclude private business. Alternatives to a state-provided court system with a well-developed body of business law can be devised: they are simply more costly. That is one of the reasons why the Russian market sector, widespread as it is, is much less efficient than the market economies of Western countries. The costs of alternative arrangements to help ensure contractual sanctity are so high that only the most valuable transactions are worth the effort, and those transactions that do pass muster must still bear the high transactions costs.

One mechanism that business people turn to in highly uncertain environments is a reliance on the reputation of their contracting partners. Businesses that develop good reputations are likely to find many other businesses that are willing to transact with them. Enterprises that acquire a bad reputation will lose business. The importance of developing a good reputation may be sufficient to induce a firm to fulfil contractual bargains, even if it could breach without incurring any legal penalties. Reputation effects are so potent that many if not most business deals in the US are not strictly legally binding.[103] The development of personal relationships between business people complements the effectiveness of reputation in enforcing contracts.

Ironically, in the pre-perestroika, Brezhnevian 'period of stagnation', reputation effects among business partners were quite strong. Extra-legal activity in those days generally involved state officials. The trading on state resources under their control was well understood and generally accepted.[104] Long-term relationships could then develop in a stable environment. Furthermore, failures to live up to a bargain could be punished by selective official enforcement of laws against economic crime.[105]

The personal relationships that developed for sub-rosa private economic activity during the Communist regime have been useful in providing the trust that helps to promote exchange in the current, less constrained atmosphere. Ministers and other former government and party officials have moved into the private sector.[106] This move has occurred not only because such officials are well-placed to become owners via spontaneous privatization, but also because they have developed valuable networks of reliable trading partners.

Pre-existing personal relationships have been particularly valuable during the Russian economic transition because other factors have helped to undermine the capacity for reputation concerns to lead to good business behaviour. For reputation to effectively protect contracts, contracting parties must believe that by behaving well in a business deal today, they will get more opportunities in the future. Uncertainty regarding the future government policies toward Russian business is so great, however, that entrepreneurs have little confidence that they will even be allowed to operate in the future. Such uncertainty creates, quite rationally, an interest in short-term profits among Russian entrepreneurs. Given a chance to breach a contract profitably, entrepreneurs might well do so, since the value of a good reputation is likely to be negligible, particularly if close personal ties have not been established. Understanding this, contracting parties avoid deals that are supported only by considerations of reputation.

Even without established reputations or personal connections, there exist avenues to extra-legal contractual protection. They are all used to some extent in the West, but are even more valuable within the legal vacuum in reforming Russia. One such avenue is what economists call 'vertical integration', in which a downstream firm and its upstream supplier merge. If the construction firm cannot trust the timber company, it could buy the timber company – or vice versa. Then both stages of the transaction would be controlled by the same parties, greatly diminishing incentives to cheat. Russian enterprises, even prior to reform, tended to display a much greater degree of vertical integration than their Western counterparts, and not simply as a consequence of central orders. Without recourse to effective alternative forms of contractual protection, Soviet firms found vertical integration a useful means to govern transactions and ensure supplies. In the current environment, vertical integration is again being pursued as a way to organize new business relationships.[107]

Another method that contracting parties use to protect contracts is to take measures that commit the parties to actually carrying out the contract terms. For example, in a loan contract the borrower could put up collateral for the loan. If the lender could actually seize the collateral in the event of default, the borrower would have powerful incentives to repay, and the lender would face little risk in making the loan.[108] Barter exchanges between enterprises, which are quite common in Russia – one estimate indicates that 15 per cent of all inter-enterprise trade in 1991 was conducted via barter[109] – are one way of arranging a transaction to minimize the possibilities for a contracting partner to breach.[110]

The importance of barter as a method to mediate transactions gives firms an incentive to produce a wide array of goods, as this will expand their opportunities for barter.[111] As a result, conglomerates have been forming in Russia. The benefits brought from pre-existing personal relationships have the effect of making the new conglomerates look similar to the old ministry structure – often the same people are in charge. Both barter and the semi-private recreation of conglomerates are often viewed as negative developments in Russia, since they seem to harken back to the planning regime.[112] But in a high uncertainty, high transaction cost environment, barter and conglomerates are generally desirable features, increasing the degree of marketization of the Russian economy.

Without a functioning state legal system, private parties may create their own alternative legal system. Western researcher Kathryn Hendley, for example, documents how 'some Russian enterprise managers are responding to the current crisis by creating internally consistent legal regimes (within their enterprises) that meet their needs'.[113] In some instances, extra-legal systems may take the form of organized crime. Just as citizens receive some benefits for their tax payments to official governments, criminal organizations often offer services in exchange for their 'tax' revenue. Contractual protection, debt collection, a reduction in official interference, or a more stable business environment are benefits that organized crime can provide, at least in some circumstances. The pervasive bribes noted earlier likewise help to grease the skids of private business, though at a high cost.

Thanks to alternatives to court-enforced contracts, business can be conducted in Russia's market economy. And thanks to spontaneous as well as official privatization, productive assets are at the disposal of private Russian citizens, who generally have strong incentives to use those assets profitably. Together, these conditions have kept the Russian economy from collapse, and even ameliorated many of the problems that existed before the Gorbachev-era spurt in private enterprise.

## AGRICULTURE

Take the case of agriculture. Throughout the 1990s there have been many reports of potential Russian famine during the wintertime. These fears have prompted calls from both Russian and Western leaders for Western food aid to Russia. Sometimes these calls are for very large amounts of food aid, and to some degree, these calls have been answered.

The agricultural problems that are often cited are not with Russian production, although the drop in grain production recorded in official statistics for 1991 is sometimes seen as a contributing factor. (The official 1992 harvest was considerably better, and 1990 brought a record grain harvest.) Rather the problems are suggested to lie in the harvesting, storage, and distribution system – the food infrastructure, if you will.[114] The food is said to rot in Russian fields and warehouses, without making it to market. In fact, the food-rotting problem may have been severe in the pre-Gorbachev Soviet Union, but de facto privatization and marketization has greatly reduced the scale of the difficulty.

Here is why. Under central planning, the farmers were paid based on their gross output (sometimes biased upwards by the weight of dirt and moisture), whether or not the food ever made it to market. Once the food entered the state distribution network and the farmers were credited with its production, they had no further interest in the crop. A similar story applied to the workers within the distribution system; as long as they were credited for moving so much food, they had little interest in the quality of the product, or whether it ever reached its intended destination. Consequently, food did rot in the field, in warehouses, and in railroad cars and trucks. Official Soviet sources indicated that at least one-third of the agricultural harvest was wasted before it reached the final consumer.[115] The free-price collective farm markets for food, though, made it likely that much of the food that was claimed to have rotted actually found an informal route to the market, just as in the current system.

Now, due to spontaneous privatization, any food that is lying around can be appropriated by someone and sold for private gain at market prices. Some of the nominally state-owned harvest can also be diverted in this fashion. Those who control the food can line their own pockets by ensuring that it gets to market. Ironically, this is particularly true if the reports of Russian food shortages are correct. If supplies are short, food will carry a high price, and people will be especially vigilant not to waste any food at their disposal.

Of course, the reports of Russian food shortages are misleading. The Russian state sector is (and in the past generally has been) experiencing food shortages, because its prices are fixed too low and state-sector suppliers would not keep the profits if there were any, at least prior to spontaneous privatization and price liberalization. But thanks to the legal free market in food, the increased production on private plots, and the large amount of food that has been shifted from the state sector to the private sector, there is not a shortage of food in the Russian economy overall.[116] The shifting of food from the state to the private sector even has public manifestations. Advertisements appeared in Russian newspapers in the fall of 1991 urging peasants to sell their crops at the private Moscow Commodity Exchange, instead of selling it to the state, and at prices ten times those the state would pay.[117] Russian farmers, both on the state-controlled collective farm fields and on the new private farms, are responding to market incentives.[118] This private activity, and not Western food aid, is why there has been no famine in Russia in the 1990s.

The agricultural sector demonstrates not just the amount of private economic activity in Russia, but also the considerable government intervention that limits the possibilities for development of the market economy. Consider some of the conditions in Russian agriculture at the end of 1993. Farmers continued to be compelled to deliver produce to state agencies at low prices. The allocation of farm inputs likewise remained to a large degree within the state sector. Access to credit is particularly important for private farmers, who incur many costs during the planting season but do not see much revenue until the harvest. Nevertheless, loans to farms were also 'monopolized by the Russian Agricultural Bank, which distributed state subsidies and shifted accounts among suppliers and buyers rather than acting as a banking system in the market-economy sense'.[119] Government officials can seize land that they determine is being used 'irrationally,' and over 162,000 hectares had been taken from peasant farmers in this fashion in the first nine months of 1993.[120] Though there has been a good deal of official 'denationalization' and privatization in the countryside – by March 1993, the state generally no longer had official title to the old state and collective farms – extensive government controls like the ones mentioned here continued to act as a brake on the transition to a normal market economy. Indeed, the controls made for a situation where many of the changes in agriculture were primarily cosmetic, and regulation had simply re-instituted the old system of central planning by other means.

## CONCLUSIONS

The tradition of private activity within the Russian economy is quite extensive. Recent official and spontaneous reforms, such as de facto privatization and increased private agriculture plots, have greatly increased the scope of free-price, private enterprise activity. High transaction costs substantially hinder, but do not preclude, the workings of the Russian market economy. Here once again is Russian economist Vitaliy Nayshul': 'If one looks at our economy in this way [i.e., focusing on the substantial private activity] it changes one's approach to reform. We don't need to build a market, since a market already exists. We need to develop the existing market.'[121]

How can the Russian government 'develop the existing market'? The key is to lower the transaction costs associated with private economic activity. A more thorough liberalization, the further dismantling of state controls in the economy, is the most important step in lowering transactions costs. In this sense, the Russian economy could greatly benefit from some benign neglect from the government. Other, active measures would also be useful; for example, the development of a workable system of contract law would facilitate private economic activity.

Another lesson for reform that is drawn from a recognition of the extensive pre-existing market activity is less optimistic: the results that can be expected from market-oriented reforms are limited, at least in the short run. The reason, again, is that the most valuable market undertakings are already being carried out in Russia. While important, reducing transactions costs will probably not create a tremendous, rapid improvement in the state of the Russian economy. This negative point is counter-balanced by a positive one, noted in the Introduction and developed in the following chapters: just as many of the gains from a market economy are already being achieved in Russia, many of the costs of a market economy are already being paid. Reform will alter the nature of these costs from implicit to explicit forms, but the total costs need not increase.

## THE RUSSIAN ECONOMIC PARADOX

Large-scale spontaneous market activity provides the answer to an old paradox that Westerners generally did not even acknowledge, much less attempt to unravel. The paradox concerned two contradictory images of Russian life, both frequently depicted on Western television and in Western newspapers during the Gorbachev years. The first image was that of Russian street scenes: seemingly well-dressed, well-fed people going about their daily business. One would have had to look hard to distinguish the pictures from those of the populace of any Western European country. The second image was that of state food stores, filled with only one item: empty glass cases.

How did Russian citizens generally dress nicely and get plenty to eat when there was little clothing or food in the state stores? The answer, of course, is that many Russian citizens did not rely extensively on state stores to procure their goods, and virtually all Russian citizens got some of their goods outside of the state sector. (The Western media focus on empty state stores was itself curious, since it could just as easily have provided photos of bustling, well-stocked, legal, and free price food markets that could generally be found just blocks from the empty state stores.) Recall that private plots accounted for approximately one-third of the agricultural products in the pre-reform system. Simultaneously, a good deal of the state-sector production was distributed outside of state stores, either directly through enterprises or through free markets. Thanks to both official and unofficial market activity, the condition of the state stores has not been a reliable indicator of the climate of the Russian economy. The Russian economic paradox was privately resolved.

## ORGANIZED CRIME

a good many economic and business principles that operate in the 'upper-world' must, with suitable modification for change in environment, operate in the underworld as well – just as a good many economic principles that operate in an advanced competitive economy operate as well in a socialist or a primitive economy.

Economist Thomas C. Schelling[122]

One of the frequently-lamented results of Russian economic reform has been the emergence of 'the Mafia'. The market economy in Russia is lawless, like the 'Wild West', and organized criminals control the distribution of commodities. The old system was destroyed and the new system was not created to replace it, allowing the Mafia to fill in the power vacuum.

Applying the general method explained in the Introduction to the phenomenon of organized crime provides a rather different perspective. First, organized crime existed in implicit form in pre-reform Russia and is now becoming explicit. Second, the extent to which organized crime continues to prevail in Russia is largely due to the partial nature of the reforms that have been undertaken so far.

Corruption and organized crime have a distinguished history in the pre-reform Soviet economy. While central planning mandated that the production and distribution of goods be largely the state's prerogative, executing the plan required human intervention. Many individuals therefore had effective control over state resources, and they could (illegally) exchange these resources, often via barter, at prices that were essentially market-determined. The examples of trading on control of state resources are well-known and virtually endless. Butchers could sell choice cuts of meat 'through the back door', and nearly all retail clerks could engage in similar activity.[123] Consumers could bribe officials to move to the front of queues for scarce commodities such as automobiles. Tolkachi, the supply expediters employed by state enterprises, used connections and bribes to secure supplies. Even housing, which was constitutionally guaranteed in the USSR to be distributed on the basis of need and with very low rents, nevertheless was allocated in large measure via formal and informal markets.[124]

As we have seen, the old system was one of near total corruption. The 'ring leaders' of this activity were party and state officials. They controlled access to the jobs (enterprise managers, for example) that led in turn to more direct access over goods. Just as important, party officials controlled the judicial system.[125] Bribes thus tended to flow up through the party and state hierarchy. Indeed, the privileges and access to goods and bribes that accompanied important state and party posts were well established, and the term 'mafia' was used freely.[126] Professor Gregory Grossman described the situation this way in 1977:

> At the very least one can deduce that the purchase and sale of positions for large sums of money signifies the profound institutionalization in the Soviet Union of a whole structure of bribery and graft, from the bottom to the top of the pyramid of power; that considerable stability of the structure of power is expected by all concerned; and that very probably there is a close organic connection between political-administrative authority, on the one hand, and a highly developed world of illegal economic activity, on the other.[127]

The systemic corruption in the former USSR thus can be characterized as an implicit form of organized crime, where the organization was provided through the Communist Party power structure. The bribes that flowed up the Communist Party hierarchy formed the tribute, the extortion money, or the informal taxes, that were a necessary part of doing business in the USSR.

Organized crime does not prosper in all environments. Mafias that are in the business of offering protection require a monopoly; otherwise, clients may be subject to competing claims for tribute, and less powerful mafias cannot actually provide protection. Organized crime likewise thrives under conditions where good substitutes for Mafia protection are not available. This is the role that illegality plays. An honest operator of a legitimate business in the US is less vulnerable to extortion because he or she can turn to the police.[129] An operator of an illegal bookmaking service cannot do likewise. The hold that organized crime had on the distribution of liquor in the Prohibition-era US did not survive the legal competition that emerged following the repeal of Prohibition.

Pre-reform Russia presented almost ideal conditions for organized crime. The Communist Party had a legal (and even supra-legal) monopoly on power and the judiciary, and there were few competitors willing to challenge it. Furthermore, virtually all private business was illegal. Bribes could thus be demanded for any private economic activity, and even legal activity within the confines of the plan was not exempt. In many instances, in order to receive timely supplies of sufficiently high quality, state enterprises had to bribe representatives of their suppliers, which were other state enterprises.

Economic reform has, to a degree, undermined both the monopoly and illegality conditions that help to promote organized crime. The expected stability of the power structure, noted by Grossman, unravelled during perestroika. The monopoly on power held by the Communist Power has disappeared. 'Private' protection rackets can now compete, among themselves and with the remnants of the old system, to attempt to gain monopoly rights. This competition is more visible – explicit – than was the

stable environment of the pre-reform system. The new competition in rac-
keteering can more accurately be described as an increase in 'disorganized'
crime, a breaking down of the old organizing structures, the Communist
Party and the central economic plan. Simultaneously, the increased visibility
of corruption is further enhanced by the new journalistic freedom.

The extent of Russian economic crime, whether organized or disorganized, is fostered by continuing controls over private enterprise, i.e., by
partial reforms. It is virtually impossible for a Russian entrepreneur to
operate entirely in accordance with the laws – in fact, the laws are themselves conflicting. While private economic activity remains to some degree
illegal, organized crime has an opportunity to exploit business people, as
they cannot generally turn to the police. And state officials continue to play
a role in organized crime. Russian economist Valeriy Rutgaizer reports on a
survey of 542 adults in Kiev, who were asked to choose one of seven
'definitions' (including 'no opinion') of the mafia. 'A criminal network with
accomplices in law-enforcement agencies and governmental organizations'
was the answer chosen by 80 per cent of the respondents, while no other
answer received more than a seven per cent share.[130] The former head of
government anti-monopoly efforts in Russia, Valery Chernogorodsky, in
comparing Russian with Western corruption, has said 'Corruption encom-
passes more people at the top [in Russia], not just a few. It goes in all
directions, from the bottom to the top of ministries – through bribes – and
from the top to the bottom – through power.'[131] State controls have tremendous staying power, owing to the large profits that powerful state officials
can glean from them.[132]

Slow movement on the development of contract law also contributes to
the prevalence of organize crime in Russia. If the state is unable to enforce
private contracts, business people must look elsewhere. Substitutes for state
enforcement include barter, collateral, or a reliance on personal connections
and reputation. Another alternative, however, is the mafia, and under some
conditions, this may be the best of the feasible options. Organized crime can
provide the contractual security that business people need to enter into deals
in the first place.

During a transition period in which the amount of private economic
activity increases sharply – despite a measure of illegality – organized
criminal activity can increase. More private economic activity means that
there are more potential victims for criminals to extort. Eventually, however,
the competition among potential extortionists – the increased difficulty in
maintaining a monopoly position – and better methods of defence for
private businesses, will reduce the amount of organized crime. The evolution of some protection rackets into Western-style security firms is already
apparent in Russia. (It should be kept in mind that in the US, the number of
private security guards far exceeds the number of public police officers.
Security is a normal, and often substantial, business expense.) With more

complete reform, private entrepreneurs will no longer be forced to behave illegally, and thus they will make less attractive mafia clients.

In at least two other respects partial reform has served to promote corruption indirectly. First, to the extent that the remaining regulations and controls make it difficult to create new businesses, the monopoly position of the old system cannot be successfully challenged. For example, the flower market in Moscow is widely rumoured to be controlled by 'the Mafia'.[133] This seems almost impossible, since there are seemingly thousands of small-scale flower sellers throughout Moscow street corners and subway stops. But the flowers are not grown in Moscow; rather, they are grown in more temperate climes, and transported to Moscow. The transportation stage is dominated by lingering monopoly elements of the old command system. By controlling the means of transportation, an organized network can set monopoly-level prices when it sells flowers to individual street corner entrepreneurs, without caring what prices are then charged by the sellers to their customers. (This account is indirectly substantiated by seasonal changes that appear to take place in the Moscow flower markets. Mafia control of the market for flowers is suspected during the winter months; in the summer, flowers can be grown in the Moscow area, undermining the transportation monopoly, and Moscow flower markets appear to be competitive.)

The second route by which partial reforms indirectly foster corruption follows from their deleterious effect on total income in Russia. While the mechanisms by which partial reforms reduce the size of the Russian economic pie will be examined later, the detrimental impact itself will encourage corruption. With low incomes and the impediments that continued state ownership place on the rapid adjustment of wages to market conditions, the temptation to augment one's income by corrupt means increases – particularly in occupations where direct non-monetary compensation is not a large part of income.[134] A traffic policeman in Moscow, in an interview where he claimed that the majority of his fellow workers took bribes, explained his own reasons for doing so[135]: 'You understand, in order not to take bribes you have to earn a normal salary. A salary that enables you to live decently so you don't have to wrack your brain about how you're going to feed your family.' The inertia of the old system ensures that the corruption continues. Even if he wanted to stop taking bribes, a policeman may not be able to refrain from doing so, as his superior will continue to expect a cut.[136]

Inertia contributes to continued corruption in one other respect as well. As corruption became institutionalized, it lost much of its moral taint. Russians are surprisingly tolerant of employee theft, for example. A December 1989 survey indicated that a majority (52 per cent) of respondents did not condemn workplace theft.[137] Sociologist Vladimir Shlapentokh notes a 1983 study showing that 79 per cent of the Moscow workers surveyed refused to condemn pilfering of state property from the workplace.[138]

Nevertheless, Russians are quite apt to believe that the mafia is the cause of their difficult economic conditions.[139] During economic reforms in which the distribution of income is changing rapidly, people who find their relative position slipping – or fear such a slip – are likely to ascribe the relative success of others to nefarious means, and the visibility of corruption suggests an obvious scapegoat. Ethnic hostilities and the perceived ethnic homogeneity of 'mafia' groups may also contribute to such charges. And the perception of extensive organized crime is itself undoubtedly harmful to the Russian economy, as potential entrepreneurs refrain from opening businesses, or limit the scope of their business activities, in order to avoid dealing with 'the Mafia'.

The presence of organized crime is virtually dictated by the continuing illegality that plagues private enterprise, the absence of contract law and the difficulty of privately challenging state monopolies. Further liberalization of economic life will leave less, not more, scope to organized criminals, dependent as they are on government monopoly and the illegality of private economic activity. Organized crime, like its companion government monopoly, will see its sphere of influence dwindling to 'normal' Western levels as reform proceeds.[140] In the meantime, a corrupt market is probably preferable to no market.

# Chapter 3

# Price liberalization and inflation

**TRANSITION ECON 101**

Free the Prices!

While not exactly the kind of slogan that is going to inspire crowds, this nostrum is a rallying cry for development and reform economists. There's an old joke that says 'If you laid all the world's economists end-to-end, they wouldn't reach a conclusion.'[141] 'Free the Prices' is one bit of economic wisdom that gives the lie to the jest. Economists differ about when in a reform prices should be liberalized (before or after privatization?), and whether some prices should remain fixed for a while (say, food and gasoline), but within the Western economics fellowship, it is widely believed that almost all prices should be free, somehow, some day.

The theoretical economic argument in favour of free prices is both compelling and now familiar, being the chief narrative of Economics 101. Controlled prices in centrally-planned economies lead to resource misallocations, most particularly, the production of the wrong goods. Such resource misallocations can be partly ameliorated through second economy activity. A more complete solution, however, lies in that most basic of reforms – freeing prices. Then the advantages to individuals of various alternatives would be related, through the invisible hand, to the usefulness of the alternatives to society.

Prices can be freed at a single stroke. All it requires is a government declaration to that effect. (The Russians came close to implementing immediate price freedom on 2 January 1992, as part of the reform measures undertaken by then Deputy Prime Minister Yegor Gaidar.[142]) With complete price freedom, the only other reform that is necessary to secure most of the benefits of free markets is that people be allowed to respond to those prices. There is no sense in freeing prices while constraining the reactions of entrepreneurs and managers to those prices. Like the former Soviet Union's contingent at the 1992 Olympics, free enterprise and free prices are a unified team, split up only at the economy's peril.

If this Transition Econ 101 wisdom is so potent, why are not all economists, politicians, and everyday people in favour of immediately freeing prices? There are two types of reasons. One is concerned with the potential distributional impact. While freeing prices may be a good thing on average, there may be some deserving or politically influential people who are made worse off by the action, and there may be some disreputable people who would benefit greatly from free prices. The other type of objection to freeing prices is the fear of inflation. If prices are free to change, then open inflation – a rise in the prices of goods generally – may occur, and typically does occur in modern market economies. Both of these objections are rendered much less powerful when the alternative of continuing to control prices during a market-oriented reform is examined closely. The thrust of the counter-argument is that the concerns of inflation and distributional impact apply, perhaps with even more force, in the pre-reform, fixed-price setting.

## INFLATION, REPRESSED AND OPEN

First, consider the inflation argument from the perspective of a Russian economic policy-maker in the fixed-price regime. In other words, play the economist's game, and assume that you did not know that Russian inflation following price liberalization approached hyper-inflationary levels. (This suspension of knowledge will become more difficult to sustain as you encounter the arguments of the next few sections. If you are impatient for a discussion of the inflation that actually did occur, you may want to skip ahead to the 'Causes of inflation' section.) What should you expect to happen following price liberalization?

The most frequent concern was, in fact, that a massive inflation, perhaps 1000 per cent or more, would immediately follow price freedom. When price controls were lifted, so the story went, Russian citizens would show up at stores, 'waving fistfuls of roubles'.[143] Their subsequent spending spree would result in too many roubles chasing too few goods, rapidly pushing up prices and fuelling inflation.

The logic behind the inflationary scenario starts with the 'rouble over-hang'.[144] The amount of roubles in the hands of the Soviet population grew substantially in the 1980s and early 1990s – much faster than the amount of goods in the state stores. Therefore, with fixed prices in the state stores, the ratio between the public's cash holdings and the total value of goods in the state stores, measured at the fixed prices, rose. Citizens of the former Soviet Union had the ready means to purchase any goods that became available in the state stores at low fixed prices. When goods were available in the low-price state sector, Soviet shoppers would rush to buy them (if only for resale at higher free prices), except for goods that were so undesirable that even at rock bottom prices, no one wanted them. The result of this rush to buy engendered by the ready cash was reduced availability of goods in the state sector, and longer queues when goods were available.

(Incidentally, on a smaller scale, a similar phenomenon sometimes occurs in Western markets. A bagel shop in Durham, North Carolina, for instance, offers free bagels to customers who say 'Happy Birthday' to the clerk on the anniversary of the store's opening. Although I am a regular customer of the store, I have yet to procure a free bagel: the queue on such days usually winds outside of the store, and a person might have to wait half an hour or more for a couple of 'free' bagels.)

Diminished availability of goods in the fixed price sector, and long queues when goods are available, are symptoms of what economists call 'repressed inflation'. It is repressed, instead of US-style open inflation, since the official Soviet prices were fixed. The inflationary concern with price liberalization is that the 'rush to buy' evidenced in the fixed price regime would suddenly get converted into a massive open inflation, with seemingly no limit on the upward path of prices.

The inflation scenario that has just been described has apparently been borne out in the reality of post-price liberalization Russia. Many prices were liberalized, and a galloping inflation ensued. But this appearance is some-what deceiving. The inflation that Russia experienced after price decontrol is not a direct result of liberalization. Liberalizing prices simply ensured that the inflationary pressures would manifest themselves in an open, as opposed to repressed, manner.

The argument that price liberalization did not create inflation turns, not surprisingly, on the understanding of the relevant prices facing Russian consumers prior to price liberalization. The actual prices for goods were not simply the nominal state prices. In general, Russian consumers were not guaranteed that goods would be available at the nominal state price. Un-certainty in the supply of goods forced consumers to engage in extensive searching, which is itself costly. These high search costs represented addi-tional payments that consumers had to make to purchase goods in the state sector, and should be included when determining the actual prices facing shoppers. Nor was finding a good in the state store the end of the story. Russian consumers, as is well-known, often had to endure long queues to purchase goods. Like searching for goods, waiting is an activity that is costly to shoppers. The costs of waiting in lines should also be considered when judging the pre-reform prices facing Russian shoppers – likewise when judging the prices of 'free' bagels facing Durham breakfast aficionados.

Virtually all goods that were occasionally in state stores were also avail-able on free markets, though at prices that customarily were higher than the nominal prices in the state stores. These free markets included both legal markets, such as the collective farm markets for food, as well as illegal but tolerated black markets. A Russian consumer interested in buying a good decided whether to purchase the good on the free market or in the state sector. If the good was cheaper to purchase in the state sector, when all the non-pecuniary costs of searching and queuing were taken into account, then no one would ever use the free market, and the free market price would fall. Since people shopped in both the state sector and the free markets, on average the free market price reflected the true costs of shopping in the state sector. This is a point worth repeating – free market prices were good indicators of the actual costs of goods facing Russian consumers, even prior to price liberalization. In the free markets, these costs were paid in roubles (or foreign currency); in the state sector, the costs were borne partly in roubles, and partly in time for searching and queuing.

What happens to actual prices when price controls are lifted? The nominal rouble prices in the state sector by and large rise. Simultaneously, though, the costs of queuing and searching nearly disappear. The actual costs of purchasing goods, measured by free market prices, need not increase with market freedom. The official price reform that occurred in the Russian state sector on 2 April 1991, raising state-controlled prices by an average of 60 per cent, bears out this contention. Free market prices did not rise when the nominal prices in the state sector were raised A similar story applies to the 2 January 1992 partial price liberalization – free market prices did not jump upward on 2 January 1992, despite large increases in the prices charged in state stores.[145] The fear of an immediate inflation accompanying price liberalization was unfounded and unrealized.

The measured rate of inflation in the Russian economy for April 1991 and January 1992 was very high (63.5 per cent and 245 per cent, respectively), reflecting the large increase in state-controlled prices.[146] Nevertheless, the actual costs of acquiring goods did not rise substantially, as witnessed by the relative price stability in free markets. The conventionally-measured rate of inflation is therefore not a good indicator of whether actual prices consumers pay are rising during a market-oriented transition. Price indices are an example of how misleading statistics can be when starting from a centrally-planned system.

## ONE-TIME PRICE INCREASES VERSUS CONTINUING INFLATION

Sometimes a distinction is drawn between a one-time price increase and a continuing inflation. If all prices were to double tomorrow in the US, and remain more-or-less constant after that, the episode would be characterized as a one-time price increase. A continuing inflation, on the other hand, consists of an ongoing increase in the price level.

A common suggestion is that price liberalization in a reforming socialist economy consists of a one-time adjustment in the price level. The trick, then, is to prevent the one-time increase from initiating a continuing inflation. The point of the previous section, however, is that price liberalization does not really represent an increase, even a one-time increase, in the price level. Nominal state prices do adjust upwards, but the relevant prices facing consumers do not. Liberalization brings a one-time measured price increase, but not a one-time actual price increase. Still, the admonition to prevent liberalization from launching a continuing inflation remains relevant, regardless of the view taken towards the initial price liberalization.

## COSTS OF OPEN INFLATION

The inflationary argument against price liberalization (or perhaps the one-time price increase argument against price liberalization) might still be compelling if the costs of pre-reform repressed inflation are lower than the costs of open inflation. But, as I hope to demonstrate, the opposite case is more likely, particularly when the amount of inflation is substantial: repressed inflation is more costly than open inflation.

What are the costs of open, Western-style inflation? Perhaps surprisingly, it is not easy to identify social costs resulting from open inflation. Here is why. Imagine you wake up tomorrow, and find that all prices in the economy have gone up by a factor of ten. Simultaneously, though, your earnings increase by the same factor. The currency that was in your pocket miraculously has a face value ten times what it was yesterday. All of your assets (and liabilities) are worth ten times as much – your car, your house, your savings account, your credit card payments, your pension, your insurance policy. What is the net result, in terms of your budget, of this virtually unprecedented inflation of 1000 per cent in one night? Precisely nothing. You can still afford the new car that you were planning to buy. Paperback books still cost about the same as movies, though the books are still better. You still make less money than your spouse. Nothing has changed, except the price level is ten times higher.

Of course, inflation does not raise the prices of everything by the same percentage, and this is where some of the difficulties enter. First, the face value on currency has an unfortunate tendency to remain unchanged even as prices rise, so inflation undermines the value of cash. The value of savings in banks, to the extent that the interest paid does not keep track with inflation, is also prone to dwindle during inflationary periods. Savers might therefore not be very pleased by inflation. The bank is a little more pleased, because it was able to use the savings when they were worth more, and when depositors withdraw money, the bank can pay out cheaper dollars. Because all prices and values do not rise by the same percentage, inflation redistributes wealth; in the example given, it redistributed some savers' wealth to the bank. The savings scenario is one example of a common redistribution brought about by inflation, that from lenders to borrowers. If loans are not indexed, i.e., the amount to be repaid is not multiplied upwards by the inflation rate, borrowers get to pay back their loans with less valuable dollars. So, the bank won't be all that pleased with inflation, even if it does gain from savings accounts, because it loses out on all of its outstanding, non-indexed loans.[147]

Because of such wealth redistributions, people will be reluctant to hold cash if they expect inflation to be high in the future. They will, rather, rapidly convert their cash into goods: both consumer goods and assets that will be expected to rise in price as the price level rises, such as stocks, gold, jewellery, and art. Alternatively, they may convert their domestic currency into foreign currencies that are not expected to suffer from high inflation. Furthermore, people will only loan money (or enter into other long-term commitments) if the agreement is indexed to the future inflation rate. (The indexing could be implicit, i.e., the interest rate charged could include a premium for expected future inflation.)

While one individual can unload cash by buying goods, the cash must go to someone else, so society as a whole will still have the same amount of cash. If the person from whom I buy jewellery is also afraid of future inflation, she will try to quickly convert her new cash holdings into some other good. This continual process of attempting to unload cash because of fears of future inflation will result in a 'run' on goods, and the run itself will cause prices to rise. The widespread expectation of future inflation results in future inflation, just as the expectation of a shortage of toilet paper will cause people to quickly stock up on toilet paper, perhaps creating (at least in the short run) the feared shortage. Extensive fears of inflation are well-grounded, because of the self-fulfilling nature of such fears.

The story above suggests another cost of inflation, namely, having to think about it. In a high-inflation environment, people have to continually evaluate how best to shield themselves from losing wealth via inflationary redistribution. This may result in minor changes such as more frequent trips to the bank to minimize cash held in hand (assuming the bank interest partially compensates for the inflation), or in major changes such as a complete abandonment of the local currency in favour of either foreign currencies or barter transactions.[148] Greater concern by individuals over matters financial then translates into more financial services firms, more of society's labour and capital are devoted to financial management under conditions of high inflation. Perhaps, as a famous economist once said of monopoly profits, the best feature of a non-inflationary environment is a quiet life.[149]

There is yet another element of a quiet life that inflation undermines. Consider again the story of the overnight rise in all prices, wages, and values by a factor of ten. The fact that nothing changes under these circumstances, other than the price level, indicates that the level of prices is not important for decision making. What is important, rather, is the relative price of goods, the price of a movie relative to the price of a paperback. Candy bars once cost a quarter, and now they cost 50 cents, but I still eat about the same number of candy bars, since the price of candy bars relative to other goods has remained roughly the same. If no other prices (or my income) had changed, but the price of candy bars increased by a factor of two, then I would eat more ice cream and fewer candy bars. In a low inflationary environment, when I walk into the store and see that the price of candy bars has increased significantly, I can be fairly sure that the price of candy bars relative to ice cream has gone up, since the general price level is stable. It is then easy to process the information concerning the increased relative price of candy bars, and appropriately adjust my consumption of ice cream and candy bars. In a situation of high and variable inflation, though, when I see that the price of candy bars has gone up, I do not know whether that increase reflects a general price rise, or whether the relative price of candy bars has indeed risen. I have to check other prices, such as those for ice cream, other food products, and even my earnings, to determine to what extent the increased nominal price for candy bars represents a relative increase. Inflation therefore undermines, to some degree, the information contained in price changes.[150] The information is still there, but it requires more effort to ferret out and process. Lives are less quiet.

The variability of inflation rates and the different timing of price increases among goods and services is the source of another cost that can be attributed to open inflation. As Western economist Rudiger Dornbusch has noted, 'An environment of high and unstable inflation deters productive economic activity. . . . Spurious gains and losses related to the vagaries of inflation rather than to effort and productivity become the rule.'[151] Why bother to work hard when the return you receive depends more on something outside your control – the 'vagaries of inflation' – than on your labour input? Investment, then, can be undermined by persistent inflation, hindering long-run economic growth.[152]

There is one more important cost associated with open inflation in a market economy, and that is the cost of reversing the inflationary process. Nothing in inflation is more unbecoming than the leaving it. Substantial reductions in inflation in market economies are generally accompanied by a recession. The costs of recessions, with their reductions in output and their increased unemployment, are quite high. It is estimated that the cost of a reduction in the US inflation rate of one per cent requires a four per cent reduction in one year's output.[153] For a meagre one per cent reduction in the inflation rate, our country, by this calculation, must pay a sum that is currently equal to nearly $230 billion.

**COSTS OF REPRESSED INFLATION**

In contrast to open inflation, repressed inflation takes various forms, all of which were present in the pre-reform Russian economy. These forms include: (1) lessened availability of goods in the state (fixed-price) sector, (2) longer queues when goods are available in the state stores; (3) deterioration in the quality of state-sector goods; (4) disappearance of low-priced varieties of the output assortment in the state stores; and (5) higher prices (i.e., open inflation) in the parallel, free markets. Lowering the quality of a good while maintaining the same fixed price (repressed inflation (3)) represents a hidden price increase. Getting rid of low-price varieties (4), for example, by representing a product that is only marginally changed as an 'improvement' and therefore deserving of a higher fixed price, is another form of hidden price increase. Along with the open inflation in the free markets (5), these varieties of hidden price rises are not uncommon in Western market economies.

Repressed inflation is costly. Lessened availability of goods in the state sector means that the time and effort devoted to search for state sector goods increases. Finding goods in the Russian state sector, in fact, became an increasingly difficult task during perestroika. 'By October 1990, of the 115 consumer goods that the State Committee on Statistics (Goskomstat) follows, not one was still freely available.'[154] Once state sector goods are located, the time spent waiting in queues to purchase them expands with an increase in repressed inflation. A large amount of repressed inflation results in almost mind-boggling shopping costs. An unofficial Soviet source estimated that, on average, 25 per cent of the waking time of every Soviet adult was spent in queues.[155] Repressed inflation in the state sector therefore results in an enormous waste of time, as searching and queuing costs rise. The simultaneous open inflation in the free market sector of centrally-planned economies has costs similar to the costs of open inflation in market economies discussed above. The incentive to get rid of currency by shifting into goods and assets, a characteristic of open inflation, also occurs under repressed inflation. Not only does currency lose its value as free market prices rise, but the longer queues and dwindling availability in the state sector induce consumers to buy as large a quantity as possible when they finally get the opportunity to make a state-sector purchase. While the incentive to buy in bulk is a feature of the economy whenever state-sector prices are fixed below market-clearing levels, it becomes more prominent as repressed inflation increases the differential between state and free market prices. Inventories move out of state warehouses and retail outlets into private homes and apartments. A frequently-cited paradox of the Russian economy was that the stores were empty but refrigerators were filled.

One additional feature of repressed inflation worth noting is the increase in corruption that accompanies it. As the fixed prices in the state stores fall further and further behind prices in the free market sector, the incentives for individuals to divert goods from the state to the free market sector increase. Misappropriation of state goods and assets – a form of spontaneous privatization – increases in situations of continuing repressed inflation.

The existence of channels to evade state price controls has some interesting implications for the costs of repressed inflation associated with the time wasted on searching and queuing for goods. Some goods such as cigarettes, meat, clothing, and most other everyday consumer goods, can be fairly easily, if illegally, diverted into the free-price sector. Other goods are more difficult to divert. It is not easy, for example, to resell electricity supplied to your home, even if the electricity would command a high price in a free market. (Electricity could be implicitly resold, though, through the production and sale of goods produced using the cheap electricity, à la energy prices and Polish tropical flowers.) Nor can many services, such as haircuts, be resold, though perhaps the providers of services can spontaneously privatize.

As repressed inflation becomes severe, two competing effects emerge. In the markets for goods where diversion is not extremely costly, more and more diversion will occur, until the state sector becomes largely irrelevant.[156] In these markets, the 'time' costs of repressed inflation are shaped like the Gateway Arch in St. Louis, when plotted against the degree of repressed inflation. Low levels of repressed inflation are not that costly (one end of the arch) because the queues are short. Moderate levels of repressed inflation become quite costly (the middle of the arch) because of the long queues and search costs imposed on shoppers. High levels of repressed inflation do not carry high time costs, however (the other end of the arch). At high levels of repressed inflation, the goods disappear from the state sector, so the queues also disappear, and the repressed inflation is informally converted into open inflation. Of course, the costs of diverting these goods out of the state sector must also be borne. These costs are not inconsequential, else the diversion would have occurred even at low levels of repressed inflation.[157]

For goods that cannot easily be diverted out of the state sector, however, the situation is different. Higher levels of repressed inflation impose higher and higher costs in terms of the misallocation of resources. People continue to use electricity as if the costs were, say, one rouble per kilowatt hour (the fixed nominal price), when the actual costs are, say, 100 roubles per KWH. The state subsidy that is required for the electric utility to remain operating continues to increase as repressed inflation increases. While the information carried by relative prices in a market economy is a bit noisier with open inflation than with a stable price level, at least the information is there. With repressed inflation, the official relative prices cannot adjust at all, and resources become increasingly misallocated.

## INFLATION COSTS AND PRICE LIBERALIZATION

Price liberalization, i.e., freeing state sector prices (as opposed to simply raising their fixed levels), converts repressed inflation into open inflation. Will such a conversion increase the social costs of inflation? The 'flight from domestic currency' is similar under both regimes. The unquiet life, the necessity to think about strategies to best shield oneself from inflation, and the difficulties in assessing relative prices, are likewise similar in situations of repressed and open inflation. The major differences between these two types of inflation, in terms of net social cost, are the time and other resources wasted under repressed inflation. A conversion from repressed to open inflation frees up most of the hours spent in an effort to procure consumer goods. This time can then be put to other productive uses, which include remunerative employment as well as relaxation with friends or family. A switch from repressed to open inflation also reduces the misallocation of resources endemic to fixed price regimes. Putting aside potential effects on the distribution of income, an economy is better off with open inflation than with the equivalent amount of repressed inflation, at least when the rate of inflation is moderate to high.

## DISTRIBUTIONAL IMPACTS

While the argument above suggests that society as a whole is better off with open rather than repressed inflation, some (and perhaps even most) individuals may be better off in a regime of repressed inflation than they would be in a regime of open inflation. In the pre-reform Russian state sector, the full price of a consumer good was paid partly in roubles and partly in time spent searching and queuing for goods. Under free prices, almost the entire cost of goods is paid in roubles. People with few roubles but with a good deal of time are therefore likely to be better off (at least in the short run) with fixed prices than they would be with free prices. Given the enormous movement away from the state sector that occurs at high levels of repressed inflation, and given that those who choose to wait in state sector queues have the lowest-valued alternative uses of their time, possibly even a majority of the remaining state store shoppers may find that they are temporarily made worse off by a movement to market prices.

For consumer goods that can be easily diverted into free markets, the distributional impact of moving from repressed to open inflation is less pronounced the higher the rate of repressed inflation. Perhaps this is why the much feared social unrest that was predicted to follow price liberalization never took place in Russia, following the 2 January 1992 price liberalization. In fact, the popularity of President Boris Yeltsin's economic programme rose after the price reform.[158] Repressed inflation had reached such proportions, and goods were so widely unavailable in the state shops, that relatively few people actually lost in the conversion to open inflation, at least in the realm of consumer goods. Simultaneously, the large resource misallocation costs that occur for those goods that cannot be easily diverted are such an obvious hindrance to economic growth that popular support for price freedom increases. It was claimed at the beginning of this chapter that the slogan 'Free the Prices' was not likely to inspire crowds. But in late 1991 there were demonstrations in Moscow by supporters of radical reform who favoured price liberalization.

Still, price liberalization hurts some people. While it is impossible to know precisely who will be hurt by price liberalization, some groups are more likely to suffer than others.[159] People with low monetary incomes, those without access to consumer goods through channels other than retail shops, and those who had a relatively large amount of time available for state-sector shopping, were liable to be hurt by the move to free prices. Retirees, known as 'pensioners' in Russia, were particularly likely to exhibit these characteristics. (Individuals who were able to make large profits by diverting state sector goods to the free market also benefited from repressed inflation.) Low official state sector prices therefore served as a safety net, albeit a frustrating one in light of the searching and queuing costs, for those with low monetary incomes – an implicit welfare system. The conversion to open inflation will leave these people in dire circumstances, unless this implicit welfare system is replaced with an explicit system. As noted in the introduction, moving from implicit to explicit inflation requires a movement from an implicit to explicit welfare system, if the poorer and most vulnerable members of society are to see their living standards protected.

## ALTERNATIVES TO PRICE LIBERALIZATION

Repressed inflation occurs when the fixed state sector prices fall ever further behind market-clearing levels. In these circumstances, the demand for goods by consumers (measured at the fixed prices) is growing faster than the supply, creating shortages in the state sector. Price liberalization, the elimination of price controls, almost immediately ends the bulk of repressed inflation by replacing it with its open sibling. State-sector nominal prices increase until demands and supplies balance. The movement to free prices is a necessity in nurturing a productive and above-ground market economy, and the Russians and Eastern Europeans have indeed largely embraced price liberalization. But there are strategies other than price liberalization that can be employed to reduce repressed inflation, and the Soviet government tried at least three of them in 1991.

One obvious method of reducing repressed inflation is to increase the supply of goods, as opposed to decreasing the demand. Not surprisingly, in the Soviet Union there was continuous pressure on workers and enterprises to increase output. Exhortations to accelerate production, which were once able to motivate dedicated Communists to tremendous efforts, had with time lost most of their impact. (Incidentally, Stalin noted that the pressure to produce brought about by repressed inflation had its advantages: 'The increase of mass consumption [purchasing power] constantly outstrips the growth of production and pushes it forward.'[160]) Without material rewards for doing so, or punishment for failure to do so, workers had little incentive to increase output. Material incentives, in the form of paying workers more money for greater output, were also insufficient, since without corresponding increases in the supply of consumer goods, the higher wages simply fuelled repressed inflation. Furthermore, increased output is not always good, if the output that is being produced is not particularly valuable. Thus, the opportunities to battle repressed inflation under the planning system through increased state sector production were fairly limited by the time of the Gorbachev era. The eventual emphasis on price liberalization and privatization in Russian reform is partly explained by the dearth of palatable alternatives.

Two other strategies adopted by the Soviet government in 1991 to battle repressed inflation focused on the demand for goods in the state sector. One strategy involved raising the state-sector prices, and the second strategy entailed an effort to reduce the level of market-clearing prices.

The Soviet government raised (but did not liberalize) the fixed prices in the state shops by an average of 60 per cent on 2 April 1991. Simultaneously, savings accounts, pensions, student stipends, and other nominal accounts were indexed upwards to partially compensate for the higher prices.[161] For example, savings account balances were increased by 40 per cent.[162] This reform was somewhat successful in reducing repressed inflation. Queues in the state shops were fewer and shorter, the availability of goods increased, and there were many complaints about high prices. Continued inflation (brought about by factors discussed later in this chapter), however, undermined these temporary gains in the battle against repressed inflation, and by the fall of 1991 the condition of the state shops was as bad as it was prior to the 2 April price reform.

The controlled price rise of April 1991 was actually the second reform made by the Soviet government that year attempting to reduce the amount of repressed inflation. The earlier effort was aimed at lowering the level of market-clearing prices by taking purchasing power out of the hands of Soviet citizens. In January 1991, a monetary reform sought to withdraw from circulation all 50 and 100 rouble notes. (These were the highest denominations at the time.) Individuals who had more than a small number of these bills had to verify that their currency was legally obtained in order to exchange it for other denominations of roubles. Since many black marketeers were suspected of having high rouble balances that were illegally earned, there were hopes that this reform would eliminate some 40 billion roubles from circulation. The monetary confiscation was an abject failure, however. Only seven billion roubles were collected (about one per cent of the existing money stock), and what little faith there had been in the rouble was undermined.[163] And as with the 2 April 1991 price rise, even had the monetary confiscation been more successful, the achievement would have been short-lived, as the continual printing of roubles throughout 1991 guaranteed further inflation.[164]

## COMPARING STRATEGIES TO COMBAT REPRESSED INFLATION

Reducing repressed inflation by controlled price increases or monetary reforms shares one desirable feature with price liberalization. All of these reforms tend to reduce the demand for goods. Price liberalization and controlled price rises reduce demand simply because nominal state sector prices are higher. A well-designed and implemented monetary reform (unlike the Soviet attempt at currency confiscation) reduces demand because with fewer roubles and the same amount of goods, each of the existing roubles is more valuable. With each rouble worth more, the old fixed prices appear more expensive. (An important qualifying point is that the monetary reform must be viewed as a one-time adjustment, lest people think that the government will confiscate their currency again in the future, reducing the incentive to hold the currency.)

Despite the similar impact on the demand for goods, in other respects price liberalization is preferable to price or monetary reform. Controlled increases in prices do not allow relative prices to adjust, so resources are still misallocated as people respond to the economically-meaningless fixed relative prices. State-owned enterprises, to the extent that their behaviour remains centrally-controlled, may not even be able to respond to the price changes at all. Continuing price controls imply that desirable future changes in the answers to the 'what goods to produce' question will not be forthcoming. The higher prices that result from price or monetary reform do reduce demand, but there is little supply response, and what response there is may not be beneficial, since relative prices remain inappropriate. Alternatively, price liberalization coupled with free enterprise provides strong incentives for producers to respond to the higher prices in socially-valuable ways.

One interesting comparison between price liberalization and other price reforms is with respect to the distributional impact. Presumably, raising state-controlled prices on 2 April 1991 harmed the same people who were later harmed by the 2 January 1992 partial price liberalization – primarily those who had relatively more time than roubles.[165] Alternatively, the distributional impacts of the January 1991 monetary confiscation were quite arbitrary. While ostensibly aimed at black marketeers and shady foreigners who allegedly (and nonsensically) had spirited hoards of roubles abroad, those who were harmed were likely to be just average citizens who, through thrift and hard work, had managed to garner some savings. The black marketeers had probably diversified into jewellery, art, foreign currency, etc., long before the 50 and 100 rouble note confiscation. At the Rezina plant in Moscow, American researchers Michael Burawoy and Kathryn Hendley noted that 'For three days, the enterprise almost came to a standstill while everyone worried about how they were going to change their money.'[166] The two eventually useless 1991 reforms aimed at combating repressed inflation without price liberalization were not exempt from generating distributional changes, and yet they were implemented. Arguments against price liberalization based on its potentially adverse distributional impacts were therefore somewhat undermined in Russia. The Soviet government had already demonstrated its willingness to impose distributional costs in hopeless reform attempts.

It is far from obvious that price liberalization is any more unpopular than the alternative methods of combating repressed inflation. The prolonged Soviet experience with fixed prices conditioned Russians to believe that nominal state-sector prices were simply decided by the government, because, of course, they were. High prices, then, were perceived as being due to bad government decisions. When the price of a good rises in the West, people do not usually blame the government.[167] But in the Soviet Union, people did, and the government was so fearful of this blame that it generally avoided increasing the prices of important consumer goods.[168] A reform plan announced in May of 1990 by then Soviet Prime Minister Nikolai Ryzhkov proposed future increases in the price of bread. The plan was quickly scuttled due to the hoarding and popular discontent that it prompted. Without the supply response and improved resource allocation that price liberalization offers, the demand reduction that accompanies administered price rises has limited popular appeal. Swedish Sovietologist Anders Åslund quotes a prominent Soviet journalist: 'An increase in prices has never led to anything good.'[169] While some people may rally behind a 'Free the Prices' banner, 'Raise the Prices' is unlikely to attract comparable support.

The perception that higher prices are simply a result of bad government policy poses a problem for price liberalization as well, since the first obvious effect of price liberalization is a large increase in most state-sector nominal prices. In the city of Barnaul in Siberia, President Yeltsin felt compelled to explain to shoppers who were distressed by higher prices a few months after the price liberalization, 'As for the prices – Moscow does not dictate them any more. It is the market price.'[170] A well-implemented price liberalization should highlight this message – before the liberalization. The message may carry more weight if liberalization is viewed by the populace as a dramatic break with the past, as was the case in the Polish 'big bang' of 1 January 1990. Government responsibility for prices can then be relegated, in the minds of consumers, to the dustbin of history, a feature of the 'old system'. Nevertheless, the Soviet administered price rise of 2 April 1991 and the Russian partial price liberalization of 2 January 1992, were not met with widespread protests. As noted, this suggests that the pre-reform situation had itself become intolerable, and that some of the benefits of price liberalization, such as the ending of queues and the return of goods to the shops, were themselves advantageous enough to limit popular discontent.

## CAUSES OF INFLATION

If inflation, either open or repressed, is so bad, why is it so common? In a market economy, continuing inflation is fuelled by government monetary policy.[171] In attempting to reduce unemployment and keep interest rates low, the government may increase the money supply so quickly that inflation eventually results. But a short-term economic stimulus is indeed likely. So one cause of inflation is government monetary policies that, consciously or not, trade off perceived short-term gains for long-run inflation. There is also a pro-inflation constituency. The redistributions created by inflation imply that many individuals, such as borrowers, may benefit from an unanticipated inflation. As a large borrower, the government may itself have an additional incentive to inflate, in order to reduce the real value of its loan repayments.

The monetary policies that lead to inflation can be artefacts of a government's fiscal policy. Governments require resources in order to operate. To gain control over resources, the government in a market economy has three basic weapons – other than direct confiscation – at its disposal. First, it can collect taxes from private citizens.[172] Second, it can borrow money from the public (including foreigners) through the issue and sale of government bonds. (To pay back the money in the future, the government can again resort to one of the three methods of gaining control over resources.) Third, the government can print new money, and spend the money on goods from the private sector. This printing of money will allow the government to gain the resources, and the loss of resources coupled with the increased cash held by the private sector results in inflation. The money that people hold will be worth less as the government prints new money for its own purposes. This sort of inflation is an implicit tax, and it may be a particularly attractive tax from a government's point of view, in that it does not require the passage of a tax bill in order to take effect.[173]

If a government collects enough money from explicit tax revenues to cover its expenditures, then it will not be compelled to fuel inflation by printing additional currency.[174] (It may still choose to inflate, perhaps to influence the unemployment rate or interest rates.) But if government expenditures exceed government revenue, that is, if the government runs a budget deficit, then the shortfall will have to made up either by borrowing or by printing money. If the government elects to print money, then the budget deficit will lead to inflation.

## BUDGET DEFICITS AND INFLATION DURING TRANSITION

Why should there be a budget deficit, money creation, and inflation in a fixed-price, centrally-planned economy? The government would seem to be able to control the value of goods relative to the amount of money in the economy by fixing wages and prices at the appropriate levels. The government's needs for additional money can be met simply by raising the prices of the goods its enterprises sell to consumers, or by lowering the wages of its employees. Consequently, there is no apparent reason for the government of a centrally-planned economy to run a budget deficit.

Nevertheless, budget deficits existed in the former Soviet Union throughout the 1980s, and probably a good deal earlier.[175] Even in Communist societies leaders are not eager to take measures that are sure to be unpopular, such as raising the prices of consumer goods or lowering wages. The tendency in the USSR was for wages to grow over time, and for official consumer good prices to be held nearly constant. (Some prices were even occasionally lowered.) If the productivity of workers increased sufficiently quickly, the upward wage drift would not have created a problem, since the higher total wages would have been matched by the higher total value of consumer goods at official prices. But productivity in consumer goods production did not match the wage increases, partly because of the Soviet emphasis on the production of defence and other non-consumer goods.[176]

The total wage bill in the Soviet Union therefore tended to increase over time, more quickly than the total amount of money spent on consumer goods at official prices. One manifestation of this process was increased nominal savings on the part of the Soviet population. More important, though, was the effect on the government budget. Since wages are a cost to the government and the prices paid for state-sector consumer goods are revenues to the government, Soviet budget deficits tended to increase.

Not surprisingly, budget deficits in the pre-reform Soviet system can be characterized as implicit. Fixed prices imply that calculating real government revenues and expenditures is impossible, but even employing those fixed prices the deficit was hidden. Gorbachev himself said that 'The heaviest burden we have inherited from the past is the budget deficit, which was carefully concealed from society, but nevertheless existed.'[177] Though the existence of budget deficits in the Soviet Union was hidden, the economic effects of those deficits was tangible.

As noted, deficits that are financed via borrowing, the issuing of bonds, need not be inflationary. But the budget deficits in the former Soviet Union were not compensated for by the issuing of bonds.[178] Instead, deficits were 'monetized', i.e., the government essentially printed new roubles to cover its budget deficits. With each rouble less valuable, free prices would tend to increase as more roubles were printed. Since state-sector prices were fixed, the inflation resulting from Soviet monetized budget deficits was of the repressed variety, with reduced availability of goods in the state sector.

Russian economic reform converted budget deficits from implicit to explicit form. But the changes of perestroika increased the size as well as the visibility of budget deficits. The culprit was – again no surprise – partial reform. Because reforms that would lower government expenditures and increase (or at least limit the decrease in) government revenues were not sufficiently pursued, Soviet budget deficits worsened during the Gorbachev years.[179]

On the government revenue side of the economic ledger, the problem was that the main element of pre-reform taxation consisted of the earnings of state enterprises above their costs. Higher retail prices for state-produced goods would increase state enterprise revenue, which was largely appropriated for the government budget. In this sense, a higher price for a state good was simply an implicit increase in taxes. As perestroika gave state enterprises more autonomy, the enterprises themselves were able to keep more of their own revenue (with which they could, for example, increase the wages of their workers.) Similar changes occurred in the agricultural sector.[180]

The increased autonomy of enterprises undermined another implicit tax as well, one based on foreign exchange. In the pre-reform Soviet economy, any foreign currency that a state-owned firm earned by exporting its product went to the government. In exchange for its foreign currency, a firm received roubles, with the amount it received based on the official (centrally-controlled) exchange rate. This rate greatly overvalued the rouble, so that the foreign currency the government received was worth considerably more than the roubles that the enterprises received in exchange. This system of confiscating foreign exchange earnings was an implicit tax on the enterprise. With reform, firms received increased rights to retain their foreign currency earnings, further diluting the state's system of implicit taxation.[181]

One feature of a transition to a market economy, increased autonomy for state-owned enterprises, thus directly undermined the implicit tax system.[182] To maintain its revenues during reform, the Soviet government would have had to effectively implement, at an early stage, new, explicit taxes – a step it failed to take.[183] To be fair, this is a difficult step to take, since the entities that become available for new taxes are largely in the emerging private sector. The pre-reform government apparatus had almost no experience with taxing private businesses, so the administration of new private-sector taxes must start from ground zero.

Increased budget deficits could have been avoided, despite the fall in government revenues, had government expenditures been similarly reduced. The reforms that would have accomplished reductions in government expenditures would have been to cut or eliminate subsidies to state-owned enterprises, perhaps in concert with privatization. In other words, if the increased autonomy for state-owned enterprises, which was responsible for reducing government tax revenues, had been matched by more enterprise accountability for their financial situation, increased budget deficits could have been avoided. Reductions in the investment and defence components of the government budget would also have been helpful, and were to some degree implemented.[184] These expenditure reductions, however, were offset by continued subsidies to state-owned enterprises: by the end of 1992, no large state enterprise had yet been forced to close for financial reasons.[185]

In fact, partial reforms tended to increase government expenditures at the same time that the decay of the implicit taxation system was reducing government revenues. Under the Soviet system, new roubles were added to the money supply when workers received their wages. Transfers of goods within the state sector did not add to the money supply; while the supplying firm acquired an accounting credit and the receiving firm's financial balance changed by the corresponding debit, no actual money changed hands. In other words, official exchanges within the state sector were non-monetary, except for payments to workers. Early reforms such as the Law on Co-operatives, however, expanded the possibilities for money creation within the state sector. New businesses as well as parts of state-owned enterprises could be organized as cooperatives. Purchases by state-owned firms from cooperatives involved money creation. The purchasing firm would provide a receipt to the cooperative, which then could legally acquire the corresponding rouble payment from the state. Exchanges that in the old system did not involve the use of money thereby became monetized during perestroika. In allowing state-owned enterprises to deal with private cooperatives, without subjecting the enterprises to strict financial discipline, perestroika led to large monetary emissions and inflation.

## CREDIBLE DISINFLATION

Inflation is not an inevitable accompaniment of a transition to capitalism. It was the failure to fully reform, in the sense of effectively implementing an explicit taxation system or of limiting government subsidies to enterprises, that resulted in new inflation during Russia's economic transformation.

Russia is now faced with the task of reducing its inflation, which has largely been converted from repressed to open form. (In some localities, however, extensive controls on prices remain.) As noted, getting rid of inflation can be a costly endeavour. Recent high levels of inflation create expectations of continued high inflation in the future. Since inflationary expectations tend to be self-fulfilling, Russia appears to be caught in a cycle of high inflation.

The situation is not hopeless, however, and some policies could help smooth the transition to a lower inflationary path. The key is to alter the expectations of high inflation. And the way to lower inflationary expectations is for the government to clearly embark on an economic plan that is non-inflationary. In Russian circumstances, a non-inflationary economic programme requires a balanced (or nearly balanced) government budget. The more apparent it is that the government is committed to such a plan, the more quickly inflationary expectations will be revised downwards, and the less costly the disinflationary episode.

The first order of business, then, is to commit to reducing the government budget deficit, presumably by a combination of increased tax revenues and lowered spending. Other policies could complement the deficit reduction package. A currency reform, for example, wherein 'old' roubles are exchanged for new ones, perhaps at a ratio of 1000 old roubles to one new rouble, could in these circumstances have an effect beyond reducing nominal prices by a factor of 1000. Combined with a credible government budget deficit reduction package, the new currency might not carry the weight of the old currency's inflationary expectations. The path to a low inflation regime could then be accomplished without the severe output declines that often accompany disinflationary policies.[186] Currency reforms tied to credible regime shifts have worked elsewhere, with the German monetary reform of 1948 being one of the most conspicuous successes.[187] Another success was the Soviet NEP-era currency reform of 1922, which introduced a gold-backed parallel currency, the 'chervonets'. Combined with tax increases, the monetary restraint derived from the gold-backed currency resulted in a balanced government budget by 1923-4, following years of high and even hyperinflation.[188]

How can a deficit reduction policy be made credible? After all, the government can always resort to printing more roubles, old or new, tomorrow, and it would even appear to have incentives to do so. Under these circumstances, no disinflationary programme can be completely credible. Nevertheless, some plans are more believable than others. One way to enhance credibility of a plan to reduce the deficit is to tie the currency reform to privatization. Once in private hands, enterprises no longer have claims to government subsidies – or at least their claims are less compelling. Privatization, therefore, is in itself a disinflationary policy.[189]

There are other means of achieving credibility of a disinflationary policy, such as a commitment to a conditional International Monetary Fund aid and reform programme.[190] Poland had been experiencing large budget deficits in the late 1980s. The Polish 'big bang' reforms of 1 January 1990, which liberalized prices and made the Polish currency, the zloty, convertible, also resulted in a government budget surplus in 1990, without a currency reform.[191] The Polish experience indicates that a currency reform is not an essential element of a transition to a market economy. What is essential is some reform that will introduce a believable disinflationary regime. By making a very visible break with the past (in the manner of the Polish big bang), a currency reform combined with deficit-reducing policies has the potential to quickly erase inflationary expectations.[192]

## PARKING AND PERESTROIKA

It is difficult for Westerners to understand the nature of some of the changes accompanying economic reform in Russia. Strange as it may sound, one area of Western life that presents a useful analogy to conditions in centrally-planned economies is that of automobile parking in major metropolitan areas. Consumer behaviour responds to similar circumstances in pre-reform Russia as in Western parking.

On-street public parking in the West generally involves either no monetary payment, or a relatively small fee collected via parking meters. It often takes a long time to find a public parking space in crowded downtown areas because the price is fixed below market clearing-levels. This is the Western analogue to the search for goods and long queues that awaited Russian shoppers in pre-reform state stores, where the monetary costs of goods were also held artificially low.

Once a driver finds a parking space, moreover, he or she can generally not claim it for ever. There is usually some time limit, ranging from a few minutes to a few hours, beyond which the same car cannot remain legally parked, even if the meter price is continuously paid. The Russian analogy here is with the quantity restrictions that await shoppers when they finally get to the front of the line in the state stores. They cannot buy all they want of the good at the low fixed price, but instead are often limited to a certain small quantity. (Incidentally, this is another illustration of the tendency for economic controls to snowball. Since higher prices cannot be used to ration the demand, quantity controls become necessary.)

Public parking on the street at below market rates is only one parking option. An alternative is to park in privately-operated parking lots and garages that charge whatever the market will bear. Here, the waiting time is generally minimal, but the price can be many multiples of the price for public street parking. In Russia, goods sold in state stores were also available at free market prices in 'parallel' markets, which are now largely legal, and in the case of food have been legal for decades. Russian consumers buying food, like Westerners attempting to park, could use the subsidized public sector or the free market private sector.

An important difference between the public and private parking alternatives should be noted. When a driver pays a private garage owner, the driver gets the parking and loses the cash, but the garage owner receives the cash. That is, the cash payment for the parking space is a transfer of purchasing power from the driver to the garage owner. In the state sector, the time that goes into searching for a space is 'spent' by the driver, but does not benefit anyone else. Instead of a transfer of resources, time spent in search uses up a valuable resource: the driver's time. By using up resources, the allocation of goods by low fixed prices and waiting lines is more costly to a society than free markets. Thus repressed inflation tends to be more costly than open inflation, and the blatant waste of resources is partly to blame for the frustration that often accompanies the search for a parking space.

Reform has witnessed an increase in the process of 'spontaneous privat-ization' in Russia. This activity occurs when private citizens (workers and managers) simply usurp the state ownership rights – quasi-legally, at best – and operate enterprises for their own profit. Interestingly, spontaneous privatization also occurs in particularly congested Western parking markets. Large men will step into public parking spaces when automobiles leave and then 'offer' the spaces at market prices to others wishing to park. The driver can either pay the market price, continue to search for another parking place, or attempt to park anyway – a strategy that will likely be met with violence (or at least the implicit threat of violence) either to the car or the driver. An alternative device to achieve the same ends involves a protection racket. Here a private citizen will offer, for a fee, to keep an eye on the car of a newly-parked driver.[193] (Thus the protection rackets that have become widely remarked upon in Russia also have their – pardon the pun – parking parallels.) If these sorts of spontaneous privatizations seem disreputable, imagine how the Russians feel about their similar, and much more widespread, phenomenon.

One point that the parking analogy suggests, however, is that spontaneous privatization can occur in situations of excessive shortage, even without reform. Much of the spontaneous privatization now under way in Russia represents a more visible version of a long-standing practice, that of diverting state sector goods to private markets: once more, the implicit–explicit distinction. (A similar point applies to protection rackets.) While state-sector shortages increased during perestroika, and thus the incentive to spontaneously privatize also increased – and reform measures simultaneously reduced the costs of such privatizations – reform did not directly cause spontaneous privatization.

Information plays a key role in parking. A local who knows the location of difficult-to-find public parking spaces can more easily discover a place to park at the low fixed price than can a tourist. Businesses that trade on this information can even spring up, by offering 'valet' parking in public spaces. Information about local 'market' conditions is likewise invaluable to Russian shoppers. By knowing which state stores are likely to have which goods at which times, local consumers can often procure the goods, and perhaps without large amounts of time spent in searching and queuing. Specialists become professional shoppers, collecting fees for buying goods for others in the state sector.

Now consider Russian economic reform. Full reform will mean that state sector prices will match the parallel market prices, and searching and queuing will largely disappear. For those who have relatively more time than roubles, and who have good information about the current state sector, the reforms will be unwelcome. The social costs of time wasted waiting in queues, however, will virtually disappear, and quantity restrictions will become unnecessary.

Likewise, imagine a reform to raise the prices for all public parking to market levels. (In some areas, this could involve a more than ten-fold increase in prices.) Again, for those with relatively less money than time, and with relatively good information about the availability of public parking spaces, parking will become more onerous. Simultaneously, however, the search for parking would be virtually eliminated, as would the restrictions on the amount of time in a parking space.[194] Suddenly, drivers would have no trouble finding parking, and no socially wasteful time would be spent searching for parking spaces! Such a reform would raise the quality of life for many drivers, even if it came at a higher monetary price. But the Russians put up with the equivalent of parking problems in virtually all of their everyday, state sector transactions. For many Russians, full price liberalization offers a very significant increase in welfare.

## ARE ROUBLES WORTHLESS?

The question 'Are roubles worthless?' has been answered in the affirmative so many times in the Western media and by Western economists that there seems to be little reason to pursue the issue further.[195] The worthlessness of roubles is viewed as being responsible for the rise in barter and the lack of incentive to work – why work if the roubles that you are paid cannot buy anything? Nevertheless, the notion that roubles are worthless is a complete myth. It has been the case throughout the reform era that you could buy virtually anything you desired in Russia, including dollars, with roubles, if you had enough of them. Roubles are valuable. In his seminal paper on the Soviet second economy in 1977, Gregory Grossman noted that he had been told by a Moscow resident that 'In this city you can get anything for money, though sometimes it takes a lot.'[196] This characterization of the Russian market economy remains accurate, and the money involved need not be foreign currency.

The perpetuation of the myth that roubles are worthless stems from an over-emphasis on the official component of the Russian economy. The low fixed prices in the state sector and the accompanying shortages gave the appearance that the binding constraint on Russian shoppers was not the number of roubles that they had, but rather the amount of time that they were willing to invest to procure goods. This appearance matched reality only within the fixed-price state sector, however. Parallel markets with free prices also existed, and Russians could buy goods in these outlets as well. Many Russians did not purchase a substantial amount of their goods on the free market because of the high prices. (Young people, however, were reported to buy 40 per cent of their goods on the black market.[197]) But this is precisely the point. High prices only deter shoppers if they cannot afford the high prices, i.e, if additional roubles would be valuable to them.

After the recent reforms that increased state sector prices, complaints concerning high prices were voiced by many Russian shoppers. Nevertheless, the 'roubles are worthless' myth continued to be perpetuated, sometimes even in articles that simultaneously reported discontent over high prices![198]

The related myth that Russians have no interest in working hard in order to earn their worthless roubles has also proved persistent. Actually, the incentives to work for roubles are quite intense, and perhaps ironically, the more difficult the economic situation, the greater these incentives become. Indeed, the amount of effort devoted to earning roubles in cities like Moscow is eye-opening. Entrepreneurs have been running enormous risks in Russia – in 1988–9, 34,000 Soviets were punished for 'speculation'[199] – to earn roubles. Of course, workers are happy to work directly for consumer goods as well – maybe even happier. But they will also willingly work for roubles, if they are paid enough of them. They are less eager to work in state-sector jobs that pay only low rouble wages, or if they get paid the same amount whether they work hard or not.

The notion that roubles are worthless is connected to the idea of a rouble overhang, which has its origins in the concept of 'unsatisfied demand' in the Soviet economics discipline. Unsatisfied demand is calculated as the amount by which the value of consumer goods produced in the economy, measured at fixed state prices, exceeds the income earned by households, minus a small amount of desired savings. If households have more income than there are consumer goods, they will be forced to save the money, or so the theory goes. The total amount of such forced savings, accumulated year after year, represents the ominous-sounding rouble overhang.

Again, the difficulty with the concepts of unsatisfied demand, forced savings, and the rouble overhang is that they ignore the free price, parallel markets. 'Forced' savings are actually voluntary; individuals choose not to pay the high prices on the free markets, and save the money instead.[200] Westerners engage in similar behaviour; for example, shoppers might wait until a sale before making a desired purchase. This is the Western equivalent of a Russian postponing a purchase until he or she luckily comes across some low-priced goods in a state-sector shop.

The concept of a rouble overhang is not itself worthless, because it represents a good indicator of repressed inflation. The greater the rouble overhang, the greater (in general) the amount of repressed inflation, and the greater the difference between free market prices and the official state-sector prices. But the rouble overhang does not directly portend doom. As a measure of repressed inflation, the rouble overhang gives some indication of the amount by which fixed state sector prices will rise with price liberalization, though prices in existing free markets probably provide a better guide. The rouble overhang does not create any new inflation, however. Russians will not suddenly show up 'waving fistfuls of roubles', because they could have done so before in the free market sector but chose not to. And in fact, the rouble overhang came crashing down after the 2 January 1992 partial price liberalization with barely a whimper. There is always a new crisis on the horizon, though. The crisis following the partial price liberalization was a tremendous *shortage* of roubles that was preventing Russian workers from getting paid![201]

# Chapter 4

# Employment and unemployment

Our unemployment is the highest in the world. But unfortunately, all our unemployed get salaries.

Russian economist Pavel Bunich[202]

It is no secret that even now many people get their pay only for reporting to work and hold positions regardless of their actual labour contribution. And the most surprising thing is that this hardly worries anyone.

Mikhail Gorbachev[203]

## INTRODUCTION

For Russians long accustomed to a high degree of price stability in the state shops, the rapid increases in prices during the reform era must have come as something of a shock. But that shock may be relatively minor compared with what transition holds in store for them with respect to employment. Finding a job was not difficult in the Soviet Union, maybe even easier than finding desirable consumer goods. Western-style unemployment was virtually unknown. A transition to a market economy will end this situation, and many Russians will be faced with potentially long periods of involuntary unemployment for the first time in their lives. Government assurances that basic needs will be met and that eventually everyone will be better off might provide little solace. A rough US analogy might be a reform to quickly eliminate the Social Security system. Given the amount of controversy engendered by minor proposed changes in Social Security, sudden abolition of the programme could ignite a revolution. Will a rising unemployment rate cause Russians to man the barricades?

The themes that emerged during the discussion of price liberalization – pre-existing markets, misleading statistics, implicit versus explicit phenomena, and the dangers of partial reform – re-emerge in the transitional employment sphere. For example, implementation of the Soviet government's full-employment policy resulted in substantial underemployment, or 'repressed unemployment', as evidenced by the quotations that open this chapter. Such repressed unemployment continues in present day Russia. Wages are also partly hidden, as Russian enterprises generally provide scarce goods and social services to their employees, in addition to monetary compensation. These benefits, combined with the full employment mandate, formed part of the implicit welfare system in the pre-reform setting, complementing the low fixed prices in state stores for most everyday consumer goods. There was no system of unemployment benefits under the Soviet regime, because there was little need for one. But during market-oriented reform, the repressed unemployment becomes open unemployment, and the implicit welfare system formed in the employment sphere ceases to operate. An explicit unemployment benefits system therefore becomes a high priority during reform. The economic costs of the new open unemployment need not exceed the costs of the old repressed unemployment, however, and the implicit social welfare system can be replaced with an explicit one that includes unemployment benefits: conclusions familiar from the examination of price liberalization and inflation.

The major benefits from market-oriented reforms of state-owned enterprises derive from changes in the answers to the 'what goods to produce?' question. Making the right goods will require that workers who are currently making the *wrong* goods change their jobs. Finding a new job is not always easy, though, particularly in a society where people have little experience in searching for work while unemployed. Some of the people who have to change jobs, and some new entrants to the Russian labour force, will go through spells, perhaps prolonged spells, of open unemployment. This is standard operating procedure in Western market economies; some unemployment is accepted as necessary to allocate labour efficiently, though governments typically try to cushion the adverse economic consequences of unemployment for out-of-work individuals. Such acceptance of open unemployment cannot be taken for granted in Russia, however; polls indicate that most Russians believe that it is the duty of the government to provide everyone with a job,[204] and the cushions in the form of unemployment benefits are not yet well developed. But a reluctance to generate open unemployment during transition carries a cost beyond the continued misallocation of labour. If enterprise reform does not keep pace with price reform, the potential benefits of market prices are themselves partially undermined. In disbanding the 'unified team' of free prices and free enterprise, the entire reform process runs the risk of being run aground.

## THE LABOUR SECTOR UNDER THE ANCIEN RÉGIME

'Implicit contract theory' is a branch of Western macroeconomics and labour economics theory that bears some relationship to conditions in the pre-reform Russian economy. Implicit contract theory is based on the notion that workers tend to be more averse to risk in the amount of their pay than firms are to risk in the amount of their profits.[205] In these circumstances, firms might provide implicit insurance to workers, by maintaining wages and salaries even during economic downturns, at the cost of sharing fewer of their profits with workers during an upswing. The Russian state employment sector operated roughly in accordance with implicit contract theory. Workers were implicitly insured in the form of near guarantees of employment and relatively stable pay.

The Soviet government announced the official end of unemployment in October 1930, and there was no mass open unemployment during the years of central planning.[206] (This provided quite a contrast with Western market economies during the Great Depression, and to a lesser degree since.) A small amount of unemployment did exist, however, due to what economists call 'frictional factors', These include situations that are specific to individuals, and that result in temporary unemployment: quitting, getting fired, or newly entering the job force. Unemployment due to more widespread factors, such as the decline of an entire industry or an economy-wide recession, was not a feature of the centrally-planned system. Typical estimates of the Soviet pre-perestroika frictional unemployment rate are on the order of 2–3 per cent.[207]

The maintenance of full employment was an explicit goal of the Soviet regime. The Soviet constitution recognized the right and duty of a citizen to work, and the duty of the state to provide citizens with jobs.[208] Able-bodied adults without a working spouse or family responsibilities who did not have an official job were potentially subject to prosecution under 'anti-parasite' laws.[209]

Participation in the Soviet labour force greatly exceeded typical Western levels: about 80 per cent of adults of working age were active in the labour force, as compared to approximately 70 per cent in the US[210] This relative labour force activity was most pronounced for Soviet women, who held jobs at a higher rate than women in any other industrialized country.[211] Part-time work, at least officially, was virtually unknown: almost all Soviet workers held full-time jobs. Unofficially, though, opportunities to work less than 40 hours a week were widely available.[212] In contrast to the high labour participation rates, official retirement ages were relatively young. Most Soviet workers could retire with a state-provided pension at the age of 60 for men and 55 for women.[213] Many pensioners continued to hold formal or informal jobs, however.[214]

The Soviet employment realm was an amalgam of planned and market elements, and the conditions that arose from this combination have continued into the post-planning period in Russia. At a general level, planners determined the allocation of labourers between occupations and enterprises – how many workers were needed in what jobs requiring what skills in what industries.[215] The official 'demand' for labour was thus guided, though not precisely determined, by the plan. Wage rates were centrally determined, varying with job classifications. Other aspects of the employment relationship, such as the working conditions, were also centrally regulated.

The planning system exerted less influence over the supply of labour than it did over the demand for labour. The leverage over labour supply operated through the anti-parasite laws, official education and training opportunities, retirement policies, military service, and, alas, forced labour camps. The distribution of workers among individual enterprises, however, generally involved the conscious decisions of individual Russian citizens. The great majority of Soviet workers were hired simply by applying at the local factory, without any centralized allocation.[216] (The major exception involved initial jobs for school graduates, who were often placed in employment.) To some degree, despite the anti-parasite laws, there was even a choice over whether or not to enter the work force.[217] (The relative freedom that workers had in the labour market became particularly important in the post-Stalin era. Under Stalin, labour was 'militarized', and during the war, a single late arrival or absence from work could result in a five-year term in a labour camp.)

Because of the relative freedom in labour supply, planners had to respond to workers' preferences by raising wages or bonuses for jobs in which it was otherwise difficult to attract workers, such as those in remote areas.[218] Planners in Moscow had limited information on local conditions and limited control over individual enterprises, though, so their actions alone could not come close to matching labour supply with labour demand. Action on the part of the managers of individual enterprises was therefore necessary to attract good workers. Since the official wage rates were fixed by the planners, it was impossible for managers to directly raise wages in response to local conditions. Enterprise managers had to find ways to circumvent the central wage controls in order to attract and retain workers.[219] Among the devices for informally increasing compensation were spurious upgrades of positions, management complicity in the mis-appropriation of time or materials from work, and the distribution of highly sought-after goods through the work place.[220] The amount of such informal compensation was surprisingly extensive; one conservative estimate indicates that 12 per cent of total working time was 'stolen' from state employers in the late 1970s.[221] Large enterprises took on the role of benevolent company towns, supplying food, consumer goods, housing, schools, and even vacation retreats to their employees.

Soviet planners understood the opportunities for informal compensation on the job, and they responded, perhaps unintentionally, by fixing lower official wages for jobs that offered particularly lucrative additional sources of funds – another case where planning followed practice rather than vice versa. Butchers and retail trade employees, for example, had fairly low official wages, implicitly recognizing the opportunities in these professions for informal wage supplements. Retail trade workers could easily supplement their official pay by selling state-sector goods 'through the back door', at free market prices paid either in roubles, gifts, or favours.[222]

Soviet state-owned enterprises, unlike private Western firms, were not motivated to earn high profits. Their main official goal was simply to fulfil, and if possible to overfulfil, their output plan, which as previously noted, could be revised downwards if they were in real danger of severe under-fulfilment. Lacking a strong profit motive, enterprises also lacked incentives to ensure that they operated efficiently and at low cost, or that they produced high quality output.

The relative unimportance of profits was perfectly reasonable in a fixed-price regime. If prices are centrally-determined, then profits are, to a large extent, also centrally-determined. By raising the price of a firm's output or lowering the price of its inputs, the planners could generally raise a firm's profits. High profits in a Western economy are a signal that a firm is pro-viding something that its customers find particularly attractive. In a centrally-planned economy, high profits signal planners' whims, not consumer satisfaction. Indeed, urging enterprises to increase profits in a fixed-price regime is dangerous – it is the Polish tropical flowers story, or the feeding bread to livestock tale. By focusing on output rather than profits, the centrally-planned system maintained a degree of internal consistency.

The internal consistency of the pre-reform system is also demonstrated by the seeming lack of work place discipline. Workers would drink, steal goods and time, and generally lack industriousness at their official jobs at levels that apparently far exceeded those of the West. Why would managers tolerate and even in some cases condone such behaviour? Much of the answer lies in the official reward structure. Since plan fulfillment was the most meaningful success indicator, managers could primarily focus on meeting their output plan. As long as the plan was fulfilled, management had little interest in controlling other aspects of employee behaviour.[223]

With few incentives to minimize costs but strong incentives to fulfil the gross output requirements of the plan, enterprise managers had a tendency to demand more labour, as well as more of other inputs, than the planners deemed necessary.[224] This incentive reflects the situation of 'soft budget constraints', whereby firms that lost money simply received state subsidies; that is, there was no bankruptcy.[225] Again, subsidizing money-losing firms is perfectly reasonable, even essential, in a fixed-price economy, since profits are largely determined by the pricing decisions of the planners.

The general result of soft budget constraints has been a situation in which a firm, at the official wage rates, wanted to hire more workers than the enterprise could actually entice at that wage. From a firm's point of view, labour was another good that was in chronic shortage in the USSR. These strong enterprise incentives to hire workers in the Soviet economy played a major role in implementing the stated goal of full employment.[226] Even in the absence of excessive firm hunger to accumulate labour, though, an aggre-gate labour shortage probably would have existed, as total planned man-power requirements consistently exceeded the supply of labour.[227]

Soft budget constraints therefore led Soviet state-owned firms, in general, to hire more workers than a similar private firm in a market economy would have chosen to hire. This tendency was particularly apparent in Soviet factories that were purchased from the West, and thus had nearly identical Western analogues:[228]

> in 1969 it was reported that the [Soviet] chemical plants bought from abroad employed considerably more workers than needed in the countries of purchase: one and a half times as many in the case of basic blue-collar workers, three and a half times as many in the case of white collar workers, and eight times as many in the case of auxiliary blue collar workers.

The giant Magnitogorsk steel mill employed 60 thousand employees to produce sixteen million tons of steel per year, while USX's modern plant in Gary, Indiana produced eight million tons with only seven thousand workers.[229] This relative overstaffing of enterprises was reinforced by legal barriers that firms faced in getting rid of unwanted employees. While workers could be fired for disciplinary reasons, workers who simply were not needed were more difficult to let go. Legally, enterprises had a duty to find a new job for a redundant employee.[230]

It is easy to overestimate the amount of overstaffing in Soviet firms, however, because many seemingly excess workers were actually producing inputs or goods unrelated to a firm's main line of production for distribution to employees or for barter, or were engaged in second economy activity.[231] Furthermore, relative to Western market economies, the USSR was labour-rich and capital-poor, at least with respect to modern capital goods. A higher labour intensity therefore may have been sensible. Despite these reservations concerning the interpretation of statistics, though, Soviet enterprises probably were overstaffed relative to the employment levels that would have existed under private ownership and market conditions.

The Soviet full employment system and overstaffing brought with them underemployment, which took many forms, such as frequent periods of idleness and worker over-qualification. Since the choice of what goods to produce in the state sector was not driven by market prices, many workers produced goods that were not valuable to consumers. These workers were also underemployed relative to their potential productivity in market settings. (Perhaps the frequent periods of idleness were, in some instances, socially beneficial. More industrious workers may simply have turned out an increased supply of useless goods – another example of the internal consistency of the centrally-planned system?)

Incentives to work hard were notoriously paltry within the Soviet state sector. With near guarantees of employment, relatively low official pay differentials between employment grades, and official compensation that was tied mainly to plan fulfilment, employees had little reason to exert much effort at work.[232] Nor could workers easily turn to alternative employers when they were dissatisfied with their jobs, despite the usual Soviet condition of 'excess demand' for labour. It was generally illegal for workers to move to major cities like Moscow and St. Petersburg to look for work: the Catch-22 was that they already had to have a job offer in order to move there.[233] The chronic housing shortage further limited worker movement, since arranging for housing in a new area was extremely difficult. In-kind benefits that were distributed through the work place, often including housing, served as another barrier to changing jobs, because the potential loss of such benefits (unless they could be quickly replaced by similar benefits from the new enterprise) was nearly intolerable. Even the *possibility* of in-kind benefits limited worker mobility. Workers at an enterprise often had a place on a waiting list for enterprise-provided housing; waits of more than 10 years were not uncommon.[234] By leaving their enterprise, workers would also lose their place on the waiting list. Similarly, the importance of networks of personal connections for informal and corrupt activity served as a barrier against shifting jobs or location. And the option of openly entering business for oneself was available only in a few trades.[235]

Constraints on outside opportunities available to good workers diminished incentives for employees to distinguish themselves at their current jobs. Amid these difficulties, the amount of labour turnover, while lower than US levels, was surprisingly extensive, with 12 per cent of industrial workers leaving their jobs in 1987.[236] Simultaneously, absenteeism far exceeded Western levels.[237] The effects of substantial turnover and absenteeism on the value of production may not have been particularly severe, however, given the overstaffing and mis-production within the state sector.[238]

## FROM IMPLICIT TO EXPLICIT UNEMPLOYMENT

In moving to a market economy, Russia will have to force most state owned enterprises to make it (or not) on their own: in economics jargon, to face a hard budget constraint. The essential reform is that subsidies to state-owned enterprises cease (or at least be severely restricted), whether or not the enterprises are formally privatized. This reform is only sensible, however, if prices are liberalized and firm managers' decisions are not controlled by the state. Under these circumstances, profits become a function of enterprise behaviour and not planner decree: once again, free prices and free enterprise are a unified team.

The ending of subsidies to enterprises will be accompanied by the possibility, indeed, the near certainty, judging from East European experience, of widespread open unemployment. Without the implicit subsidies (low prices on inputs, including subsidized credit) and explicit subsidies (direct transfers from the state budget) that they currently receive, many enterprises will become bankrupt.[239] But prior to the cut-off of subsidies and the freeing of prices it cannot be determined which enterprises or how many enterprises will be unable to cope in a market setting, since only then will profits be a good measure of a firm's solvency. And even those enterprises that can make it under market conditions may need to reduce their work force, further adding to open unemployment.[240] As state-owned enterprises lose their access to state subsidies, the state-guaranteed 'implicit contract' will no longer operate. Instead, the employment sector will be marked by the familiar Western situation where workers bear some of the risk of economic downturns, by possibly becoming unemployed during recessions.

What is the potential size of the open unemployment that could accompany reform? An unemployment rate of 10 per cent, similar to that prevailing in some East European countries in the years following the implementation of major reforms, would leave more than seven million Russian citizens unemployed.[241] Other estimates of Russian unemployment can be generated by measuring the extent of pre-reform overstaffing. Relying on an over-staffing figure of 25 per cent drawn from a survey of more than 500 factories, the International Labour Organization suggested that 15–45 million workers in the former USSR could become unemployed during reform.[242] Such a large amount of unemployment would not be in accord with Eastern European experience. Nevertheless, even much lower levels of unemployment appear daunting, particularly since there were so few openly unemployed Russians in the pre-reform situation.

If the Russian labour force participation rate were to decrease to levels more typical of Western market economies, the increase in open unemployment during reform could be lessened. This may already be happening, as employment has already begun to fall, even without significant increases in official unemployment.[243] Participation rates may not fall sharply, though. Expanded opportunities for part-time work may attract some new workers into the labour force – though some workers who now hold full-time jobs may elect to reduce their work hours.

In any event, reform is quite likely to result in a substantial increase in open unemployment. Open unemployment is economically detrimental for two reasons. First, unemployed workers are not producing goods and services that other members of society can enjoy. This is a cost that society as a whole pays for unemployment. Second are costs that the unemployed workers themselves must bear. These include reduced income, as well as the psychological costs that often accompany the state of unemployment.

The social costs of open unemployment, though, are already being borne in the unreformed Russian economy. Consider a firm that becomes bankrupt post-reform. Bankruptcy in a market economy indicates that the firm's inputs are more valuable than its outputs. A Russian enterprise that is forced to close during market-oriented reform therefore reveals that it was being subsidized prior to the reform. The subsidy may have been implicit, being hidden in favourable pricing or priority access to inputs. Indeed, the firm may even have made positive 'profits', calculated according to the fixed state sector prices. Whether the pre-reform subsidies were explicit or implicit, closing the firm and ending the subsidies represent a net benefit to society; in other words, the economic pie gets bigger.

A rise in measured unemployment in Russia during the transition therefore need not represent a rise in de facto unemployment; the increase in the measured unemployment rate is misleading in terms of costs imposed on the economy, because the pre-reform unemployment rate failed to capture the repressed unemployment. As Nobel Prize-winning economist James Tobin once noted, 'If people are at unproductive work, whether as hired wage earners, family farm hands, or self-employed, the best statistical symptom of this social malady is low per capita income, not unemployment.'[244]

Shutting down unprofitable firms is just one of the routes to social gains via labour market reform. Another benefit that will accompany the introduction of hard budget constraints is the improved incentives to work on the part of those who remain employed. Even absenteeism can be expected to fall abruptly, as it has elsewhere when workers were faced with the prospect of reform.[245] In the longer run, the switch to the production of goods that are highly desired by consumers will also increase the size of the social pie.

Some job opportunities for newly (and openly) unemployed workers will continue to arise in the nascent legal private sector, particularly as burdensome government restrictions are removed.[246] As noted earlier, some 50 per cent of the Russian work force was employed in the private sector by mid-1994.[247] The process of privatization, both spontaneous and official, whereby state assets have been converted to private use, has allowed many workers and managers to supplement their wages with de facto profit shares.[248] Private employment may rise particularly quickly in those areas that were relatively neglected under Soviet central planning. Housing construction and maintenance, and the service and consumer goods sectors are candidates for rapid growth. The former Soviet Union had only one third the number of workers in trade occupations as the US had in retail trade alone.[249] The retail sales kiosks that have sprung up on busy street corners throughout Russia can thus be seen as filling a particularly wide niche left unfilled in the old system.

It is likely that the total social costs in the Russian employment realm will go down during a comprehensive market-based reform, even as open unemployment rises. But the decrease in total social costs is largely irrelevant to those individuals who are forced to newly bear the costs of open unemployment. To shift some of the costs of unemployment that otherwise fall on the unemployed, Western governments typically provide explicit unemployment insurance, in the form of benefits to laid-off workers. The Russian government should do likewise during the transition, explicitly restoring, in part, the previous implicit contract. And indeed, the Russian government is attempting to implement a new system of explicit unemployment benefits.[250] Shifting the costs of unemployment away from the unemployed individual involves a difficult trade-off, though. The higher the level of unemployment benefits, the less unemployed workers suffer, but the lower the impetus to find work and stay employed. The incentive to work hard fuelled by the threat of potential unemployment becomes attenuated as unemployment benefits rise. Simultaneously, employers may be more willing to let workers go if the employers know that substantial unemployment benefits are available.

Payments to 'unemployed' workers are basically a fixed cost in the Russian economy.[251] These payments can be made just as easily to explicitly unemployed workers post-reform, in the form of unemployment benefits, as they can be made to implicitly unemployed workers pre-reform, in the form of wages and in-kind benefits. The unemployment benefits of Russian workers who lose their jobs during a full market-oriented reform do not represent new costs for society to bear. Since Russia can afford its pre-reform, implicit social safety net, which was relatively inefficient because it required wasteful production and was not targeted at the most needy individuals, it can easily afford a targeted, explicit social safety net during transition to a market economy. With labour costs only some 20 per cent of total production costs, the gains from eliminating wasteful production while paying explicit unemployment benefits are in fact quite substantial.[251*] Boris Fedorov, then the Russian Minister of Finance, estimated in 1993 that it cost three times as much to keep a person employed at an unproductive job through industry subsidies than it would cost to pay unemployment benefits.[252]

The argument that unemployment and its costs simply change from implicit to explicit form during the transition may understate the difficulties that reform poses in the employment sector. There are two potential sources of new costs – i.e., costs that were not already being borne in the unreformed system – associated with open unemployment. One is the non-monetary strains suffered by unemployed workers. Other new costs, examined in the next section, may arise as a result of partial reforms.

One Western expert on Soviet labour lists some of the individual non-pecuniary consequences of open unemployment[253]:

> a change in role and status, changes in social contacts outside the home and in the sphere of intrafamilial relationships, an increase in free time, idleness, a lack of purpose, boredom, the feeling of not being wanted, a sense of deprivation and alienation, demoralization, resignation, despair, apathy, hatred of immigrants, and enmity between the sexes.

These non-pecuniary costs can be quite substantial, as anyone knows who is familiar with unemployment in Western industrialized nations. But the extent to which these represent new costs in the Russian employment sphere is uncertain. Many of these negative consequences of open unemployment are 'reproduced' in the full employment Russian setting.[254] People can generally tell when they are engaged in unproductive work. The implicitly unemployed are therefore already susceptible to the non-monetary costs of open unemployment. Taking the general disappearance of job security into account makes it likely that the non-pecuniary costs of open unemployment during transition will exceed the analogous costs of repressed unemployment in the pre-reform Russian system. But the magnitude of the additional costs is not calculable.

## PARTIAL REFORMS AND ECONOMIC DISTORTIONS

Beyond the psychological costs of open unemployment, there is a host of other potential sources of economic distress that could accompany a market-oriented reform of the enterprise sector. For the most part, the roots of increased costs in the employment realm during transition can be characterized as partial reform measures. This section examines two of the potentially most damaging partial reforms, those associated with incomplete price liberalization and credit market restrictions.

Consider the difficulties that partial price liberalization brings to the employment realm. As noted, in market economies without major distortions, a firm becomes bankrupt when the value of the inputs the firm uses – e.g., raw materials, machinery, and labour – exceed the value of its outputs. When the firm goes out of business, the inputs can be redeployed to other, more highly-valued activities. Bankruptcies, then, are beneficial to the economy as a whole, even as they are quite painful to the workers, owners, and creditors of the defunct company. This logic, though, rests on the assumed lack of major 'distortions' in the economy.

An economic distortion is a departure from competitive conditions. Common distortions include unregulated externalities such as pollution, monopoly power, and anti-competitive government regulations such as tariffs. All economies are distorted, and there is no theoretical reason why a 'more' distorted economy should work less well than a 'less' distorted economy, because additional distortions could in some sense be offsetting.[255] A previous example illustrates this point: given the distortions caused by fixed prices in centrally-planned economies, restrictions on private enterprise were necessary to prevent individuals from responding to the distorted price signals. Nevertheless, as conditions in centrally-planned societies indicate, economies that are extremely far removed from competitive conditions are unlikely to perform as well as those that rely primarily on the market mechanism for answers to the what to produce, how to produce, and for whom to produce questions.

One important source of distortions, particularly in centrally-planned economies, is fixed prices. The distortions generated by fixed prices can result in substantial costs in the employment realm during reform. When some prices remain fixed, profits, which are a noisy indicator of the social valuation of productive activity under the best conditions, will be unreliable signals of which firms are and which are not socially viable. Then the wrong firms, and perhaps too many firms, will go bankrupt. Thus Polish tropical flowers formed a viable industry when the energy price was subsidized.

Excessive layoffs may have occurred in Eastern Germany, where real wages – the price of labour – were maintained at artificially high levels after reunification.[256]

Distortions related to the price of labour may be common, even in market economies. A key feature of Keynesian economics is the presumed difficulty money wages have in falling – the 'downward rigidity' in wages. Since wages represent a price, if there is some mechanism that prevents them from fully adjusting to market conditions, then wages resemble the fixed prices of centrally-planned economies. If wages are not flexible downward, insufficient demand for goods and services can lead to increased unemployment.[257] The Russian economy has two features, though, that lessen the relevance of this Keynesian predicament. First, recall that Russian workers receive a large amount of employment compensation in non-monetary and informal fashion. Even if monetary wages are not flexible downwards, such informal elements of compensation are generally more adaptable. Second, inflation remains rampant in the Russian economy, and a high inflation rate will exist for the foreseeable future. In an inflationary environment, monetary wages can rise even as their purchasing power – real wages – decline.

Another potential distortion that is frequently cited as a source of additional unemployment during reform stems from the credit market. In a well-functioning market economy, productive firms do not have to continuously generate enough cash to pay their current bills; rather, if they are temporarily short of funds, they can borrow money from banks, and repay the loan later. Banks are willing to make such loans if they are confident that the firm will eventually be able to settle its accounts, because the loans are repaid with interest. In a well-functioning market economy, temporary illiquidity does not force an otherwise valuable firm to close down.

Russia does not have a well-functioning market economy, though. Consider the plight of a Russian enterprise that has to change its product mix to survive under market conditions – presumably, a very common situation. Such changes are costly, and they have to be borne now, whereas the benefits of the adjustments will not occur until later.[258] Adjustment costs may cause temporary illiquidity in some firms that would be solvent in the long-run. The problem is that in the absence of a well-developed banking sector, such firms may not be able to secure bank loans. Without credit, these potentially viable firms may nevertheless close when their budget constraints are hardened.

While the theoretical point that credit market imperfections can lead to increased bankruptcies and economic distress is compelling, the empirical relevance of this potential problem remains unknown. Though there is not a well-developed capital market in Russia, the private banking sector is growing, and should increase with further reform. The large conglomerate enterprises that are springing up in Russia also help to ease the credit crunch, because they can internally allocate funds to the branches of the firm that offer the best returns.[259] Barter deals and inter-enterprise credits can also allay liquidity constraints during the transition. It is therefore not clear that illiquid but otherwise solvent firms will be unable to borrow. Certainly many new firms have been able to open and grow during the reform years, despite any credit market imperfections.[259*]

Concerns have been raised about the presumably high price of credit – the interest rate – as well as credit availability. While nominal interest rates have been high – in late 1992, over 100 per cent per annum – after adjusting for inflation, real interest rates have not been particularly high, and were even negative until November 1993.[260] As long as interest rates are market-determined in the absence of other major distortions, it is not clear that the price of credit is a problem. If interest rates are high, that reflects the real costs of borrowing money in Russia – precisely what free interest rates are supposed to do to achieve the best mix between current consumption and investment. The expectation of continued inflation implies that market-determined nominal interest rates will remain high (by US standards) in the near future, but this does not in itself portend doom for the Russian economy.

## ENTERPRISE DEBT

As opposed to shortages of credit, the more salient concern in the reforming Russian economy is an *excessive* amount of credit, either explicitly or implicitly provided by the government, and interest rates that are too low. For the most part, interest rates and access to credit in Russia have been determined by political, not economic, factors. Credit is therefore likely to be used to sustain state-sector firms that should be downsized or eliminated, as opposed to being channelled to the emerging market-oriented firms.[260*]

The Russian government can avoid closing state-owned enterprises by providing loans to money-losing firms, either through banks, other enterprises, or to the troubled firms directly. Inter-enterprise loans suddenly became widespread in Russia during the early months of 1992 (i.e., following price liberalization): debts between state-owned enterprises rose by a factor of 80 between January and July 1992.[261] While market-based credit is generally a good development, these non-market loans, which may never be repaid, have the same effect as direct state subsidies – postponing the day of reckoning, when firms have to make a go of it (or fail to) in the marketplace. Furthermore, the interest rates applied to loans backed by the Russian Central Bank are held below the market-clearing levels, and real interest rates, as noted, were actually negative throughout 1992.[262] With subsidized interest rates, it is not surprising that credit must be administratively rationed. What enterprise would not want to borrow money if it was getting paid to do so, which in effect is the situation when real interest rates are negative?

There is little risk to individual banks or enterprises in dispensing such credit, provided that the practice is widespread, even if there is no explicit government insurance. When most state enterprises have debts they cannot repay, the state almost certainly will step in with additional funds, rather than risk massive shutdowns. Such considerations are one key to the build-up of trillions of roubles in credit.[263] Another important factor in dispensing inter-enterprise credits is that a firm that does so, and is not repaid, does not appear to suffer any major negative consequences. Even if the firm is not being paid by its customers, it generally is given access by the state to funds with which to pay the wages of its own employees.

Banking in the pre-reform Russian economy was passive – dare I say implicit? – and was largely devoted to accounting for the flows of goods and services that were determined by the plans.[264] Soviet banks were not in the business of evaluating potential borrowers and making loans for those projects that appeared most promising. During the transition, independent commercial banks should emerge that will explicitly take on the job of funnelling investment funds to high-valued users. But the unwillingness to impose hard budget constraints on enterprises slowed the development of the commercial banking sector. Writing in early 1993, Russian researchers Sergei Aukutsenek and Elena Belyanova concluded that 'in many respects the Russian financial system has not changed since the reforms began. . . . [T]he old system of credit allocation by the state continues to exist and is concealed behind the visible credit market.'[265] Also in 1993, the Russian government affirmed the right of privatized firms to receive access to sub-sidized state credits on an equal footing with state-owned enterprises, thereby indicating that privatization alone would not lead to a market allocation of credit.

Whether funnelled through banks or state enterprises, low interest, state-provided credits have the unfortunate end result of the printing of roubles to make good the loans, and the continued fuelling of inflation. This is another instance of the damage that can be caused by partial reforms; in this case, reforms that do not harden budget constraints and produce market interest rates. With the continuing availability of state-subsidized credit, which is often assured through personal connections between enterprise managers and bank officers (the bank may even have been established by the enter-prise, ensuring its access to loans), enterprises that continue to produce even useless output receive the financial means necessary for production.

A goal of price liberalization and free enterprise is that profits become useful indicators of the social value of the activities of enterprises. But if subsidies remain available and budget constraints remain soft, profits during the transition become even more unreliable signals of a firm's performance than they were under central planning. Firms can have profits on paper at the same time that they are not being paid by their customers. The real value of an enterprise's accumulated accounts receivable is unknown, and prob-ably unknowable. If the money to match the accounts receivable is forth-coming from the central bank (and the value of the roubles to be paid has not been undermined, relative to expenses, by inflation), then the firm may indeed be profitable, but perhaps only because its customers are being propped up. If the funds are not forthcoming, then the enterprise's paper profits are worthless.

## LESSONS FOR REFORM

The recognition that the unreformed Russian employment regime involved repressed unemployment and an enterprise-centred social welfare system bolsters one conclusion from the examination of price liberalization: to implement a successful reform, an explicit unemployment and welfare system must be created, since the rise in open unemployment that will accompany reform undermines the old enterprise-based social welfare system. This explicit welfare system will take a different form than the old implicit system, but it can be substantially less costly, as subsidies can be made available only to those individuals who are truly needy.

Other lessons for reform also emerge from examining the employment sector. For example, unemployment benefits should not be tied to past wages, because of the tremendous uncertainty as to what actually constitutes the wage rate in Russia. Given that official and unofficial wage components were generally inversely related – butchers had low state wages but high informal compensation – basing unemployment benefits on only the official portion of the previous wage would result in new inequities among workers from different industries. Brookings Institution economist Clifford Gaddy has argued that labour unrest during the reform era by coal miners, who traditionally have the highest official wages of any category of Russian industrial workers, has been sparked by the limited opportunities for coal miners to earn additional income informally. There is little to steal in a coal mine, and literally underground workers have a tough time producing for the 'underground' economy during official working hours.[266]

The extent of open unemployment can be minimized if reforms are led by freeing new economic activity. Emerging private enterprise can attract workers away from the state sector on a significant scale, as has happened in China and Eastern Europe, and is already taking place in Russia. The state sector can then wither away (as opposed to attempts at rapid privatization) as long as the government can resist demands for higher state wages. Resisting such demands may be quite difficult, however. Wages for employees in private businesses are typically 1.5 to 3 times the wages of comparable state employees.[267] Much of this difference can be explained by the non-wage compensation available in the state sector, but it is still probably the case that private-sector employees have higher real earnings, on average, than comparable state employees. (Part of the differential may also represent a 'risk premium', since private-sector employees may still enjoy less job security than state-sector employees.) If Russia were to remove the substantial legal barriers to entry into private enterprise, these wage differentials would draw labour out of the state sector until the wage rates equalized. But in the meantime, the remaining state sector workers are likely to press demands for higher wages, which if met will contribute to the government budget deficit and inflation, and slow down the withering away of the state sector.

Instead of raising state wages, the government may choose to limit private incomes in order to maintain the existing relationship in the remuneration between private and state employment. Like raising state-sector pay, though, wage limitations on the private sector, whether they take the form of direct wage controls or indirect levers on earnings such as high income tax rates, would prevent the gradual development of the private enterprise economy. To encourage the movement of labour into the private sector, therefore, the wage controls that are applied to state-owned enterprises should not be extended to private firms.[268] This is another instance of the undesirability of partial reforms, or rather policies that run counter to market-oriented reform.

The main danger of partial reforms in the employment realm, however, has already been discussed: partial reforms that maintain pre-existing economic distortions could result in the wrong firms adjusting, and adjusting in ways that are not socially beneficial. To prevent the costs of unemployment from rising, most market restrictions should be lifted before state enterprises are given unlimited managerial discretion and are cut off entirely from state subsidies. Price liberalization makes for a good start, and tariffs that remain fixed by the state, such as energy prices, should be raised to reduce or eliminate subsidies. Enterprise profits will then be a strong guide as to which firms will be solvent in the marketplace.

Freeing prices is the easy part. It is the next step, that of cutting state-owned enterprises off from government subsidies and tolerating the open unemployment, that has proved more difficult. Of course, for political purposes, after imposing hard budget constraints, the Russian government can elect to subsidize some of the insolvent firms. As long as this is not a pervasive phenomenon, it need not be particularly costly to the economy – at least not as costly as the unreformed system, where the government propped up all insolvent state-owned enterprises, without even knowing which firms were net recipients of subsidies.

The partial reform of price liberalization in the absence of hard budget constraints on state-owned enterprises, as occurred in Russia in 1992, also generates new problems. Under these circumstances, thanks to the easy availability of loans, enterprises do not have to alter their behaviour in response to the free prices. 'Free' prices then are similar to higher but administratively fixed prices, in that they discourage demand but induce little supply response, at least from the state sector. (The private sector, not dependent on subsidies, may respond to free prices all the more quickly, if the potential state sector competitors are not interested, particularly if government constraints do not severely limit or preclude private market activity.)

The final implication of the implicit/explicit approach in the employment realm echoes an earlier contention: the initial gains to even a well-designed reform are not monumental. Just as many of the costs of unemployment were already being borne in the unreformed economy, many of the benefits of reform were already being captured. The large amount of de facto private activity, which has increased markedly in the Gorbachev–Yeltsin years through spontaneous privatization, implies that the most flagrant wastes of labour were informally curtailed long ago. While the partially reformed nature of the Russian economy channels some activity into endeavours that are not socially valuable – e.g., the continuing energy subsidies lead to great waste in that area – the existing private market ameliorates the problem. People are not likely to waste even subsidized gasoline if they can easily sell it at high market prices.

## DISTRIBUTION AGAIN

It must be remembered that there is nothing more difficult to plan, more doubtful of success, nor more dangerous to manage than the creation of a new system. For the initiator has the enmity of all who would profit by the preservation of the old institutions and merely lukewarm defenders in those who would gain by the new ones.

Machiavelli[269]

Increasing the size of the social pie is not necessarily a good thing if the slices of the pie that some individuals receive get smaller. Workers who lose their current jobs because of enterprise bankruptcies or downsizing are strong candidates to be among those who are harmed by reforms – though sensing this, many Russian workers have already left enterprises with poor prospects. It is important to (at least partially) compensate unemployed workers, if only to ensure that popular discontent with reform does not become sufficient to scuttle reform efforts. Markets may well be viewed as being unfair if some industrious workers lose their jobs and incomes while others prosper post-reform, merely as an artefact – albeit an important artefact – of market prices. Of course, the pre-reform fixed-price system created economically-arbitrary winners and losers. With reform, alternatively, 'strong' enterprises and industries will be those that efficiently produce socially-valuable products.[270] Nevertheless, unfavourable movements from the status quo for some people surely will be perceived as particularly unfair, providing yet another reason to create an explicit social welfare system.[271]

There has been concern expressed about the rise of an ownership class, on the grounds that Russians are not ready to accept such a development.[272] Reform will allow some entrepreneurs to earn large profits: there is already a Russian millionaires' club. (That is a million dollars, not a million roubles.) A significant share of total income will then represent a return to the ownership of capital (interest and profits). Capital income seemingly entails a profound change from the pre-reform situation, when almost all household income was earned as a payment to labour in the form of wages, bonuses, and in-kind compensation. There were no (open) capitalists collecting profits or interest payments. Once again, though, the unreformed system is misleading when taken at face value. Productive assets were controlled by individuals, even if they were not the 'owners'. Often, these individuals could extract a return from their control of capital, via bribes, favours, or simply free market sales. Capital did earn some positive return (even above the low nominal interest rates applied to individual savings accounts), and there were millionaires in the pre-perestroika Russian economy.[273] Still, reform is likely to increase the number of individuals who are substantially more wealthy than the average. Under the planning regime, the necessity of keeping illegal private economic activity fairly well hidden limited the scale of such endeavours – hired labour, for example, constituted only a small fraction of labour inputs into the pre-reform second economy.[274] With reform, the scale of successful private enterprises will increase, and the owners should therefore reap greater returns.

The return to various skills will undergo a tremendous re-alignment during transition. Some professions that require substantial education and training, such as the medical profession, were poorly paid under the Soviet regime, though again, informal mechanisms for increasing the pay of doctors abounded.[275] The hours invested in Marxian studies or the Marxian version of social sciences, which were well rewarded under the old system, will become relatively worthless. Simultaneously, highly-trained engineers and technical workers may increase their standing, perhaps by participating in joint ventures with Western firms, though the relative over-supply of technical workers may make some engineering skills less valuable under free markets.[276] Incentives to accumulate human capital in business fields such as accounting and finance are already increasing dramatically. Traders skilled in the ways of free markets can also reap large returns, as the new system of free relative prices develops and stabilizes.[277]

Just as the elimination of Social Security in the West would tend to harm older citizens relative to younger citizens, Russian reforms are biased towards the young. Younger people will have more time to enjoy the eventually increased living standards, and they have committed fewer resources to the pre-reform system. They have more time and incentive to invest in high-return education and training. Not surprisingly, younger Russians are much more prepared to enter the private sector than older workers.[278] A 1993 survey indicated that younger people were more likely to have seen an improvement in their economic situation from the previous year, and to be more optimistic about their future economic prospects.[279] Older Russians, particularly those on fixed incomes, may find themselves relatively worse off with reform. One mitigating factor is that older people have generally been able to accumulate some wealth in the form of housing and durable consumer goods. Difficulties that arise during transition can then be overcome by liquidating some of this wealth, an option that younger people, most of whom did not have an opportunity to acquire a substantial holding of consumer goods, do not share.

## REAL WAGES

What is the wage of an average Russian worker? Thanks to the wide-scale provision of goods like housing and food through the work place and informal opportunities to supplement the basic wage and bonuses by taking bribes or stealing time, calculations of a Russian worker's compensation are complex. Inflation further complicates the determination of a worker's wage.

When there is inflation, wages tend to go up along with other prices, though not by the same percentage. Higher wages and higher prices are not necessarily preferable to constant wages and constant prices, because a dollar of wages will buy less as the prices of goods in the shops inflate. Increases in wages that only match the price inflation do not make workers better off.

Economists attempt to account for the illusion of prosperity when inflation raises wages by taking out the component of wage increases that reflect generally higher prices. The resulting wage statistic is called the 'real wage', and it serves to measure the actual purchasing power of wages, simultaneously providing a proxy for the standard of living of a worker. The real wage is calculated by dividing the nominal money level of wages (what a worker actually receives in his or her pay cheque) by a price index that measures inflation. The price index equals 100 in some specified base year, so real wages are expressed in dollars (or roubles) of that year. As an example, US wages in private nonagricultural industries averaged $7.68 per hour in 1982, and averaged $10.50 per hour in December 1991. If the US price level is defined to be 100 in 1982, it would be about 140 in 1991: in other words, prices on average went up 40 per cent in the US between 1982 and 1991. Real wages in December 1991 were $10.50/140 = 7.48 per hour measured in 1982 dollars – actually lower, in real terms, than they were in 1982.[280]

While the procedure for determining real wages is straightforward, the results can be quite misleading in the circumstances of a reforming socialist economy. The numerator of the real wage calculation, the nominal monetary wage, is rendered nearly meaningless unless in-kind and informal components of compensation are also included. The denominator, the price index, is even more problematic. Price indices capture the change from repressed to open inflation as though it represented new inflation, because the original (base year) prices are understated when the official state prices are used: for example, the costs of searching and queuing for goods are not reflected in the pre-reform price

Average annual rate of growth (%) of the average real wage, USSR

| Year | Growth rate |
| --- | --- |
| 1986 | 0.9 |
| 1987 | 2.4 |
| 1988 | 7.7 |
| 1989 | 7.2 |
| 1990 | 8.2 |
| 1991 | −2.1 |

Source: IMF (1992a, p. 62)

index. But even if corrections for this understatement could be made, deter-mining the pre-reform price level is exceedingly difficult, since there were multiple official prices for each good. The prices that a person had to pay depended on the person's official position, with high official positions generally associated with lower prices.[281]

Thanks to all of these complications, the calculation of real wages in Russia using the official price and wage data is ludicrous. (See the table above.) The early years of perestroika (1988-90), according to the official statistics, were marked by tremendous increases in the real wage. These large increases in real wages should have been associated with a tremendous economic boom. Later, the sharp drop in real wages in 1991 would seem to signal an economic crash.

In reality, neither the boom nor the crash took place.[282] Actual prices facing consumers during the early years of perestroika increased much faster than the official price index, because of the increased amount of repressed inflation. This trend was reversed in 1991 and 1992, when the repressed inflation was largely converted to open inflation. The total growth in real wages evidenced by the table is more than 25 per cent between 1986 and 1992 – an equally nonsensical figure, signalling an elusive prosperity. Nor can the usual association of real wages with living standards be maintained during the Russian transition, as moonlighting and multiple job holdings increased significantly. The real wage is a textbook example of how statistics from an economy undergoing a transition from socialism to capitalism can be particularly misleading.

## MISLEADING UNEMPLOYMENT STATISTICS

Price indices and the real wage are not the only statistics that tend to be misleading during transitions. Changes in unemployment rates are also suspect. The large rise in measured unemployment that will accompany a successful reform does not signal economic deterioration; rather, it reflects a shift in unemployment from the repressed to the open variety.

Not only is the change in the measured unemployment rate during reform not indicative of actual economic changes, the level of unemployment may itself be misleading. Officially unemployed workers often hold jobs in the informal economy. Anecdotal evidence suggests that unrecorded second economy jobs in transitional economies can result in immensely overstated measured unemployment rates. A leading spokeswoman for the poverty lobby in Hungary reportedly has said that eight out of 10 registered unemployed Hungarians have other sources of income. The same report tells of a Hungarian agricultural cooperative that declared its work force 'unemployed', bussed them to the unemployment benefits office, and then bussed them directly back to work.[283] The official unemployment rate in Poland is thought to overstate unemployment by approximately one-third.[284]

The effects of increasing second economy activity on economic indicators such as the unemployment rate can have serious and deleterious ramifications. Policy-makers will be tempted to change policies in response to a perceived worsening economic situation, even as the actual situation is not deteriorating.[285] This is particularly true of transforming socialist economies, as the initial levels of the indicators are themselves quite distorted.

While unfavourable statistics can sometimes mask positive developments, favourable statistics can likewise conceal less favourable movements. Potentially, one such statistic is the exceedingly low official unemployment rate in Russia, remaining under two per cent throughout 1993.[286] This figure could be understated for a variety of reasons, including the fact that Russian citizens have little incentive to register as unemployed, when unemployment benefits are relatively modest. A person registered as unemployed is also subject to government efforts to place the worker in a new job, which some people view more as a penalty than a service. Furthermore, the official unemployment rate excludes workers who are on short time or forced variations, or who are not paid their full salary in a timely fashion. But the most likely cause of the low unemployment rate is that decisive restructuring has yet to take place within state-owned enterprises – a conclusion bolstered by the almost total lack of plant closings. Of course, important gradual changes have occurred since perestroika began, both in the new private sector and the privatized state enterprises. But the transition from repressed to open unemployment that is almost sure to accompany the imperative state-sector restructuring has yet to appear. As one Russian economist, perhaps overly pessimistic, told me in the summer of 1992, 'Reform cannot be said to have begun until the unemployment rate is three per cent'.

Finally, it is the effect of unemployment on human welfare, and not the amount of unemployment in itself, that matters most. For this reason, Western economists often focus on the duration of unemployment, and persistently high unemployment rates among socio-economic groups such as minority teenagers. In transitional Russia, the welfare losses from un-employment have tended to be low. It is extremely rare for a Russian household not to contain at least one employed person, even if some member of the household is unemployed. (This could change, however, if large firms in 'company towns' close down.) Participation in informal economic activities, such as self-provision of food, also limits the impact of unemployment. Based on annual surveys of Russians conducted since 1992, British economist Richard Rose concludes that in Russia, 'the effect of unemployment upon a household's economy tends to be temporary and marginal'.[287]

# Chapter 5

# Privatization

In this sense, the theory of the Communists may be summed up in the single phrase: Abolition of private property.

Karl Marx and Friedrich Engels, *The Communist Manifesto* [288]

## INTRODUCTION

Socialism is frequently defined as an economic system in which capital goods, the 'means of production', are state-owned, as opposed to capitalism, where private individuals own capital and can employ it for their own gain. Accordingly, the privatization of capital goods is a leading issue in the Russian transformation from socialism to capitalism, and an official privatization programme is ongoing. Treatises on economic reform in formerly socialist countries typically devote a good deal of attention to such privatization programmes.

The discussion here has so far been notable for almost completely skirting the issue of official privatization. Voucher schemes, auctions, multi-coloured coupons and the other paraphernalia of various official privatization schemes have been honoured here only in the breach, while the somewhat shady spontaneous version of privatization has uncustomarily received the observance. This madness is partly thrust upon, as Russian reality had seen a good deal of spontaneous privatization prior to any official privatization; and it is partly achieved of method, reflecting my view that official privatization is not an indispensable element, particularly in the early stages, of a successful transformation. What is indispensable, as previously argued, is the freeing of *new* economic activity and the provision of a relatively undistorted economic environment. Combined with the privatization of small-scale state-owned enterprises such as restaurants and retail outlets, new private endeavours and the emergence of pre-existing market activity have already created a substantial open market economy in Russia. With time, this emerging private activity can swamp the state-owned sector, so that official privatization of large state-owned industries becomes a desirable but not too pressing policy. The state-owned sector can wither away instead of being 'big-banged' out of existence.

At the same time, within the traditionally state-owned sector, what matters is not so much whether assets are state-owned or privately-owned, but rather the environment in which the ownership claims exist and the performance incentives that accompany ownership. State ownership is not prima facie 'worse' than private ownership. Under Soviet conditions, though, state ownership and fixed prices resulted in poor incentives to create economic wealth.

The improved economic environment in Russia, most particularly the liberalization of prices and the partial hardening of enterprise budget constraints, has led to improved performance from many state-owned enterprises even prior to privatization. Recall that during 1991 and 1992, one survey indicated that 80 per cent of enterprises had changed their suppliers or customers to some extent.[289] Product innovations and the shedding of excess labour have also been common.[290] A new concern with the sale of output, as opposed to the production of output, has become widespread.[290*]

Nevertheless, at some point privatization of the 'commanding heights' of the economy, those large-scale industrial enterprises, must be addressed. Once again, the issue of privatization is clarified by understanding the pre-reform situation. Not surprisingly, the ownership structure in Russia during the pre-reform era involved many implicit, repressed elements. As discussed in the previous chapter, de facto ownership claims by individuals over capital goods existed under Russian socialism, despite de jure state ownership. Since the de facto property rights were not recognized in pre-reform official statistics, assessments of reform based on the number of state-owned firms that have been 'privatized' are inadequate and even misleading indicators of the extent of private ownership and marketization in the Russian economy.

Partial reform measures in the privatization sphere, as elsewhere, can raise the costs of transition. Privatization is not a desirable policy unless accompanied by complementary reforms. Recall that a partial reform that includes privatization and free foreign trade but not price liberalization, for example, would be dangerous. Entrepreneurs would purchase goods that are underpriced in Russia – oil, for instance – and export them, reaping the economic rent created by the price controls while the Russian government pays the subsidy. Or, they might purchase a cheap input like energy, and produce a final product like tropical flowers for export. A reform that includes privatization but does not include the establishment of an explicit social safety net may also be undesirable, as newly unemployed workers may suffer unduly.

## PRIVATIZATION GUIDELINES

By enlisting the aid of various partial reforms, it is comparatively easy to design detrimental, even disastrous privatization schemes. But what properties should be exhibited by a potentially successful privatization programme for large-scale industrial enterprises? I will mention five such properties, though not all would receive universal assent, nor would a failure to exhibit all of these properties clearly spell doom for a privatization programme: they are desirable, not essential. Two of the features concern the destination of enterprise reform. The first, near to the heart of economists, is that at the end of the process, clear, explicit property rights should be established. Informality (of property rights) breeds contracting problems, so informality should be limited by reducing ownership un- certainty. A second desirable property for the destination of a privatization programme is related to the first: not only should clear ownership claims be established, but the owners should in general have strong incentives to take socially-valuable actions. A law that stipulates that everyone gets paid an identical amount no matter what his or her actions would surely provide poor incentives for 'owners' and, for that matter, everyone else.

Three other markers of successful privatization concern the nature of the transition path to private ownership. First, the privatization scheme should largely validate pre-existing ownership claims. Taking away what people regard (often for good reason) as their property is bound to generate resent- ment and opposition. (There may be competing 'ownership' claims pre- reform, but the system was so well-established and stable in Russia that I believe this complication is relatively unimportant.) It can be argued that the pre-existing ownership structure is unfair, and should not be respected. But it can also be argued that the pre-existing claims are no more unfair than other distributions, and that there are better ways of dealing with unfairness than through the privatization scheme – with progressive taxation, for instance, or an improved social safety net.[291]

Beyond the respect for pre-existing claims, I believe that 'fair' access is a second desirable property for the transition to private ownership. A privat- ization programme should not be systematically biased against classes of people who are identifiable prior to the programme. (After the fact, there are bound to be relative winners and losers.) In general this property would seem to require widespread access to the privatization programme, so that pensioners, for example, are not sure to be excluded from the benefits of privatization. And the final desirable feature of ownership transition is that the privatization programme be relatively swift, both to generate improved enterprise performance and to limit the amount of special pleading that enterprises and individuals can engage in to try to garner more of the benefits for themselves.

## PRE-REFORM PROPERTY RIGHTS

By informal property right we mean legally unsanctioned and even illegal, yet in reality effective, control over assets for private profit or other form of access to future streams of informal/illegal income and consequent wealth. Such an informal right may be an expected and de facto accepted by-product of a legitimate job (a very common situation).

Gregory Grossman[292]

'State ownership' of the means of production, in itself, leaves a host of questions unanswered. (So does 'private ownership'.) Sometimes it is said that state ownership of an asset means that everybody owns it, which means that nobody owns it: ownership, like 'priority', cannot accrue equally to all without eviscerating the concept in the process. But it is not really the case that state ownership is the same as no ownership. Some person or group of people controls the uses and returns to capital goods, even in a socialist society. Economist Yoram Barzel makes this point quite emphatically:[293]

> The distinction between the private and the public sectors is not a distinction between the presence and absence of private property rights. Such rights are necessarily present in both systems. The distinction lies in organization, and particularly in the incentives and rewards under which producers tend to operate. In the private sector, producers are more readily given the opportunity to assume the entire direct effects of their actions. In the government sector, people assume a smaller portion of the direct effects of their actions.

State ownership, then, is associated with relatively weak incentives for the owners, whomever they are, to take actions that are socially valuable, since the owners' rewards are not tied closely to 'the direct effects of their actions'. It is these poor incentives that have sullied the reputation of state ownership. But this is not to say that state ownership *requires* poor incentives.

As an example of state ownership, it might be useful to broaden the earlier discussion of the operation of a Russian state-owned restaurant to state-owned enterprises more generally. Under an ideal version of central planning, an enterprise would receive its output plan and requisite inputs from the state, and hire workers at wages that were state-controlled. It would then deliver the planned output to the centrally-specified downstream customers, at prices – accounting entries, basically – that were also state-controlled. If the enterprise happened to make a profit (measured at the fixed state prices), then the profit would be returned to the state. Under this ideal centrally-planned system, workers have the property right to their centrally-determined wages: a fixed payment, largely independent of the 'direct effects of their actions'. Downstream customers have property rights to their share of the planned output at the fixed prices, and the state is the 'residual claimant', receiving whatever is left over after the claims of the other parties are satisfied.

The official Soviet system did not attempt to implement such an extreme form of central planning. Rather, official compensation was tied somewhat more directly to the effects of employees' actions, at least as measured by the plan indicators. To provide better incentives for workers, bonuses were available for above-plan output, with the bonus fund depending on a host of indicators of enterprise performance.[294] Similarly, some profits could be retained by enterprises for investment purposes.[295] Wages were supplemented in areas with poor working or living conditions, such as for coal miners or for jobs in the Far North. The administratively-set prices were, in general and relative terms, not inconsistent with market-based scarcity prices.[296]

Of course, the actual operation of a state-owned enterprise in Russia bore little relationship to either the ideal version of central planning or the de jure system. Extra-plan, informal activity generally moved the economy towards the form of organization associated with private property, with compensation tied more closely to the direct effects of actions. (And the measures of the effects of action in the informal economy were no longer plan indicators, but real market values, and hence more in tune with consumer preferences.) Bribes to official and unofficial suppliers, theft of goods and time from work, second economy production on the official job, bribes from customers, and bribes to secure employment: all formed the part and parcel of 'really existing' socialism.

The de facto system of property rights therefore differed considerably from the de jure system. Workers and managers were, to a degree, residual claimants of their enterprises' profits – in some sense, owners. The central government was likely to receive close to a fixed payment, the 'planned profit' for the enterprise. High officials in the planning or party networks, who controlled either supplies or the jobs that controlled supplies, received bribes, and presumably higher bribes for increased supplies. Customers generally could not convert roubles to goods at the fixed prices, but could do so at higher prices, paid either in roubles or partly in time and partly in roubles. There was even a substantial, illegal 'capital market', where underground firms could be bought and sold.[297] And of course, the shadow system of property rights was closely tied to Communist Party positions.

The pre-reform system thus had many elements of a private ownership, market economy, where producers had opportunities to serve as residual claimants. As Gregory Grossman noted in 1977, the Soviet second economy was 'a kind of spontaneous surrogate economic reform that imparts a necessary modicum of flexibility, adaptability, and responsiveness to a formal setup that is too often paralyzing in its rigidity, slowness, and inefficiency. It represents a de facto decentralization, with overtones of the market.'[298]

## THE REFORM PERIOD

The market overtones of the Soviet second economy amplified considerably during the Gorbachev era via spontaneous privatization. Three factors helped to promote marketization during the perestroika years. First, the degree of repressed inflation increased, simultaneously raising the benefits available from diverting state-sector goods to the private sector, since the free prices in the private sector rose, while the state prices remained, for the most part, fixed. In the language of property rights theory, the value of assets that were previously 'in the public domain' appreciated, increasing the incentives for private individuals to garner control of those assets, legally or illegally.[299] The second factor promoting marketization was that legal routes to garner control of state goods and assets were expanded. For example, the Law on Cooperatives provided one quasi-legal route to divert state-sector goods into private hands. Reform provisions thereby lowered the costs of diverting state-sector goods to free markets at the same time that the benefits from so doing were increasing. The third factor driving spontaneous privatization might be termed an 'insurance incentive'. As the stability of the old system began to be undermined during the late 1980s, individuals saw that their implicit property rights were threatened by reform. They had an incentive, then, to insure their ownership claims by converting their implicit property rights into explicit rights that would be more likely to survive the reform process. Together, these three factors led to marketizations that in many cases were complete enough to merit the now familiar term 'spontaneous privatization'.

But the increasingly formal private property rights in Russia did not translate into an efficient economy. High transaction costs, as discussed in Chapter 2, are a major impediment. Furthermore, the extent to which reform has brought rewards that are closely related to the direct effects of actions has been limited by government policy. The owners of privatized firms do not necessarily become residual claimants. Because the Russian government has been unwilling to cut off subsidies to unprofitable enterprises, owners do not face significant penalties for failure.[300] The up-side potential for private activity within the former state-owned enterprises may also be limited, as it was in the pre-reform system, to the extent that successful enterprises will be the source of subsidies for the unsuccessful firms. The 'partial reform' of continuing state subsidies has reduced the value of the shift from repressed to open private property rights.

This reflects the more general point noted above, that privatization is not an end in itself. (For that matter, neither is a Western-style market economy, but it appears to be the best means to the higher living standards that presumably are an end.) The important conditions for the efficient operation of a market economy are generally free prices, and strong incentives to respond to those free prices. Residual claimant status provides the strong incentives for owners, and free prices enhance the probability that the privately profitable decisions will be socially valuable, whether the state or an individual is the official owner. In the absence of generally free prices and strong incentives to respond, the Russian economy is unlikely to markedly improve, irrespective of the extent of privatization. Indeed, some privatized firms operate exactly as they did under state ownership.[301]

## OFFICIAL RUSSIAN PRIVATIZATION

The ongoing Russian privatization plan includes three variants for large enterprises.[302] Under two of the variants, large firms (more than 1000 employees or a book value exceeding 50 million roubles) are being converted into capitalist-style joint-stock companies. Ownership shares are then distributed, with the two variants distinguished by the amount, type (preferred or common), and price of stock available to employees and management. In each of these distributions, no less than 25 per cent of the stock would go to 'insiders', the workers and managers of the enterprise. A third, considerably less popular, alternative is for the employees of part or all of an enterprise to submit a reorganization plan that requires some additional investment on their part. After one year, if they have lived up to the terms of the agreement, employees then have some priority in purchasing common stock. Remaining shares are slated to be auctioned off to the general public. In practice, workers and managers of a privatized enterprise are likely to control no less than 40 per cent of the shares under any of the privatization schemes, and early results indicated that some 70 per cent of shares were initially procured by enterprise insiders.

Not all of the shares are being sold for roubles, however. By early 1993, nearly every Russian citizen had received a 'privatization cheque', a small piece of paper with a serial number and a face value of 10,000 roubles printed on it. At least 29 per cent of the shares of large enterprises are slated to be auctioned off using privatization cheques.[303] The purpose of privatization cheques is to widen the scope of privatization and render it more fair. Teachers, doctors, pensioners, and others who do not work for privatizing state-owned enterprises can still take part in privatization, and at no monetary cost, by purchasing ownership shares of an enterprise with their privatization cheques.

Privatization cheques counter the bias towards enterprise insiders in the privatization process, but they certainly do not eliminate insider advantages. Indeed, there are further aspects of privatization that favour existing workers and managers, beyond the privileged access to ownership shares. Employees who spontaneously privatized their enterprises by leasing their assets prior to 3 July, 1991, the date of the original Russian Federation law on privatization, can now become employee-owned. Firms in fields such as R&D and defence are exempt from mandatory privatization, though spontaneous privatizations are taking place among enterprises in these industries. Finally, the auctions of the remaining shares of enterprise stock, whether for privatization cheques or cash, are tainted by a seemingly large informational advantage of insiders. How can an outsider have a good sense of the value of a privatizing firm, relative to insiders? One mechanism that helps outside investors is the development of a 'market for information'. Russians can sell their privatization cheques to other individuals or for shares of mutual funds, that then invest the collected cheques on the funds behalf. The funds – there are more than 500 in Russia – presumably are better positioned to learn about the enterprises in which they invest than are individual shareholders. Still, insider advantages are not overcome by these contrivances, and the remaining insider bias may be large enough to chill the competitive nature of the share auctions.[304] A similar phenomenon exists in the West, where it is feared that widespread insider trading makes stock market transactions less attractive to outside investors.

How does the Russian official privatization programme measure up against the privatization 'success indicators' promulgated earlier in this chapter? As for creating clear ownership claims, the official Russian programme appears to accomplish this goal straightforwardly: the shareholders are the owners of firms. The protection of pre-existing de facto ownership claims is also largely achieved in the privatization programme, via the preferences given to enterprise workers and management. Thanks to this policy, there has been virtually universal voluntary compliance with the privatization programme. And except for the desirable bias towards existing workers and managers, there appears to be little discrimination against identifiable social groups in privatization. The mass distribution of vouchers gives all Russians a stake in privatization, though worker-manager control appears to be the likely short-term outcome. Furthermore, the speed of the Russian privatization programme compares favourably with that of Eastern Europe. By privatizing most non-defence state-owned enterprises more-or-less simultaneously, special pleading has been held to a minimum. Creating privatization cheques and stock markets out of thin air has required some time, of course, particularly in comparison with the alternative of simply turning firms over to their workers, but the generally perceived increase in fairness may have been worth the extra time.[305]

It is with respect to the incentives for the new owners that the Russian privatization programme is most vulnerable. The first obstacle, familiar in the West, is that in the absence of a single controlling owner, individual shareholders have limited incentives to actually monitor the activities of the firms that they 'own'. Most employees in the US who own shares of firms via their pension plans do not pay close attention to the management decisions in the firms in which their pensions are invested, though perhaps the pension fund managers do. Wide distribution of vouchers virtually rules out a controlling owner in the short term. Again, however, much of the ownership is accruing to workers and managers, who should have the interest, information, and ability to exercise effective ownership control. Incentives for worker-owners should be fairly 'high-powered', since their wages and profit shares will directly depend on the performance of the enterprise – unless continuing state subsidies provide adequate compensation irrespective of performance.

Worker ownership is not necessarily ideal, however. Workers do not have the same incentives that outside owners might have; in particular, workers might be reluctant to hire more employees, since another employee not only receives wages but also dilutes the ownership shares of those already working. (An outside owner would not be similarly reluctant since the new worker would not get a stake in ownership.) Worker-owners also face some diversification problems, since both their labour income (their wages) and their investment income are tied up in the same firm. In general it might be thought that individuals would prefer to invest in firms other than the one in which they work, to minimize their exposure to bankruptcy of the firm.

The empirical evidence on worker ownership is not encouraging. First, the practice was institutionalized in Yugoslavia, without much success. Second, worker ownership is rare in Western market economies, where it is perfectly legal and feasible. If worker ownership were economically beneficial, would there not be more of it in the West?

Perhaps. But the West is not undergoing a transition from socialism. As Harvard economist Martin Weitzman argues, during transitions worker ownership can play a valuable role, particularly in maintaining employment.[306] With relatively free stock markets, over time more efficient ownership structures can evolve to replace worker ownership – workers can sell their ownership shares to outsiders. The official Russian privatization programme therefore has the virtue of not fixing a final ownership pattern – unlike the Yugoslavian precedent – but rather allows for the evolution of the form of 'normal market economy' that best suits Russian conditions.

The Russian privatization programme, taken in isolation, seems to offer fairly good incentives for new enterprise owners. But privatization is not taking place in isolation. It may well be the environment created by other policies not directly related to the privatization scheme that could undermine the programme. One such policy would be an unwillingness, perhaps because of concerns with extensive monopoly power, to extricate the government from its old duty of price setting. Whatever the incentives that the owners would then have, there would be little reason to suspect that they would be well aligned with social benefits. A second stumbling block has already been mentioned, that of continuing government subsidies to privatized firms because of fears of open unemployment: in 1993, the Russian government indicated that privatized firms would receive the same access to subsidized state credits as state-owned enterprises![307] Without penalties for failure, incentives to respond well to free prices are reduced, though not necessarily eliminated. Third, excessive taxation of successful enterprises, perhaps to raise revenue for subsidies to poorly-performing firms, will similarly limit the incentives for private sector firms to engage in socially valuable activities. Fourth, slow movement on the development of state-enforced contract law will keep transaction costs high. Finally, it is competitive markets that seem to provide good incentives. Constraints on new private activity, such as the onerous licensing requirements, will reduce the degree of competition faced by privatized firms in the Russian market economy, and thereby reduce the benefits of privatization.

# Chapter 6

# Monopoly

## INTRODUCTION

Monopoly, the control of an industry by a single seller (or perhaps a small group of sellers) is one situation in which free markets are likely to result in socially undesirable outcomes. Monopolists in market economies produce too little output from a social point of view, in order to sustain high prices and profits, and so they at least partially deserve their bad public image. The high profits, in turn, attract competitors. Unless there is some barrier preventing the entry of new firms, monopolies in market economies tend to be short-lived.

Central planning in Russia, however, was invested with the legal authority to sustain a highly monopolistic industrial structure. Thirty to forty per cent of manufactured products, including sewing machines, freezers, and colour-photography paper, had a single producing enterprise within the USSR.[308] Presumably, the planning task was made easier by dealing with a relatively small number of big firms than with a host of little firms: the enforcement of price controls and centralized rationing could be streamlined. Market-oriented reform in Russia, it is often argued, holds the danger of creating an economic system dominated by large monopoly producers. Some observers suggest that privatization should be postponed until after the forced de-monopolization of Russian industry, in order to forestall the detrimental effects of monopoly firms operating in a market environment.[309]

The existence of monopoly in the pre-reform Russian economy holds implications for the analysis of reform and the role of demonopolization. Monopoly 'rents', or excess profits, were available in the pre-reform Russian system, though not in the usual market economy form of excessive profits arising from prices that are high relative to costs.[310] Rather than focusing on how best to combat post-reform monopoly or on how to demonopolize prior to reform, the initial question for reform becomes whether the social costs attributed to mono-poly are higher in the pre- or post-reform setting. In other words, to what extent is monopoly a *reform* problem? This chapter argues that the costs of monopoly were substantially greater in the pre-reform Russian economy than they will be in the fully reformed system, though the reduction in the costs of monopoly that will accompany reform can be slowed or reversed if anti-competitive measures – partial reforms – are adopted. From this perspective, excessive industrial concentration is not an important issue for a comprehensive market reform, irrespective of concentration's detrimental impact on the Russian economy. Russia would be lucky indeed if the only economic problem that it had to worry about was monopoly.[311]

## MEASURING MONOPOLY

For a change of pace, I would like to begin this section by talking about the ease in interpreting the reliable Soviet statistics on monopoly power. But, of course, I can't. Plus ça change . . . As with inflation and unemployment, measures of the degree of monopoly power in Russian industry may be misleading. Consider, first, measures based on 'concentration ratios', the percentage of a good's production that derives from the one, two, three (or more) largest producing enterprises. (Concentration ratios are typical measures of monopoly power employed in the West.) In 1988, the market share of the single largest Soviet producer exceeded 50 per cent for over 60 per cent of product groups; for the US in 1982, the four largest producers exceeded a 50 per cent market share in less than 30 per cent of manufacturing industries.[312] This appears to be rather unambiguous evidence that the pre-reform Soviet economy was more concentrated than the US economy.

One problem with concentration ratios, however, derives from the extreme amount of vertical integration in Russian firms.[313] Because of the near-impossibility of disciplining state-owned monopoly suppliers, Russian enterprises (and ministries) produced many of their own inputs, as noted earlier. Dr Ed Hewett wrote that in the planned Soviet economy, 'the successful enterprise is the vertically integrated enterprise, and the successful ministry, the vertically integrated ministry'.[314] As a result, in the situations where an enterprise (or a ministry) was particularly dependent on a single supplier, vertical integration (perhaps conducted informally) probably occurred prior to reform. A second factor suggesting that concentration statistics yield a distorted view of the extent of monopoly power in the pre-reform system consists of the defence sector. Production in the defence complex was virtually a black box, with what happened inside a fairly closely guarded secret. Goods that were produced by a single civilian seller may also have been produced in the defence sector, though the defence production would generally not be reflected in official concentration statistics. And in making comparisons between Russia and Western market economies, it should be kept in mind that the planned imports in Russia – the state had an official monopoly on foreign trade – rarely offered effective competition to domestic producers in the Soviet system, whereas imports often provide important competitive elements in the West.

Another type of statistic that is used to document the extent of monopoly power in the pre-reform Russian economy focuses on the large size of enterprises, often as measured by the number of employees. For example, 73.4 per cent of the (Soviet) work force was employed in enterprises with more than 1000 employees.[315] The average size of industrial enterprises in Soviet-type economies, in terms of number of employees, exceeded that of developed market economies by more than a factor of ten.[316] The interpretation of such statistics must be conditioned on the range of activities that occurred within Russian enterprises, however. The extent of horizontal conglomeration, as with vertical integration, was immense in the pre-reform Russian economy. As previously noted, an industrial enterprise was often involved in providing its workers with food, schools, hospitals, apartments, and a host of other goods and services that were outside the enterprise's main line of business. Concentration statistics that are based on the number of employees at average enterprises are then particularly suspect, as many of the employees were engaged in these sideline activities.

Incidentally, it is perhaps worth noting that the size of individual enterprises is not directly related to monopoly power, at least as monopoly is understood in the West. Monopoly power has to do with the extent of competition in the market for a firm's output, not with how big the company is. Duke University is a large employer (the biggest in Durham, North Carolina!), but its students choose among many competing schools, so Duke is not a monopolist. In the former Soviet Union, however, the monopoly problem associated with capitalism consisted of more than just high prices for the monopolist's output. Another problem associated with monopoly was the propensity of big, powerful enterprises to exploit their workers through low wages and benefits and poor working conditions. The number of employees at a firm is a useful indicator of these kinds of 'monopoly' problems, which approximates the Western notion of 'monopsony'. A monopsonist is a firm that represents the only purchaser of a good. Large firms may have monopsony power in the purchase of labour, as in the case of company towns (like Durham?). Nevertheless, the association of large enterprises with monopoly may be lingering into the post-Soviet era.[317]

The discussion so far indicates potential biases in the usual measures of monopoly power, but the difficulties of using the 'usual measures' in centrally-planned systems are even more fundamental. Concentration ratios or employment ratios calculated at the enterprise level are inappropriate measures of monopoly power in the pre-reform Russian setting, since the former industrial branch ministries provided a built-in cartel structure for the production of many goods.[318] Five producing enterprises that were all subordinated to a single ministry may have had as much monopoly power as a single firm, if the ministry could effectively act as a cartel ringleader. The number of competing ministries in the production of a good probably provides a more accurate guide to the degree of monopoly power than the number of producing enterprises. There was also a good deal of regional specialization, where a geographical area was supplied with a commodity from a single enterprise in the region. (A relatively poor transport infrastructure continues to provide more geographical insulation than is typical in Western market economies.) The number of producing enterprises nationwide would then serve as a poor indicator of the extent of competition.

Most importantly, however, the nature of the central planning system itself renders any statistic irrelevant as a measure of the extent of monopoly. Under Russian planning, virtually all producers were monopoly providers from the point of view of their customers. Downstream users were tied to individual suppliers by the plan. If an enterprise was dissatisfied with the performance of one of its suppliers, and the firm could not vertically integrate, it had little recourse.[319] At another level this was even the condition in retail trade. While Russian citizens could choose to shop at different outlets, the state was generally the only legal seller.[320] Monopoly power, though 'repressed', was nevertheless extensive.

The Russian planned economy therefore resulted in an industrial sector that was much more monopolized – irrespective of industrial concentration statistics – than its Western counterparts. How does the existence of monopoly pre-reform influence the Russian transition to capitalism?

## MONOPOLY RENTS, PRE- AND POST-REFORM

The 'dead-weight loss', the net social value of output that monopolists choose not to produce but that would be produced under competitive conditions, is the usual focus in identifying the social losses from monopolies in market economies. (Other social losses may arise from the money that enterprises spend on lawyers and lobbyists in an effort to obtain government support for a monopoly position.[321]) High prices relative to costs are then the most important indicators of social losses from monopoly. Under central planning, alternatively, almost all prices in the Russian state sector deviated significantly from real costs, which can not even be ascertained without free prices, anyway.[322] Fixed prices result in their own dead-weight losses; in fact, the inefficiencies of the fixed-price system are probably the major reason that Russia is undergoing economic reform. But the fixed-price regime indicates that the criterion of the deviation of price from (marginal) cost cannot easily be applied in assessing monopoly power in pre-reform Russia. The dead-weight loss of monopoly can not be distinguished from the efficiency losses and misallocations associated with fixed prices.

The social costs of Russian monopoly are indirectly indicated, however, by the nature and extent of the excess profits, 'rents', that accrue to monopolists. In a centrally-planned setting, monopoly rents take on different (and perhaps less visible) forms than in market economies. Large state monopolies in the pre-reform setting had a great deal of bargaining power in dealing with planners. They were therefore in a position to receive more inputs and lower output targets than firms in worse bargaining positions. Likewise, such firms had bargaining power with respect to customers, even those who were legally entitled via the plan (and the corresponding contract) to the monopolist's output. Large monopoly suppliers could then perform poorly with impunity, letting quality, output assortment, or delivery schedules slip.[323] Alternatively, the monopolists could informally solicit payments in cash or kind for their output – those high prices generally associated with monopoly. The inefficiencies of excessive vertical integration brought on by a firm's attempts to shield itself from unreliable suppliers should also be counted as a cost of monopoly in the pre-reform system. As Ed Hewett noted, 'The result [of excessive vertical integration] is costly for society: large quantities of goods and services produced in small batches at very high cost and probably of variable quality.'[324]

With privatization and price liberalization, monopoly assumes its market economy guise of reduced output (relative to hypothetical competitive levels). Monopoly rents will be generated by prices that are higher than costs. But now the familiar argument applies: the new form of monopoly during transition does not imply higher social costs. Indeed, the emergence of competitors (including imports) will almost certainly mean that the social costs of monopoly will be lower post-reform than pre-reform, even in the absence of any official anti-trust activity.

The basic reason is that the Russian economy can hardly become less competitive during reform, since it started with so little competition relative to that in market economies. With free enterprise, barriers to entry will disappear. Suppliers who dissatisfy their customers will see competitors spring up to take away their business. The Russian economy is quite large, making the prospects for the development of competitors bright relative to those in smaller, closed economies. With the 'emergence' and conversion of military industries, defence enterprises may surface as new competitors. Competition will also be given a boost to the extent that reform increases the participation of foreign firms in the Russian economy. The only monopolies that seem destined to survive reform will be natural monopolies – those monopolies that can produce any given level of output at lower cost than could competitive firms. Temporarily, perhaps some collusion among enterprises could restrict competition in sectors that are not natural monopolies. (Such collusion is difficult to sustain because it is generally in any individual firm's best interest to quietly break the collusive agreement.) But in any case, the post-reform situation will represent quite a departure from the pre-reform system, where nearly every producer was invested with a degree of monopoly power.

Of course, partial reform measures contain the possibility of worsening the monopoly situation during reform. First, some prices, particularly those of the outputs of producers deemed to be monopolists, could be controlled, undermining the incentive for competitors to emerge. Simultaneously, the combination of enterprise autonomy (making it possible for firms to respond to prices) and some fixed prices (as for energy) can result in the Polish tropical flowers problem. Second, government barriers to legal entry, such as a complex licensing system, could likewise prevent competitive pressures from coming to bear. (Private barriers to entry, perhaps due to organized crime, could also limit competition.) Third, the possibility of legal action against firms that raise their prices 'unfairly' could also act to 'fix' prices, and bring on the associated resource misallocations. In other words, government anti- monopoly policy could itself sustain monopoly. With a fairly comprehensive reform, however, monopoly power and the associated costs will fall.

## MONOPOLY AND PRIVATIZATION

Since the social costs of monopoly will automatically be reduced during a comprehensive reform, anti-trust activity would appear to have a low priority on the reform agenda. The best policy would seem to be to implement reasonably complete market-oriented reforms, let competition develop and conditions improve, and then tinker around the edges with regulations and anti-trust legislation for the few remaining monopolists. One potential problem with this happy scenario, though, is that the existence of monopolies may itself hinder the reform process. A common contention is that privatization is made more difficult by the presence of monopolies, implying that demonopolization must precede privatization.[325]

There are three main arguments. The first is that privatization, especially through sale, is more difficult for large enterprises than for small enterprises. The second is that demonopolization may be more inconvenient post-reform, and reform itself may increase industrial concentration. The third argument suggesting that industrial concentration hinders reform is that a large enterprise has bargaining power. Enough large enterprises may be able to bargain exceptions for themselves that privatization becomes meaningless.

Why should larger enterprises be more difficult to privatize than small enterprises? The possibility generally considered is that there are not enough wealthy citizens to become owners of huge enterprises. Of course, the enterprises will be sold in shares, not as indivisible units. The new owners do not have to consist of a few wealthy individuals. Another consideration is that the social consequences of bankruptcy are much greater for large enterprises than for small enterprises, so that privatization and the imposition of hard budget constraints are not credible policies. Government bailouts of major corporations in the US, for example, have occurred precisely because of the perceived social consequences of bankruptcy. Once again, however, this monopoly problem – actually a problem of large enterprises, not necessarily monopolists – is worse in the unreformed Russian economy.

No doubt many large enterprises are candidates for bankruptcy, but until prices are free and private ownership is established, it cannot be determined which ones. Now, all of the potentially bankrupt companies are being sustained by the government. Post-reform, failing companies that are deemed worthy may see increased infusions of cash from the private sector. Those that will still be non-viable will then become known. As previously noted, the government can then choose on an individual basis which ones to aid and which ones to let falter.

The concern that monopoly will increase during reform is prompted by reports of enterprises attempting vertical integration and horizontal conglomeration during the transition. In general, however, these types of transactions do not increase monopoly power. If large previously-competing producers attempt to merge, then perhaps some government oversight is desirable, but I know of no evidence of this occurring in Russia. So far, the concern that monopoly power will increase with transition appears to be empirically unjustified.

Preceding privatization with demonopolization may be sensible if the ability to implement anti-trust measures is likely to be greater in the pre-reform setting than after private ownership is established. In market economies, it appears that it is easier to prevent mergers from occurring than it is to break up firms that have already merged.[326] But in Russia, to the extent that new competition-reducing mergers are not taking place, the choice is between breaking up existing monopolies before or after reform. Since market-oriented reforms would seem to do much of this work automatically, and expose those firms that are truly viable monopolists, postponing anti-trust activity until after privatization would appear to be a more efficient strategy for combating monopoly. This point is amplified by a consideration of the limited number of trained personnel available to help manage the transition. Given the importance of such tasks as privatization and military conversion, devoting significant human resources to antitrust policy during the early stages of reform comes at a high cost.[327]

The argument that large enterprises may bargain exceptions for themselves to avoid privatization may well be correct. It is perhaps even more likely, however, that the exceptions they bargain for will be better terms for privatization or continued subsidies. In any case, the bargaining power already exists, and it might also prevent the implementation of demonopolization decrees. Reform and the increased competitive pressures are the best way of counteracting this bargaining power. As Russian economist G. Kazakevich has said, 'Every act of privatization is simultaneously an act of demonopolization.'[328]

Political and nationalistic problems are creating barriers to interregional trade in the former USSR. Regional economic policies that restrict the 'export' of locally-produced goods to other parts of Russia present another barrier.[329] By keeping out competitors, these trade barriers help sustain monopoly power. (The possibility that such barriers reduce trade and output, irrespective of their effect on monopoly power, is probably more significant.) But again, the increase in monopoly power due to trade disruptions is neither caused by economic reform nor worsened by reform, and some of the decreased competitiveness is clearly the result of local anti-reform policies. Political barriers to trade are unfortunate, but are not a problem for market-oriented reform per se.

Finally, two elements of monopoly may actually be beneficial for reform efforts. First, if monopoly pricing practices would generally be available after reform, and these high prices translate into high profits, then sales of monopoly firms during privatization should find plenty of buyers. Foreign firms should also be relatively eager to enter such potentially lucrative markets. (The high profits of monopolies also present a trade-off with the concern over the increase in open unemployment, as profitable monopolies will not go bankrupt.) Second, the breakdown in economic coordination that is sometimes feared from reform is ameliorated by industrial concentration. Downstream firms know precisely what supplier they will have to continue to deal with, and new enterprises should also be able to quickly learn where inputs are available.

## ANTI-MONOPOLY POLICY

It has been argued here that anti-trust policy should be accorded low priority in the design of market-oriented reform policies in Russia, and that the more appropriate time to consider anti-trust action is after market reform has been fully implemented and new competitors have had a chance to emerge.

There are two anti-trust measures that may be appropriate for the transitional era, however. First, a watchful eye could be kept on mergers of previously-competing enterprises. In cases where such mergers can be shown to involve large social costs, they should be prevented. Second, price fixing among competitors should be proscribed.

Anti-monopoly policy in Russia during reform has gone well beyond the relatively limited role that I think is desirable. Subsequent to the 2 January 1992 price liberalization, lists of enterprises designated as monopolists were established, at both the national and local levels. An enterprise was eligible for the anti-monopoly list if it produced more than 35 per cent of the output of a good, though in practice inclusion was rather arbitrary.[330] This criterion was even applied at local levels, where almost any large firm would exceed 35 per cent of the locally-produced output of its main products. Note also that the lists were based on local production, not on local sales. So vodka producers, for example, who faced stiff competition from many other vodka makers, including importers, were frequently on local anti-monopoly lists.

The outputs of an enterprise deemed to be a monopolist are subject to price regulation, and overall profitability limits can also be established. An enterprise that exceeds those limits can have its excess profits confiscated, even if they are not attributable to the goods for which it is considered to have a monopoly position. Since most large enterprises are considered monopolists, anti-monopoly policy has provided a mechanism to continue price controls and other features of the planning mechanism. Depending on the level of the price controls and profit ceilings, the monopolists may have little incentive to increase output. Other firms may also be reluctant to increase their market share for fear of being labelled a monopolist. Furthermore, price controls provide a rationale for money-losing firms to demand state subsidies. On balance, Russian anti-monopoly policies seem to be effectively serving as anti-reform measures.

# Chapter 7

# Income and living standards

if you can know but one fact about a man, knowledge of his income will probably reveal most about him. Then you can roughly guess his political opinions, his tastes, and education, his age, and even his life expectancy.
Nobel Prize-winning economist Paul A. Samuelson[331]

## CRISIS, CHAOS, COLLAPSE . . .

and Consensus. Virtually all observers in recent years appear to agree that the Russian economy is or will soon be in a state of crisis, chaos, and collapse:

> The economy is in a free fall with no prospects for reversal in sight. Severe economic conditions, including substantial shortages of food and fuel in some areas, the disintegration of the armed forces and ongoing ethnic conflict will combine this winter [1991–92] to produce the most significant disorder in the former U.S.S.R. since the Bolsheviks consolidated power.[332]
>
> Robert M. Gates, Director of the CIA in 1991–2

> The collapse of the Soviet Economy following the August coup is an event all but unprecedented in recent economic history. . . . The rapidity of the upheaval and the magnitude of the Soviet economic decline have been especially spectacular. In two to three years' time, the economy moved from positive growth to a drop in the GNP exceeding 20 percent and from relative price stability to a yearly inflation rate approaching 1000 percent.[333]
>
> Marshall I. Goldman, Associate Director of the Russian Research Center at Harvard University

This [Soviet] crisis is often described as a deeper version of the Great Depression in America. In fact, the ex-Soviet Union is in much worse condition, nearer to that of post-World War II Germany and Japan. Its infrastructure is crumbling. Aeroflot no longer has adequate fuel, its planes decrepit and disintegrating; the collapse of the railroads is not far off; the oil industry is in a similar shambles.[334]

> Martin Malia, professor of Russian history at the
> University of California, Berkeley

the situation of the real economy remains grave. The depression has deepened and is already much worse with respect to output reduction than the Great Depression in the West; living standards have fallen sharply; officially registered foreign trade has been greatly reduced; the foreign debt is increasing; and income distribution has become very unequal.[335]

> Michael Ellman, professor of economics at Amsterdam University and a
> specialist on the Russian economy

And finally, former President Richard Nixon:

Russia is going through an economic downturn worse than the Great Depression of the 1930's in the United States. In 1992 inflation was 25 percent a month, the gross national product was down 20 percent, and living standards were down 50 percent.[336]

Nor are the reports of economic crisis new. Marshall Goldman's 1983 book, *USSR in Crisis*, subtitled 'The Failure of an Economic System', had already pointed to economic deterioration, as had many predecessors. And in some sense, a crisis began with the introduction of central planning in the late 1920s, as suggested by the previous discussion of the resource mis-allocations endemic to centrally-planned systems. As time passed and the czarist productive legacy became less relevant, the state-sector difficulties perhaps increased, though simultaneously, second economy activity expanded. But there is remarkably little evidence to indicate that average material living standards in Russia have declined significantly, if at all, in the recent years of reform. The consensus view of Russian economic collapse, like virtually every other aspect of the conventional Russian economic story, is misleading.

Exponents of the collapse scenario muster both theoretical and empirical arguments to support their views. The empirical evidence centres on the large fall in measured GNP, and includes secondary phenomena such as declining industrial production, high inflation, and barter. The bulk of this chapter will be devoted to a closer examination of the fall in GNP and the other empirical evidence offered in support of the view that Russian living standards have fallen drastically.

The theoretical arguments cited by the purveyors of Russian doom often focus on coordination problems (a.k.a. 'chaos' or 'anarchy') that arise during reform. These problems are rarely spelled out, but the arguments typically invoke either the costs incurred in changing long-term economic relationships (the adjustment costs discussed earlier), or the lack of individual, private incentives to take actions that, collectively, would result in an improved economy.[337] Neither of these forms of coordination problems provides a persuasive source of economic collapse, however.

First, consider again the costs involved in changing existing connections among enterprises. When will the established relations be severed? Existing economic relationships will not be changed on the whole, unless the new relationships are more efficient. (Political problems associated with the dissolution of the Soviet Union have caused inefficient breakdowns, but these unfortunate developments are not the consequence of economic reform.) A breakdown in existing economic relationships is not a necessary by-product of reform, and as long as partial reform measures do not result in the wrong relationships being severed, the economy is helped by the rearrangement of economic ties. The benefits of the rearrangement may not accrue until the future, though, while the costs of establishing the new economic relationships are borne immediately. But exchanging immediate costs for future benefits is the profile of any investment. And just as with any other investments, the immediate costs should not be viewed as signalling a worsening of economic conditions. Freely choosing to save and invest (your own resources, at least!) in the hope of higher consumption in the future does not make a person, or an economy, worse off, even at the cost of a reduction in current consumption. For this reason, investment expenditures are included in calculations of GNP.

The second type of perceived coordination problems are those associated with situations where the private incentives of individuals result in poor social outcomes. For example, in escaping a burning building, any individual viewed in isolation should get out as quickly as possible. (Economic game theorists might say that there is a 'first-mover advantage'.) Applied to all individuals, however, these incentives can cause panic and tragedy. In the case of economic reform, there may be a 'second-mover advantage'. While society might be better off if people embraced capitalism, the first individuals to do so might, for example, find their personal gains expropriated by the government through selective taxation. Everyone has an incentive to let others go first, and capitalism never takes root. The problem with this argument (and its siblings) is that it just is not so. There are plenty of incentives to be successful in the free market sector in reforming Russia, though the incentive is less for state-owned enterprises, which through 1993 basically remained immune to bankruptcy. The 'second-mover advantage' is a theoretical possibility, but not a major practical concern.

While coordination problems are unlikely suspects, other factors may work to reduce Russian incomes during reform. As argued in the previous chapters, economic reform threatens living standards in two respects. First is the difficulty in expeditiously replacing the implicit tax and social welfare systems with explicit counterparts. Second is the problems that accompany partial economic reforms, such as free enterprise combined with some fixed prices. Partial reforms, for example, weaken the link between enterprise profits and the social desirability of production. Increases in unemployment may then represent more than simply a movement from repressed to open unemployment.

Many Russians are apprehensive that lower incomes will accompany reform. A September 1990 survey of Soviet citizens indicated that 75 per cent feared that their material well-being would fall during the transition.[338] These fears have not been put to rest by the experiences of Eastern Europe, nor by the further economic reforms in Russia.[339] In 1994, a majority of Russians surveyed indicated that they believed their living standards had fallen during the previous five years.[340]

## MEASURING LIVING STANDARDS

As with inflation and unemployment, the initial step in understanding the effects of economic reform on living standards is to evaluate the pre-reform situation. But first we must investigate how to measure living standards. Incomes, perhaps the premier data in assessing a society (or a person, as Paul Samuelson suggests in the opening quotation), must be determined – and there is the rub. The measurement of income is full of pitfalls, even in market economies, and is much more problematic in centrally-planned economies.

Of the frequently-employed indicators of income, perhaps the single most comprehensive statistic is *Gross National Product* (GNP), particularly in per capita terms.[341] A nation's GNP measures the total market value of all final goods and services produced in the nation during a given time period, typically one year.[342] Since for every good sold there is a payment to someone, there are two avenues to computing GNP. One route, the income method, is to measure the incomes accruing to workers and owners; alternatively, the product method consists of adding up the value of the final goods sold, capital investment and additions to inventory, government outlays, and net exports.[343] This approach results in the well known identity $Y \equiv C+I+G+(X-M)$: GNP (Y) equals the consumption expenditures of households (C) plus investment (I) plus government expenditures (G) plus net exports (X–M).[344] Price indices are used to offset the effects that rising price levels (inflation) have on GNP measured in current values of the national currency; i.e., real GNP is calculated by deflating nominal GNP by the relevant price index.[345]

Of course, income is just one element of the standard of living. Defining and measuring the quality of life is notoriously difficult, resulting in a panoply of indicators being employed to provide a more-or-less satisfactory portrait of living standards. Important indicators include life expectancy, literacy rates, and rates of infant mortality.[346] The 'noise' inherent in using GNP as a signal of living standards must be borne in mind. Some of the shortcomings associated with the use of real GNP to measure welfare were eloquently addressed by Robert F. Kennedy[347]:

> For the gross national product includes our pollution and advertising for cigarettes, and ambulances to clear our highways of carnage. It counts special locks for our doors and jails for the people who break them. The gross national product includes the destruction of the redwoods, and the death of Lake Superior. It grows with the production of napalm and missiles and nuclear warheads, and it even includes research on the improved dissemination of bubonic plague. The gross national product swells with equipment for the police to put down riots in our cities; and though it is not diminished by the damage these riots do, still it goes up as slums are rebuilt on their ashes . . .

One other important component of social welfare that is inherently absent from aggregate measures such as GNP is the distribution of income. A nation can have a relatively high GNP if all the people enjoy moderate earnings, or if a small number of people have phenomenally high incomes while everyone else is poor. The quality of life is likely to differ markedly between these two scenarios, even as per capita GNP is unchanged.

Interpreting GNP simply as a yardstick of economic output or income or material living standards, as opposed to an indicator of human welfare, does not avoid difficulties. Measuring economic output is hard. Major issues include: (1) market vs non-market output; (2) final vs intermediate production; (3) the constituents of 'investment'; and (4) the valuation of output.[348] These issues, discussed here in the context of market economies, will later be shown to be even more germane with respect to pre-reform Russia.

The national product accounts are geared towards transactions that occur in legal markets. Needless to say, many activities that generate economic benefits are thereby excluded from the calculations. Illegal transactions such as those involving contraband drugs, prostitution, or illegal gambling are not counted. Off-the-books employment, often paid for in cash, also are ignored. Barter agreements, such as when a dentist treats the teeth of an investment broker in exchange for financial counselling, are missed. Housework, which provides large benefits in terms of cleaner homes and laundry, is not counted, except if you hire someone to do your housework for you – and the transaction is properly reported and taxed.[349] Above all, the benefits of leisure time are not directly included in the national accounts.

Theoretically, only 'final' goods and services should be included in GNP. Sales of new automobiles are included, but the steel that goes into the car door is not directly counted. 'Intermediate' goods, i.e., those goods (like steel) that are used to produce other goods, are excluded, because otherwise they would be double-counted. The value of the steel is captured in the value of the car. To count the steel separately is to count it twice. Many goods that in practice are included in GNP nevertheless appear to have a large 'intermediate' component; a common example is the gasoline that is consumed in commuting to work. The government sector is particularly susceptible to the intermediate goods problem. Government expenditures (excluding transfer payments such as unemployment benefits) are included in the calculation of GNP, yet many of these expenditures are for intermediate goods and services. The nearly $300 billion US defence budget, for example, provides national security, which primarily represents an intermediate good that helps to promote the enjoyment of other goods and services such as birthday parties, beach vacations, and deodorants. Alternatively, some intermediate goods, such as services provided by businesses to their employees, are in reality final goods, and should be included in theoretically-pure calculations of GNP.

'Investment' goods are problematic in calculating GNP because many transactions that represent investment are either excluded from GNP calculations, or counted in other categories such as household consumption or government purchases.[350] When you buy a new car, it counts as a consumption good in this year's GNP, even though it will provide you with driving services for many years: i.e., it is largely an investment (and, a large investment!). Cars, like washing machines and other durable goods, are counted as consumption goods if purchased by households, are counted as government expenditures if purchased by the government, and are intermediate goods and thus excluded (directly) from GNP if purchased by businesses (laundromats or taxi companies, say). Expenditures for education and training also are generally not considered to be 'investment' in national income accounting. And the investments that do get counted are risky, in the sense that they are not guaranteed to bring future rewards.[351]

Market prices are used to aggregate GNP. But what is a market price? Taxes, subsidies, monopoly, and unpriced externalities all drive prices away from the Econ 101 conceptual ideal of prices formed in perfectly competitive markets. But that is only part of the problem. Seemingly identical goods (say, boxes of Tide laundry detergent) often have different prices even among stores in the same supermarket chain in nearby locations, though in competitive markets such price differences are generally small. The opposite problem is also a concern in calculating GNP; specifically, goods that differ in terms of consumer satisfaction may have the same measured price. Consider, for example, the benefits of shopping in pleasant surroundings with polite salespeople, as opposed to shopping in a dingy and hostile environment. The same pomegranate purchased for the same money price in the pleasant store as in the uncongenial store represents varying 'output', due to the differential quality of the shopping experience. But the addition to GNP is the same regardless of which store you buy your pomegranate in. (Alternatively, this 'market price problem' may be viewed as resulting from the 'non-marketed' production of service quality – a positive externality.)

This concludes our brief tour of major obstacles in measuring the nominal or 'dollar' value of economic output. There is one further piece of potentially disappointing news, however. The dollar value of GNP, as it happens, is not particularly useful in itself. The problem is that a rise in dollar GNP (or, in France, franc GNP) could be due either to inflation or to more output or to a combination of the two. In order to remove the effects of inflation and thereby get a better measure of changes in output, dollar GNP must be divided by a price index to generate 'real GNP'. The price indices used to convert dollar GNP to real values can be very inaccurate, though, as was demonstrated in the discussion of real wages. For inflation to be accurately reflected in real GNP, prices of goods and the quantities produced in some 'base year' must be known, as well as the current prices and quantities. But many common items such as microwave ovens, VCRs and personal computers did not exist twenty years ago, and hence had no relevant prices, making it hard to account for these items in price indices. It was noted in the discussion of real wages that in the US, real wages in manufacturing jobs fell slightly between 1982 and 1991. Hardly any of the people holding those manufacturing jobs in 1982 owned microwave ovens, CD players, or laptop computers, but today, many do. While measured real wages have fallen, it is not clear that the real consumption those wages buy has also fallen, because access to new products is not adequately accounted for.

The problems that new products cause for the measurement of real GNP arise in less drastic form for products that undergo quality improvements. Higher prices may reflect, well, higher prices for the same goods, or higher prices for better quality goods. Consider a bottom-of-the-line 1993 car, and a bottom-of-the-line 1972 car, both in their brand-new, showroom-floor incarnations. Though the price in real terms for the 1972 car in 1972 and the 1993 car in 1993 are likely to be about the same, the 1993 car is undoubtedly higher quality. Such quality improvements are often missing from GNP statistics, since separating out the quality-increase component of a price rise is hard.[352] As quality improves over time, measures of real GNP will generally understate the actual increases (or overstate the decreases) in the value of output, as some quality improvement is masked while the corresponding price rises enter the price deflator.

Thus far the discussion has focused on measures of GNP that count the value of outputs. As noted, it is also possible to generate GNP by counting the payments to workers, owners, and lenders, since every dollar spent by one person goes into another person's pocket. These 'income-side' calculations of GNP are, not surprisingly, also full of complications. Please permit just one example. Measuring income requires that the compensation received by workers be recorded. The problem is that a good deal of compensation takes place not as simple wage payments, but rather in some non-monetary forms, such as fringe benefits. The value of non-wage compensation, though, is hard to accurately measure. How much is it worth to an employee to get an office with a big window? How much is it worth to an employee to make personal calls at work, or to 're-allocate' office supplies to home use?

No matter how you calculate it, on the output side or the income side, GNP (or any related measure) is pretty hard to interpret, for all the reasons given above, and more. But often the next step is still more risky: comparing one country's GNP with another country's GNP. The most obvious problem is that they will be measured in different currencies, so direct comparisons are of the apples and oranges variety. Fortunately, there are (imperfect, of course) methods to convert GNPs to the same currency, resulting in a comparison more akin to Mackintosh apples and Delicious apples.[353] A second problem is that a GNP of $100 billion means one thing in a country with good roads, plenty of streetlights, an efficient government, and a large stock of other public goods, but $100 billion means another thing in nations less favourably bestowed. Still more difficulties in cross-country comparisons of GNP are likely to crop up in the pages ahead . . . (an old soap opera ploy!)

## GNP AND LIVING STANDARDS IN THE FORMER SOVIET UNION[354]

It is at least as hard to assess the standard of living in the former Soviet Union as in Western market economies. Nevertheless, a useful first step is to calculate GNP. Only shortly before its demise did the Soviet Union begin to provide an annual estimate of GNP, however. The main measure of aggregate economic activity that the Soviets employed was called 'Net Material Product'. This statistic includes final material goods but excludes 'unproductive' activities such as most services.[355] The West therefore had to rely on its own statisticians to compute GNP for the Soviet Union. The major source of estimates was the US Central Intelligence Agency, which was particularly interested in Soviet military potential. The CIA's annual calculations included the USSR/US GNP ratio; for 1989, the CIA estimate of this figure stood at 51 per cent.

Throughout the 1980s CIA estimates of Soviet GNP became increasingly controversial, with most critics suggesting that the CIA estimation approach overstated, perhaps by a large margin, Soviet GNP relative to US GNP.[356] The report on the Soviet economy prepared at the request of the G7 summit in Houston in 1990 estimated the USSR/US GNP ratio at 8.5 per cent, though this estimate employed a rather dubious method of converting Soviet GNP measured in roubles to a dollar figure using the then-prevailing 'market' exchange rate.[357] Nevertheless, many other observers have provided estimates well below that of the CIA. Russian economist Victor Belkin, for example, estimated the USSR/US GNP ratio at 14 per cent.[358]

The CIA methodology in calculating Soviet GNP in roubles was based on 'adjusted (average) factor costs'.[359] These costs, for labour and other inputs, take the fixed state-sector prices as their starting point. The effects of explicit Soviet taxes and subsidies were then removed. Because Soviet enterprises received machinery and equipment without paying market prices, the costs of using these machines were not included in the official Soviet prices. So, the CIA methodology imputed payments (interest charges) for the use of capital goods, and added them into the factor costs.[360] Adjustments were also made to reflect the fact that many Soviet goods had multiple prices, with preferred customers like heavy industry or the defence sector typically paying lower prices.[361] The adjustments to the fixed Soviet prices generally did not make a large difference, however; that is, estimates of Soviet GNP based on official costs and those based on adjusted factor costs are similar.[362]

Given an estimate of Soviet GNP, common currency units must still be employed to make international comparisons. The CIA used a 'purchasing power parity' approach. The dollar estimate of Soviet GNP was prepared by examining Soviet production, and asking how much it would have cost in the US, in dollars, to produce the same things. Comparing this figure with US GNP measured in dollars resulted in one US/USSR GNP ratio. Alternatively, the cost in roubles that the Soviets would have faced in generating US output, and comparing this with Soviet GNP measured in roubles, provided a second estimate.

The dollar approach to the US/USSR GNP ratio gave markedly different results from the rouble approach. For example, in 1989, the dollar approach suggested that Soviet GNP was 66 per cent of US GNP, while the rouble approach yielded an estimate of 39 per cent.[363] A country's GNP tends to be overestimated when calculated in another country's prices. Goods that were relatively high priced in the US, for example, tended not to be made in large quantity in the US – the high price discouraged demand. If the same goods had relatively low prices in the Soviet Union, though, they may have been produced and consumed in great quantities there. Accounting for such Soviet goods at the high US price therefore produced a higher measure of Soviet GNP than using the lower Soviet price.

To produce its final estimate of the US/Soviet GNP ratio, the CIA simply took an average (the so-called geometric average) of the estimate calculated on the dollar side and the estimate calculated on the rouble side.[364]

Criticism of the CIA approach has focused, and rightly so, on the validity of employing Soviet official statistics, both on prices and quantities. Quality deterioration and fabricated product improvements are suggested as having led to price increases that do not reflect increases in output value; i.e., there is hidden inflation. Revelations during the years of reform have also undermined the traditional view that Soviet data expressed in physical units was basically trustworthy. Finally, the relationship between what is produced, and what is actually used, has been questioned. For example, output that spoils or is destroyed in transport is included in CIA calculations, despite being unavailable for use.[365] Some commentators suggest that these losses were staggering. 'Every year approximately 40 per cent of agricultural output . . . and half of industry's output . . . is lost.[366]

Stephen Rosefielde, an economics professor at the University of North Carolina, Chapel Hill, has reviewed the controversy between the CIA and the critics of its Soviet GNP calculations. Professor Rosefielde concludes that their differences '. . . are due almost entirely to disparate perceptions of free invention [i.e., made-up Soviet output statistics], hidden inflation, waste and forced substitution . . . [367] and that 'The problem primarily lies in our inadequate access to the facts, not in the inherent shortcoming of the national income accounting methodologies at our disposal.[368] The 'limits to knowledge' discussed in the introduction suggest that calculations of Soviet-era GNP will remain controversial.

## CENTRAL PLANNING AND THE MEASUREMENT OF GNP

Consider the situation that would arise, though, if we had access to the 'facts' that separate the CIA from its critics. Assume for a second that Soviet official statistics met world standards, and all experts agreed on the calculation of Soviet GNP. What would such a figure tell us? I believe that we would learn little or nothing of value about Soviet output or living standards. The nature of the centrally-planned system, with fixed prices, questionable investment, over-production of intermediate goods, and a large share of output traded outside official channels, inherently reduces the correlation, tenuous in the best of circumstances, between measured GNP and welfare, or even between GNP and material well-being. The obstacles, identified in the previous section, encountered when calculating GNP – market vs non-market production, final vs intermediate goods, the nature of investment, and the valuation of production – are substantially more sizeable in the pre-reform Russian economy than in Western market economies. Coupled with the actual statistical limitations and distortions, these obstacles render any calculation of Russian GNP or living standards extremely precarious, or worse, meaningless.

First and foremost is the 'legal market' criterion for the inclusion of output in GNP. Prior to reform almost all Soviet private economic activity, except for the food sold on collective farm (kolkhoz) markets, was not transacted on a legal market, and hence not counted as part of GNP. As discussed earlier, the size of this shadow economy was enormous: perhaps 25 per cent or more of Soviet GNP. While Western industrialized countries have shadow economic production as well, the phenomenon is generally on a significantly smaller scale in the West.

Another area of non-marketed 'production' is environmental degradation. A worldwide problem, pollution of the environment nevertheless achieved momentous proportions in the USSR. From the drying up of the Aral Sea to ocean dumping of nuclear waste to Chernobyl, the Soviet environmental legacy is harrowing.[369] An inclusion of the environmental impacts of economic activity into GNP statistics would surely lower the former USSR's relative standing.[370]

The second factor that makes Soviet output statistics questionable measures of aggregate economic activity is the distinction between final and intermediate production. In theory, only final goods should be included in GNP calculations, but government spending is counted even when the spending is for intermediate goods or services. An important component of government spending in the West is for defence (primarily an intermediate service); for example, defence spending represents about 4 per cent of US GNP. But this figure is dwarfed by the comparable Soviet figure, which was estimated by the CIA to be 15–17 per cent in the late 1980s. Many outside critics (including citizens of the former Soviet Union) put the defence share of Soviet GNP at even higher levels: 25 per cent is not an uncommon estimate, and some figures are as high as 40–50 per cent.[371]

Another intermediate vs final product issue arises because of Soviet fixed prices and second economy activity. Recall the feeding bread to livestock story, where price controls on bread rendered it profitable for Soviet farmers to feed bread instead of grain to livestock; for this reason some bread became an intermediate good. A similar story applies to sugar that was purchased for use in home alcohol production. Generally, inputs that go into finished products should not be counted as part of GNP. Nevertheless, the production of inputs carried great weight in CIA estimates of Soviet output.[372] This practice was particularly misleading because of the tremendous Soviet inefficiency, relative to Western standards, in turning inputs into useful outputs.[373] The Soviet Union had 'a steel output per dollar of GDP fifteen times higher than that of the United States in 1988'.[374]

A third consideration that undermines the relevance of Soviet GNP calculations is the nature of the investment component. A striking feature of the Moscow landscape to many Western visitors is the amount of building cranes that are visible in the skyline. Construction appears to be going on everywhere in Russia. And construction was everywhere: there were some 350,000 construction projects throughout the former Soviet Union in the late 1980s, though the official statistics concerning construction were quite unreliable.[375] In the absence of economic reform, it would have been likely that the building cranes would have remained in place for quite some time, since the average construction project took 10 years to complete in the planned system. With or without reform, many construction projects may never be completed. While GNP calculations included this investment at cost, the real economic value of much of the Soviet investment was questionable. Other components of investment are also dubious. Soviet payoffs from extensive research and development were notoriously small. Increases in inventories of goods during the Soviet era are similarly suspect in terms of economic value. Swedish economist Anders

Åslund quotes former Soviet Deputy Prime Minister, the economist Leonid Abalkin: 'The warehouses are overloaded with unnecessary production, and [enterprises] continue to produce more and more of it: for the sake of the growth rate!'[376] Since investment formed over 30 per cent of Soviet GNP (as measured by the CIA), versus about 15 per cent in the US in 1990, reservations concerning the value of this investment are particularly serious.[377]

(Partly because of the difficulties with intermediate production and investment goods, attention is sometimes focused on Soviet *consumption* instead of Soviet GNP. CIA figures put Soviet per-capita consumption at approximately one-third of US levels, but again, many observers believe this to be an overestimate.[378] Consumption statistics are themselves not immune to criticisms almost as severe as those levelled at GNP statistics. For example, as with investment goods, not all Soviet consumption goods were valuable.)

The fourth factor that tends to thwart the interpretation of Soviet GNP statistics is the formerly fixed prices in the state sector. Fixed prices added a good deal of arbitrariness to value calculations of Soviet output. An additional refrigerator that officially 'cost' 100 roubles to produce and sold for 150 roubles, represented a 100 rouble increase in CIA calculations of Soviet GNP (assuming that the adjustments made to official costs in calculating adjusted factor costs had no net effect). The real value of resources used in producing the refrigerator, though, may actually have been 1000 roubles. But before it is concluded that 1000 roubles is the appropriate addition to GNP, what if no one was willing to pay more than 200 roubles for the refrigerator? In the West, as noted above, an increase in crime may lead to more resources being devoted to police and security services, which could raise GNP – though welfare in the usual sense has fallen. In the USSR, fixed prices meant that many goods, perhaps even refrigerators, had this perverse property. One Soviet economist estimated that as much as 25 per cent of Soviet output was 'unnecessary'.[379]

There are other difficulties with valuation. Consider the problem of estimating household income (or the labour factor cost), which requires the calculation of wages. As previously noted, in Soviet circumstances, the determination of a 'wage' for a given occupation is as difficult as determining a 'price' for a given commodity.

Institutional differences also make GNP calculations less meaningful as welfare measures in centrally-planned economies than in market economies. Four areas where Soviet (and now, to some extent, Russian) conditions differed substantially from Western conditions are queues, quality of housing, working environments, and public transport.[380] All of these factors tend to paint a bleaker picture of Soviet living standards than the CIA's per capita GNP figures might suggest. The enormous amount of time spent searching and queuing for goods in the pre-reform situation has already been mentioned, perhaps ad nauseam. As for housing, according to one Soviet economist in an article published in 1992 (though written when the USSR was extant), 'Among industrial nations the USSR is currently among the worst regarding housing standards', and she provides many telling statistics.[381] Working conditions in ageing Soviet industrial enterprises were also a cause for concern. Soviet emigré sociologist Vladimir Shlapentokh noted a 1981 survey that found that only 34 per cent of the adult population in big Soviet cities was satisfied with conditions at work.[382] The same source reported similar dissatisfaction with public transport. Only 30 per cent of the inhabitants of large cities (and only 15 per cent in Moscow) found the mass transit acceptable – a statistic that is understandable to anyone who has spent much time crammed on to Soviet buses. While such findings add to the picture of Soviet living standards presented by GNP calculations, they provide a far from definitive representation.

For the purposes of Russian or Western policy, an inability to get an accurate reading on pre-reform Russian material welfare via the usual GNP statistics is not immediately disabling. Russia appears committed to a transition to a market economy, regardless of whether the CIA or its most strident critics are correct about the measurement of Soviet GNP. Furthermore, Western aid will be forthcoming for the reform effort, independently of the initial Russian living standards. The problems in measuring Russian pre-reform living standards, however, can lead to policy mistakes down the road, since without understanding the initial situation, assessing the welfare effects of the transition is nearly impossible.

## RUSSIAN INCOMES DURING THE TRANSITION

It has been argued above that the evaluation of Russian pre-reform living standards via the usual calculation of GNP (or per capita consumption, or any other method, for that matter) is problematic, even relative to the considerable difficulties involved in similar evaluations of Western market economies. Changing institutions such as the move to free prices implies that the complications are compounded during a transition to a market economy. With both the pre-reform and transitional positions difficult to judge, so too are the effects of reform. In the Russian case, basically unrelated events such as trade disruptions, civil unrest among the former republics, and falling world oil prices also influence living standards, making the marginal impact of economic reform even harder to disentangle.

As noted at the beginning of this chapter, there seems to be a near consensus in Russia and the West that economic conditions have worsened significantly in the past few years. Again, declining output and increased inflation are the most prominent signals of Russian economic decline.

The output and inflation statistics do not present a prima facie case for economic deterioration, however, for the by now familiar reason that during a transition, typical measures of economic activity take on entirely new meanings. Thus the change from repressed inflation to open inflation creates a large jump in price indices, even if there has been no increase in the underlying amount of inflation. This not-so-subtle point frequently goes unremarked upon. Thus the IMF reports an inflation rate of 140.7 per cent in the former USSR in 1991.[383] But the reported inflation rate for April 1991 is itself 55 per cent, due to the 2 April 1991 raising of administered state sector retail prices. This state-controlled price rise simply validated previous repressed inflation in open form; i.e., it did not represent new inflation.[384] Replacing the April 1991 inflation rate with the average monthly rate (excluding April) from 1991 changes the overall figure of 1991 inflation to 62 per cent – quite substantial, but less than half of the reported figure. And, as previously noted, determining the actual economic costs of such inflation is another matter. While there is the potential for large redistributional effects, efficiency losses are harder to pinpoint – though extremely high rates of inflation, and particularly hyperinflation, are quite costly.

Presumably the output decline is unambiguous evidence of significant economic deterioration. Measured industrial production in Russia fell by more than a third between 1990 and 1993.[385] But once again, the analysis is complicated by the pre-reform situation, which included an over-production of industrial goods, a prevalence of worthless output, the non-existence of some claimed output, and waste of output that was produced. Falling output figures alone are therefore not a sign of collapse; in fact, any successful transition will probably require a large drop in industrial output. The official statistics even indicated a six per cent increase in the production of consumption goods between 1987 and 1992.[386]

Statistics on actual consumption (as opposed to the production of consumption goods) can similarly be misleading during a transition. The Russian economy now involves widespread legal markets for most goods and services. This presents a marked change from the pre-reform situation. Different skills are being rewarded. In order to prosper in this new environment, many Russians are engaged in acquiring those skills that have seen their relative value increase: market business skills, for example. To some extent, then, a transition brings a temporary shift from consumption to investment, and hopefully to investment in skills that are both privately and socially profitable.

Many positive economic developments that arise with reform are not reflected in official statistics at all. Most obvious is the significant diminution in time spent queuing that followed the 2 January 1992 partial price liberalization. Nine-tenths of Russian households had at least one member queuing for goods at least an hour per day in early 1992; two years later, only one in six households spent that much time in line.[387] Western economist Bryan Roberts estimated the change in average welfare brought about by the price liberalization to be positive and quite substantial, with decreased queuing more than offsetting the measured fall in consumption.[388]

Increased private economic activity appears to be only partially reflected in the official statistics, which were traditionally geared to determining state sector production. Changed incentives to misreport output have also arisen with reform. Previously, virtually all parties involved in the official economy were interested in exaggerating the amount of output produced. With new taxes and relatively unrestricted wage funds, these incentives have been reduced, and in some cases replaced by motivations to understate output. Russian statistics also have a new role to play as data influences negotiations with Western aid agencies such as the IMF.

In summary, recent economic statistics that indicate severe decline in Russia in the 1990s are extremely misleading, as are the statistics indicating substantial growth in 1988-90. The regime change of economic reform results in economic statistics measuring different phenomena than they did in the pre reform economy. Changes in these statistics during reform cannot then be trusted to signify similarly changed economic circumstances.

## MOSCOW AND ST. PETERSBURG

One difficulty in judging the economic situation in Russia is that there is no single economic situation. Regions and localities differ markedly in the strength of their economy, just as they did in the pre-reform system. There have also been widely varying responses to economic reform, with local leaders often playing decisive roles in the speed and form of reforms. Nevertheless, much of the reform discussion focuses on Moscow and St. Petersburg, Russia's two largest cities.

Moscow and St. Petersburg have traditionally been better supplied with food and other goods within the official state distribution system than other regions of the former Soviet Union. This situation was not entirely accidental, as these cities were officially accorded the highest priority status within the state distribution network. (The priority standing of Moscow and St. Petersburg extended to non-economic phenomena under the old system. Former convicts, for example, could not settle in these cities.) The high priority of Moscow and St. Petersburg has been undermined in recent years, as the state distribution system has deteriorated. Residents of these cities have found their economic standing, relative to their fellow citizens, falling.[389] (In some cases, of course, their absolute standard of living has fallen as well.) Real wage statistics, as unreliable as they are in the Russian setting, seem to bear this out. Of the 76 'administrative units' in Russia, Moscow city and the Moscow region ranked 73 and 74 in terms of measured real wage growth between mid-1991 and mid-1992, with about a 35 per cent reduction. (Many regions had positive measured real wage growth.[390]) The relative decline in the prosperity of Moscow and St. Petersburg has engendered discontent among the citizens of these cities – discontent which can now find a voice in the liberalized political climate. Since the vast majority of Western foreign correspondents within the borders of the old Soviet Union are in Moscow and St. Petersburg, the complaints have been widely reported.[391]

The Moscow–St Petersburg slant on Western news from Russia is pervasive. Here is a quiz that even well-informed Westerners often have trouble with – at least I did. What is the third – or fourth, or fifth – largest city in Russia?[392]

Reform is creating other difficulties for the major Russian cities, particularly Moscow, which are then incorrectly extrapolated to the country as a whole. As the relative value of food has increased, rural areas have been prospering relative to Moscow. Smaller cities, many of which had not seen any meat from within the official state supply system for years, are no longer systematically discriminated against. Simultaneously, some of the major 'goods' produced in Moscow have seen their market dry up. Most obvious is the central management of the economy and of the Soviet empire. The reduction in the defence budget also harms Moscow and St. Petersburg relative to most other Russian regions. One-quarter of Moscow's workforce is involved in military production, accounting for a third of the city's industrial output. St. Petersburg also employs about one-quarter of its workforce in defence production.[393]

The loss of the special privileges accorded large cities in the official distribution of goods is new to Moscow. A lack of those special privileges forced remote areas long ago to find alternative methods to 'beat the system', a process that Moscow is now learning. Furthermore, the transactions costs of engaging in private business, while still quite substantial, have fallen significantly relative to the pre-reform situation in which most private activity was illegal. With high costs of doing business, it makes sense to engage only in high volume operations, since many of the transactions costs would be the same for both small and large operations. Therefore, rather than have flourishing markets in every town, big cities like Moscow became the focus of trade; people from rural areas and smaller towns would travel tremendous distances to come to Moscow to participate in both the state and private markets. (This situation was facilitated by the low fixed prices on internal travel in the Soviet Union. Farmers found it profitable to fly thousands of kilometres to large cities in order to sell a couple of bins of fruit.) As the costs of doing business fall, local markets are developing. The special status of Moscow as a trading post is therefore diminishing, particularly in the realm of consumer goods. But with the journalistic focus on Moscow, this positive development is likely to be overlooked, or worse, misperceived as a fall in living standards, as some trade that would have previously occurred in Moscow is diverted to other regions.

## DISTRIBUTION REVISITED

Along with changes in the geographic distribution of economic goods, Russian economic reform has brought changes to the distribution of income.

Once again, determining the effect of transition on income distribution requires knowledge of the pre-reform situation. This is a particularly difficult task, both because of the widespread informal activity and the former Soviet government's unwillingness to provide substantial information on the distribution of income. What does seem clear is that the Soviet Union did not have an income distribution substantially more equal than in many Western market economies. The findings of British economists Anthony Atkinson and John Micklewright, for example, indicate that the Russian household income distribution in 1986 was slightly more equal than that of Great Britain, while the distribution of individual earnings was slightly less equal in Russia than in Great Britain.[394] Since these calculations exclude second economy earnings, it is likely that Russia was comparatively even less egalitarian. Such evidence suggests that it cannot be taken for granted that economic reform will lead to wider dispersions in the Russian income distribution. It is highly probable, however, that increased legality of private economic activity is leading to more people in Russia who are very well-off relative to the average. Also, the massive inflation accompanying economic reform has led to a major change in the distribution of wealth, as the value of pre-existing rouble savings has been almost completely eliminated.

At the same time that reform influences income distribution, pre-existing income differentials are becoming more visible. The great wealth accumulated by important Party members in the pre-reform system was pretty well hidden from public view. Now, fancy restaurants, casinos, and expensive foreign cars are on open display. Repressed differences in living standards have become increasingly open; the result would likely be a perception of more inequality, even without any underlying changes.

Changes in income distribution, or the perception of changes, might create popular unrest that would scuttle reform efforts. So far, though, that does not seem to be the case in Russia. There is even some evidence that distributional concerns may not be all that great in Russia. Survey results reported in 1992 by Western Sovietologist Ellen Mickiewicz found that 84 per cent of the respondents in Russia believed that the government should not reduce differences in income among people. Comparable figures for Ukraine and Uzbekistan were 81 per cent and 58 per cent, respectively.[395]

There are also theoretical reasons for believing that distributional concerns are less compelling during large systemic changes than they are in other circumstances. With most policy changes in the West, the major distributional effects (which generally fall on a narrow group of individuals) are substantial relative to the social gains from increased efficiency, which are diffuse. For example, import barriers on Japanese automobiles are very beneficial to the relatively small number of owners and workers of US automobile companies, while the much more numerous American consumers of automobiles pay somewhat higher prices because of the trade restraints. When the entire economic system is being restructured, however, these factors can be reversed. Potential efficiency gains are large relative to the distributional effects.[396] Changes in the size of the pie become more meaningful relative to how the shares of the pie are distributed.

Distributional changes are continuously occurring, with or without reform.[397] Not all distributional changes have to be counteracted. The major concern is to ensure that the worst-off members of society do not suffer further. But protecting the worst-off citizens is comparatively inexpensive and easy, at least relative to counteracting all downward changes in distribution – though identifying the most needy represents a new task in Russia.[398] On balance, Russia appears well-equipped to provide an explicit social safety net, thanks to the existence of state stores and long experience with ration coupons.

**PERCEPTIONS OF DECLINE**

The previous sections have suggested that Western (and possibly even Russian) perceptions of the Russian economy are more pessimistic than the actual situation merits. There is indirect evidence that for many Russians, the economic situation is not as dire as many news reports imply. American economists Robert McGee and Edward Feige, writing on the US economy, note that 'Survey results suggest that individuals appear to be much more optimistic about their personal economic situation than about the general economic situation. This is precisely what would be expected when aggregate data based on false reporting produce the statistical illusion of economic malaise'.[399] Similar survey results have been reported for the transitional Russian economy. A Russian economist describes a survey in which residents of the former Soviet Union considered the economic situation of their own republic to be better than that of the union as a whole.[400] American researchers Anthony Jones and William Moskoff report on a late-1989 poll of Muscovites in which 82 per cent of the respondents thought that the overall economy had worsened under the policy of perestroika, though only 33 per cent of the respondents felt that they were personally less well off.[401] Distributional changes may help to create a perception of general decline, even if average living standards are not falling.

The limited availability and reliability of economic information in the pre-reform situation also helps to create perceptions of increasing economic misery. Russian researchers noted in an article originally published in 1991 that 'Only in the last year or two has the fact that a large number of people are living in poverty in [the Soviet Union] been recognized.[402] According to the same source, 64 per cent of the respondents to a September 1990 poll believed that there are many poor people in the Soviet Union.[403] Misinformation about living standards was surprisingly pervasive in the pre-reform Soviet Union. Sociologist Vladimir Shlapentokh reports on a late 1960s and early 1970s survey in the town of Taganrog, conducted by Boris

Grushin, 'According to Grushin's survey of Taganrog residents . . . [o]nly 2 per cent thought living standards were "very high" in the United States, France, and Great Britain; the figures for Czechoslovakia and Bulgaria were 63 and 49 per cent, respectively'.[404]

Under glasnost' there has been an upsurge of information available to citizens of the former Soviet Union, both about their own and other countries. In particular, information that paints the former Soviet Union in a negative light is newly available. The extent of environmental damage, for example, is now amply reported – there is even a Soviet branch of Greenpeace.[405] To the extent that increased reporting of negative phenomena is mistaken for an increase in the phenomena themselves, the transition may be blamed for pre-existing problems.

Perceptions of the economic situation matter, even if they do not well reflect reality. First, as mentioned, the government may respond to perceived economic problems in ways that are inappropriate for the actual situation. Second, perceptions and expectations are inter-related, and expectations influence current economic activity. What is the incentive to undertake a long term investment in an economy perceived to be on the verge of collapse? 'Real wealth', while impossible to accurately measure, surely depends to some degree on expected future income (or consumption) streams. But the perceptions of economic decline, combined with high inflation and general economic and political uncertainty, render future income streams highly uncertain, and perhaps highly discounted in current calculations of economic well-being. Economic pessimism, even when otherwise unfounded, has a disturbing propensity to be self-justifying.

## BARTER

One phenomenon that is frequently taken as a sign of Russian economic deterioration is the significant number of transactions that are conducted via barter. Yale University economist Merton Peck, for example, comments that 'The rise of bartering is the most obvious and pervasive indicator of an economic crisis.'[406] A reversion from monetary to barter exchange is harmful because the level of economic activity is almost sure to fall precipitously during such a switch. Barter is inefficient relative to the use of money to conduct exchange because there is no reason for the person who supplies the goods that I want to buy to be interested in buying the goods I can offer. My grocer may have little use for books about economic reform, even though I would like to obtain some groceries. By using money that is widely accepted, I can buy groceries without my grocer simultaneously having to buy my economic reform ramblings. The use of money makes it easier to find appropriate trading partners – in fact, it makes almost anyone an appropriate trading partner. More deals are then worth the effort, and fewer resources are devoted to arranging each exchange.

In a Western industrial economy, virtually the only circumstance in which barter would replace monetary exchange on a large scale is if people lost confidence in the currency, perhaps because of massive inflation or expected inflation. In such conditions, barter will be associated with economic collapse. But Russia has not seen a 'reversion' to barter: a good deal of barter has always been there. Furthermore, despite the substantial inflation during the reform era, there has not been an enormous movement to barter. The vast majority of transactions in Russia (and throughout the rouble zone) continue to utilize roubles. Most important, though, some of the barter that is appearing actually promotes the development of a market economy. When legal enforcement of contracts is largely unavailable, barter becomes a useful device for governing exchanges.

Barter played a substantial role in the pre-reform Soviet system, driven by legal restrictions on monetary market relationships, and the low fixed prices in the state sector. Official exchanges between state-owned enterprises did not employ direct monetary payment; rather, accounting transfers were recorded to match exchanges that took place in accordance with the state's central plan. The accounting roubles that governed these exchanges were unrelated to the roubles used to pay wages and for households to purchase consumer goods. (The accounting roubles were even called 'non-cash' roubles.) Therefore, the wholesale market, the market for capital equipment, or the market governing any official inter-enterprise trade was in essence one large barter system, separated from the rouble-employing retail market.

Recall also that informal transactions were frequently conducted through barter. Enterprise supply expediters would barter goods in order to get necessary supplies. As noted previously, workers at state enterprises would receive much of their pay in kind, and large enterprises would provide housing, kindergartens, and a host of other goods and services to workers and their families. Individuals would barter vodka for privately provided services such as plumbing or auto repair. The exchange of favours and gifts for scarce commodities has been well-documented. No description of life in the Soviet Union can be complete without a discussion of 'blat', the use of connections and gifts to obtain such goods as high quality meat or theatre tickets.[407] Soviet foreign trade with both the East and the West involved barter arrangements; for example, Pepsi Cola was provided to the USSR in exchange for Stolichnaya vodka.

The increased reports of barter that have accompanied reform are therefore not surprising: the implicit system, particularly with respect to inter-enterprise trade, is becoming explicit. And partial reform contributes to the use of barter. It remained illegal throughout 1992 for state-owned enterprises to sell intermediate goods for cash.[408]

One factor promoting barter is the enormous amount of price uncertainty, and general economic uncertainty, prevalent in Russia. Under the ancien régime there were no legal markets for outside-of-plan inter-enterprise exchanges, and hence there were no established prices for legal transactions. (And many illegal exchanges were themselves conducted via barter.) In the US, it is fairly easy to learn the approximate price of almost any traded commodity. In Russia, there may not be a 'typical' price. 'In a society where no one knows the fair value of anything, everyone suspects he is being cheated all the time', is how one journalist has described the situation in Russia.[409]

Some firms engage in barter precisely to keep the actual 'price' of a transaction hidden. Disguising prices by engaging in barter can be a way to practice what economists call 'price discrimination', which simply consists of charging different prices to different customers for an identical good. For example, airlines price discriminate when they sell seats on airplanes for high prices to business travellers, but sell at low prices to vacationers. (The familiar Saturday night stay-over requirement for a lower fare helps to implement this form of price discrimination.) It is hard to price discriminate in selling an identical good, though, if a market price is well-established, because then no customer will be willing to pay more than that price – she can always go to a competitor and pay the market price. Price discrimination is also prevented if goods can easily be resold. For example, if kids' tickets to movies were the same colour, shape, and size as adult tickets, kids would buy all the tickets at the children's price and resell to the adults. The movie theatre would then be forced to either differentiate the tickets or sell them all at the same price. Thanks to the old planning system, many enterprises in Russia have some degree of monopoly power. These firms can earn more money by engaging in price discrimination. But if the price discrimination becomes well-known, those customers that are charged the lower price will begin to resell to the other customers. Price-discriminating enterprises therefore have an incentive to conceal prices through barter deals. (Incidentally, price discrimination, even in non-barter deals, is widely practised by Russian enterprises. Traditional contracting partners are typically charged lower prices for goods than new private enterprises.[410])

The semi-reformed nature of the Russian economy contributes to barter in other ways. For example, the possibility of further currency reforms encourages barter, because the government may confiscate roubles in the future. This is not an idle threat, given the January 1991 confiscation of 50 and 100 rouble notes and the July 1993 reform that invalidated some 'old' roubles. Threats by some former republics to issue new currency operate similarly to make roubles less attractive. The continuing lack of government enforcement mechanisms for private contracts also induces barter, as such direct exchanges (particularly when conducted with long-time trading partners) enable enterprises to ensure that they are not swindled in transactions.

Finally, barter deals fall largely outside of any centralized regulation; as long as the government remains completely enmeshed in the economy, firms will engage in barter as a way of circumventing government controls. A fair number of price controls remain in place in Russia. Barter remains a means of evading such controls, and has also become useful in avoiding the value-added tax.[411]

Barter trade in the reforming Russian economy is not an unambiguous sign of economic collapse. Much of it occurred in the old system, and there are good reasons for Russian enterprises to engage in barter transactions. As reform proceeds, barter will become increasingly less common, as the factors associated with partial reforms – including the inflationary budget deficit – diminish in importance.

## THE SOCIALIST VICE

Consumption is the sole end and purpose of all production.
Adam Smith, *The Wealth of Nations*, 1776[412]

What do We Need Most of All? Most of all we need machines.
*New Russia's Primer, The Story of the Five Year Plan*, 1931[413]

quasi-humorously . . . [s]teel happens, in the minds of Communists, to be more beautiful and desirable than saucepans or even guns. This is how their minds work: the tradition has very deep roots.
Western economist PJD Wiles[414]

A friend at a party introduces you to Nina, explaining that she's a Soviet economist. Then your friend runs off to the punch bowl, and you attempt to strike up a conversation with Nina. The ambiguity of the phrase 'Soviet economist' presents a small difficulty, though. You are not sure whether Nina is an economist from the former Soviet Union, or a Western-trained economist who studies Soviet-type economic systems. Attempting not to appear too obtuse, perhaps you are unwilling to come right out and ask Nina for clarification. Fortunately, there is an indirect method of ascertaining Nina's economic background that is extremely reliable – until a few years ago, nearly 100 per cent reliable. Explain to Nina that you have heard that there is a shortage of, say, steel plate, in some exotic country, and since Nina is a professional economist, you would like her suggestion as to how this shortage should be dealt with. If Nina is a Western-trained economist, her most likely response will be 'Raise the price of steel plate.' If Nina learned economics in the former USSR, she will probably respond, 'Increase the production of steel plate.'

Production, production, production. The Soviet Union led the world in the production of steel, coal, steel, tractors, steel, nickel, steel, wheat, steel, . . . but for all its production, the Soviet official economy was clearly outperformed by many Western market economies. The focus on production was a mistake – though perhaps an inevitable mistake within a planned economy – since living standards are dependent on consumption, not production. It is this production fetish that I call 'the socialist vice'.

But surely, it might be thought, production and consumption are just two sides of the same coin. The more you produce, the more you consume, and if you do not produce, you cannot consume. Focusing on production should amount to pretty much the same thing as focusing on consumption. Production is probably easier to monitor and control than consumption, since there are relatively few producing firms and farms and relatively many consumers and mouths.

Such reasoning is fallacious. First, production and consumption are not always intimately connected. A potato that is harvested adds to production statistics, but if it rots before making it to a consumer, then it has not added to consumption. And such waste was rampant in the centrally-planned USSR; in fact, a European Bank for Reconstruction and Development report concluded in 1991 that 50 per cent of Soviet potatoes never made it to consumers.[415] Nor are all potatoes created equal. Potato quality, like 'potato' pronunciation (and spelling?), varies, and once again, low quality within the Soviet state sector was a persistent problem. But more importantly, the relationship between production and consumption depends on what goods get produced. You cannot eat steel, even if you have more of it than anyone else in the world.

But steel and other intermediate goods were accorded high priority within the Soviet production profile. Partly the over-attention paid to intermediate goods derives from the lack of a direct link between consumer satisfaction and the production of intermediate goods. Consumer satisfaction being difficult to achieve in a centrally-planned way, the planning system itself is better suited to the production of intermediate goods relative to consumer goods. Furthermore, as the opening quotation suggests, there is an ideological attachment to heavy industry in many socialist societies. In the Soviet Union, the primacy of industrial production grew from an unfortunate 'law' of socialism derived from Marx, which stated that economic growth required a more rapid expansion of industrial goods than consumer goods.[416] In a sense then, Soviet planners did eat steel, even as Soviet consumers continued to find it unappetizing. As an epigram attributed to eminent Western economist Abram Bergson put it, 'Steel was a final good to Stalin, and bread an intermediate one.[417]

The focus on industrial production was successful in producing high measured growth rates. The 1962 book by P. J. D. Wiles that has served as a source for much of the discussion in this section contains a chapter entitled 'Why They Have Grown Faster'. The relatively high Soviet growth rates continued into the 1980s, even as absolute growth rates declined. But more production does not mean higher living standards, though the output numbers may well increase – a point occasionally overlooked.[418] In fact, it is only within a market setting that production can serve as a rough proxy for consumption or living standards, since only then can it reasonably be expected that production that is not valuable will be curtailed.

Consider the situation with tractors in Russia, as described by Western economists Ed Hewett and Clifford Gaddy[419]:

> In the early 1980s the USSR produced tractors at a rate of 550,000–580,000 a year – 40 per cent of world tractor production – of which approximately 350,000 went to agriculture. US farmers purchase 50,000–60,000 tractors a year, which is one-sixth of the Soviet figure. Yet the USSR still had to devote 19 percent of its labor force, or 30 million workers, to agricultural production, and almost three-fourths of those were working manually. [Shades of Orwell's Oceania.] The apparent low productivity of tractors (and other agricultural machinery) seems linked to frequent breakdowns and long downtimes, which in turn were due to poor servicing and a shortage of spare parts. Twenty percent to 45 percent of all Soviet tractors were out of service at any one time.

Petr Aven, a Russian-trained economist, noted that in 1991 the production of tractors continued to increase, though there were insufficient numbers of tractor drivers for the existing tractor stock – itself many times the size of the stock of tractors in the US – and there was almost no demand for many brands of tractors.[420] In the Russian city of Chelyabinsk, home of a major tractor factory, parking lots and vacant areas near the factory were jammed with unsold and unsaleable tractors in 1993, while production continued. (The tractors tended to be too large for the emerging private farms.[421]) A resident of Chelyabinsk described the situation as 'a tractor hanging from every tree'.

The misplaced concentration on production permeated all facets of Soviet economic life. Economic problems were engineering problems: given a shortage, how could production be increased? Where was the bottleneck in production? If the constraint on increased production was too few trucks for transport, then the solution appeared to be to produce more trucks. Without free prices in the state sector, the cost of the increased production was neglected, though it may well have exceeded the value of the additional output. Environmental costs were particularly likely to be insufficiently taken into account.

The focus on production was not limited to officials in Gosplan, the State Planning Committee. One of the features of the Soviet planned economy was that leaders at the highest level were involved in mundane decisions concerning such issues as the number of children's shoes to produce. General Secretaries would give speeches about production problems in various industries, and initiate campaigns to increase production or decrease waste. Newspaper and television reports of production figures and plan fulfilment were a daily, mind-numbing exercise.

The early Gorbachev-era reforms also reflected the socialist vice in bringing a technological approach to economic problems. 'Intensification' and 'acceleration' were the major themes of reform in the mid-1980s. Together with the anti-alcohol campaign, they were designed to increase production – and in particular, in an echo of the socialist law concerning the primacy of industrial goods, to increase the production of machine tools, machines that could make other machines.[422]

In taking this approach, Gorbachev was applying the best wisdom available within the Soviet economics discipline, which was itself held hostage to the socialist vice. Most Soviet economists were employed in industry, and their job was to think of ways to increase production or to increase the technological efficiency of production. (Enterprise managers were not always willing customers of the economists' suggestions, however, since increased output would lead to increased plan targets in the future, and increased technological efficiency might mean fewer inputs.) The collection of official statistics also focused heavily on production, 'with distribution, consumption, and income data accorded much lower priority'.[423] Market-oriented solutions to problems were almost unthinkable, and would have branded the perpetrator as ideologically suspect. So it is unsurprising that Gorbachev's early fixation with increased production of machine tools was the pet programme of his main economic adviser at the time, Abel Aganbegyan, who had a strong reputation as a reformer.[424]

The technological approach to economic problems remains very popular in Russia.[425] In the transition another phenomenon has arisen, though, which itself is a legacy of the old regime. Under a planning system, people are likely to assign responsibility for the success or failure of the economy to decisions made by high government officials and their economic advisers. After all, such officials are explicitly responsible for all major economic decisions. (This assignment of responsibility also happens, though to a lesser extent, in market economies such as the United States, where the president has very limited influence over the economy.) Upon learning that the economies of market countries outperformed their own economy, many Russians have apparently attributed the difference to the better economists in the West, and leading Russian reform economists have emerged as popular politicians. An undue appreciation of the powers of economists is a touchingly (at least I am touched) ironic outcome of six decades of central planning.

# Chapter 8

# False hopes

The focus on implicit elements in the pre-reform economy has tended to paint a picture of Russian economic reform that is significantly rosier than that provided by the standard commentaries. The flip side of this generally positive assessment of the reforming Russian economy, however, is a greater degree of scepticism with respect to the short-term benefits from the implementation of some reform measures, such as official privatization, that are widely viewed as important for the transition to a market economy. Three reform elements that are typically deemed to be promising in lifting the Russian economy are military conversion, rouble convertibility, and Western aid. Chinese-style gradual market reforms have been similarly highly-touted. While such reforms do offer some benefits to the Russian economy, I believe that like official privatization, all have generally been overvalued. This chapter attempts to demonstrate why these reforms, for the most part, present false hopes.

## MILITARY CONVERSION

> more and more evidence points to the fact that in the area of defense expenditures, as in many other areas, the Soviet leadership operated for years and continues to operate in the dark, without a solid database.
>
> Western economist Vladimir Treml, 1992[426]

It may seem a bit disingenuous to view the defence sector of the former Soviet Union, an acknowledged military superpower, as being largely implicit, but there were a host of hidden elements. Most important was simply the burden that national security placed on the economy, which because of hidden subsidies and fixed prices was probably unknown even at the highest levels of the Soviet government – though the CIA's estimate of 15–17 per cent of GNP in the mid-1980s can serve as a lower bound. One form of hidden subsidy to defence was price discrimination: defence enterprises were charged less for some inputs, such as electricity, than non-defence enterprises. A priority system in which the defence complex received preeminent access to inputs, including skilled labour, likewise masked a subsidy. An extreme penchant for secrecy also led to other hidden attributes in the defence sector, including entire towns, comprising hundreds of thousands of people in toto, that were closed not just to foreigners but even to the rest of the Soviet population, and were omitted from Soviet maps. (Residents of these towns, which could not publish newspapers, were discouraged from venturing 'outside' the town limits, and visits from outside relatives were strictly controlled.[427])

A final, less hidden feature of the pre-reform situation in the defence sector is that the production of civilian goods has long been an important component of the activities of defence enterprises. (Any Soviet enterprise that was subordinate to one of the ministries in the 'defence complex' was typically considered to be a defence enterprise, even if it exclusively produced civilian goods.) Defence enterprises produced 100 per cent of Soviet televisions, radios, and VCRs, and the majority of washing machines, vacuum cleaners, and refrigerators.[428] Almost all high technology consumer goods were produced in the defence sector. In total, consumer goods accounted for 40 per cent or more of the output of defence enterprises, and defence enterprises accounted for some 25 per cent of all consumer goods other than food.[429]

The large percentage of Soviet output that was devoted to the military has made this sector a natural target for reformers. And indeed, the conversion of military industry to civilian production has been an important part of Soviet (and later Russian) reform efforts since Mikhail Gorbachev called for demilitarization at the United Nations in December, 1988. An official Soviet defence conversion plan was approved in December 1990. The plan was marked by two important features. The first feature was that physical 'conversion' of productive assets from military to civilian production was not the major thrust of the conversion effort. Rather, the major part of the conversion programme was a call for an increase in the production of those civilian goods that were already made within the defence complex. The second feature of the official conversion plan was, well, that it was a *plan*, i.e., it involved a centralized approach to conversion. Defence enterprises were to be told by central planners the type and quantity of consumer products to produce.

The dissolution of the Soviet Union left the fate of military conversion uncertain, and there was little progress through 1992. Furthermore, there is only a small basis for optimism concerning the outcome of conversion. Any centralized conversion plan, particularly if implemented in the absence of accompanying market-oriented reforms, can be expected to exhibit all the problems that are characteristic of centrally-planned economies. Without free prices, there is no yardstick to measure how highly consumers value goods, nor how much goods actually cost to make. As we have seen, producing more centrally-determined consumer goods does not necessarily lead to a rise in living standards. Centralized control of conversion in state-owned enterprises will also result in poor incentives to efficiently produce high quality consumer goods.

But military conversion need not be planned in Moscow; rather, it can be undertaken in a decentralized fashion. While defence enterprises were, at first, generally exempted from the official privatization programme, spontaneous privatizations still took place in the defence sector.[430] The extent of private ownership in the defence sector was further augmented by an acceleration of official privatizations in 1993.[431] Private businesses utilizing the assets of defence firms can make their own decisions concerning what to produce. As long as prices are free and the Russian government continues to adequately provide for its defence needs, there is not much that can be said against conversion of productive assets from military to civilian uses by de facto private firms. Profit-maximizing entrepreneurs in free markets have wide scope in deploying their assets, and if the 'owners' of defence firms view conversion as profitable, they should be given free rein.

Western experience with decentralized military conversion has been dismal. In the words of Martin Marietta Chairman Norman Augustine, US defence conversion efforts have been 'unblemished by success'.[432] China, alternatively, has apparently enjoyed successful military conversion during its ongoing reforms.[433] In Russia, the large amount of civilian goods already made within the defence complex might suggest that Russia is relatively well-positioned for successful military conversion. But many of these goods are the same low-quality products that are legendary in Russia: 2,000 fires a year in Moscow have been blamed on exploding colour televisions produced by defence enterprises.[434] On balance, conversion schemes that involve the actual physical conversion of assets from defence production to consumer goods production are relatively unpromising, whether undertaken in a centralized or decentralized fashion.

Nor is it the case that privatized defence enterprises are sure to be interested in the production of consumer goods. The owners may view their best opportunities to make profits as the production and export of military goods – a stance shared by many Western defence companies that are faced with similarly declining demands for their main products. Indeed, foreign trade may be the most effective way for the Russians to turn guns into butter: sell the guns and buy the butter. Privatization alone is not certain to result in physical conversion of assets to the production of civilian goods, if export opportunities exist. But the actual export options for Russian arms appear quite limited. First, Western arms producers provide formidable competition, and the Persian Gulf war has increased the perception that Western arms are higher quality than Russian weapons. Second, advanced weapons systems require ongoing maintenance and spare parts. In the midst of economic and social turmoil, Russian arms producers cannot credibly commit to being able to service weapons in the coming decades.

One conversion-type reform with the potential to improve the economy in Russia is simply to reduce the size of the defence budget. While it remains difficult to gauge the amount of resources that go to defence, there probably has been some reduction during the reform era.[435] State orders for military procurement were said to fall by two-thirds during 1992, and the number of uniformed personnel has apparently also been reduced, perhaps by 500,000 or more men.[436] The defence sector's previous priority access to material inputs and skilled labour has also been undermined during the reform era, in itself representing a diminution in the value of resources that are devoted to the Russian military.

To the extent that the resources freed by significant declines in defence expenditures are redirected towards the private sector, improvements can occur in Russian living standards. (Even if Russian military production could be sold abroad for consumer goods, a reduction in the number of troops would increase the manpower available to the civilian economy.) It still remains to be seen, however, to what extent such defence reductions actually occur and will be maintained. One commentator, writing in 1994, noted that only three million Russians were actually producing arms, and declared that military conversion had, to a large extent, already succeeded.[436*]

The expectation that military conversion in isolation can bring large improvements is unwarranted. This expectation appears to be implicit in the common view, noted in 'The myth of the plan' section, that the necessity of matching Western arms spending eventually proved so costly to the Soviet Union that the only way out was to embrace reform. If excessive military spending brought the Soviet Union down, presumably cutbacks in such spending could have revitalized the Soviet economy. As argued above, however, it was fixed prices and the concomitant paraphernalia of central planning that resulted in the resource misallocations and waste that kept Soviet living standards low. A reduction in the amount of resources devoted to defence could have postponed reform, but the underlying causes of the inefficient economy would have remained. It is systemic economic reform, not military conversion, that holds the hope for higher living standards in Russia's future.

On another level, it could be said that the entire official Soviet economy was militarized. Fixed prices, rationing, and government requisitions mark Western-style wartime economies and the official Soviet economy. The movement from a command to a market economy in Russia could be likened to converting from a wartime to a peacetime economy. In this sense, de-militarization and conversion are the essential reform elements, irrespective of the final size of the Russian defence sector.

## ROUBLE CONVERTIBILITY

Under Soviet central planning, Soviet citizens were generally not allowed to trade roubles for foreign currencies, nor could foreigners legally take roubles out of the USSR. (Tourists in both directions were allowed to exchange small amounts of currency at a rate determined by the government.) The market for foreign exchange was suppressed. In other words, the rouble was not a convertible currency: it could not be freely exchanged for other currencies.

In parallel with the currency restrictions, planners controlled virtually all Soviet foreign trade.[437] What goods to import, and what goods to export to pay for the imports, were both centrally-determined, as were the ultimate recipients of industrial imports. The primary exports to non-socialist countries were energy products (oil and natural gas) and weapons. While the Soviet Union was not a large player in world trade – even including trade with the socialist world, the immense Soviet Union was less than two Hong Kongs in terms of value of exports – as a share of its own measured GNP, Soviet foreign trade was significant.[438] In 1988, the value of imports was roughly 12 per cent of measured Soviet GNP, near the comparable US figure.[439] The actual economic value of trade with the socialist countries is difficult to interpret, however, because of the fixed prices involved, but much of this trade involved implicit Soviet subsidies to its allies. Trade with market economies of necessity relied on market prices, though concessions were made for political reasons in some cases, e.g., arms exports were frequently subsidized.

During the reform period, Russia has greatly liberalized the system of foreign trade. Trade in foreign currencies at market-determined rates is allowed, so the rouble has achieved a good deal of convertibility. Most restrictions on imports have been removed, though exports generally require a licence, and trade taxes exist for some goods.[440] Oil exports, for example, are heavily taxed, as are imports of automobiles and vodka.

The convertibility that Russia has largely adopted is referred to as 'current-account' convertibility.[440*] This means that roubles can be exchanged for foreign currencies for the purposes of trading goods and services and for tourism. It does not mean, however, that foreigners can exchange their currencies for roubles in order to buy Russian factories, or that Russians can exchange their roubles to buy foreign assets. The international exchange of asset ownership, rather, requires 'capital-account' convertibility.[441] Convertibility for capital transactions has been argued to be unwise until macro-economic stabilization is achieved.[442] One fear of capital account convertibility is that it will lead to 'capital flight', whereby assets are moved to less volatile foreign economies. Even in the absence of capital account convertibility, estimates of capital flight from Russia are in the range of $20 billion annually, possibly exceeding the aid inflows.[443]

How important has the partial liberalization of foreign trade and the foreign exchange market been to reforming Russia, and what can be expected from a more complete, current-account liberalization? Many commentators suggested that rouble convertibility would play an important, and perhaps essential, role in marketizing the Russian economy.[444] The reasoning is that convertibility, combined with a largely unrestricted trade regime, promotes three desirable consequences: increased foreign trade, increased foreign investment, and the importation of world relative prices.

Indeed, the liberalization of foreign economic relations has led to a good deal of new foreign trade with Western countries and foreign investment during the reform era.[445] Simultaneously, the break-up of the Eastern trading bloc COMECON and the dissolution of the USSR have reduced official Russian trade with countries in Eastern Europe and the other countries of the former USSR. As noted, the fixed prices involved in that trade made the value of it uncertain. On balance, the reduction in trade with the former East Bloc has probably been beneficial to Russia.[446] Breakdowns in intra-USSR trade, however, may have contributed to production declines that are not economically justified.

The trade and investment benefits that would accompany full rouble convertibility, while desirable, are not indispensable. Foreign investment generally plays a minor role in promoting economic growth, despite its potential to promote technology transfer. Foreign trade confers gains on both trading partners, so the trade-creating aspect of rouble convertibility would benefit the Russian economy. But Russia has a huge internal economy. Policies that rationalize this internal economy are almost sure to produce gains that swamp the effects of improvements in foreign trade.[447] Simultaneously, internal decontrol of economic activity, and a stable legal environment, will serve as perhaps the best attractor of foreign partners.

Beyond the trade and investment benefits, rouble convertibility is viewed as desirable because of its ability to 'get prices right', both in the direct sense of ensuring that world prices are relevant in Russia, and in the indirect sense of providing commitment to a domestic price liberalization. Russian enterprises, monopolies or otherwise, will not long be able to charge excessive prices if foreign firms can offer competition. In itself, however, the importation of world relative prices may not confer large gains on Russia. There is evidence that the state-controlled relative prices were largely consistent with world prices, though with some notable exceptions such as the prices of housing and energy.[448] Again, the more important reform is to ensure that domestic producers have strong incentives to respond to market-determined prices, as opposed to simply 'getting prices right'.

The 'commitment' argument suggests that rouble convertibility, combined with unfettered foreign trade, necessitates internal price decontrol. If prices remain fixed when trade is freed, arbitragers would purchase Russian goods that are relatively underpriced, export them, and receive the higher world price. Such arbitrage activity would result in a huge wealth giveaway by the Russian government.[449] (For this reason, the Soviets required joint ventures operating in the USSR to use world prices even for domestic transactions, as opposed to the fixed state prices.[450]) To avoid this outcome in a regime with rouble convertibility and free foreign trade, the Russians would have to free prices internally. Adopting a policy of rouble convertibility, so the story goes, therefore commits the Russians to price liberalization.

The significant degree of price liberalization that has occurred since the beginning of 1992 renders this credibility argument largely moot in a policy sense. But there were good reasons to distrust this 'convertibility-implies-price liberalization' logic anyway. If the Russians truly were committed to full price liberalization, they could achieve this convincingly without rouble convertibility, simply by decontrolling prices. Without governmental commitment to price liberalization, a policy of rouble convertibility is not credible – the government will simply back off from convertibility as its losses mount – so convertibility cannot provide any commitment to a price liberalization policy.

Rouble convertibility has often been tied to Western aid programmes. The logic is that if foreign trade is to be liberalized and the rouble made convertible at a fixed exchange rate, balance-of-payments assistance (i.e., provision of foreign exchange or other measures to subsidize Russian imports) or a 'rouble stabilization fund', or both, may be necessary to maintain the exchange rate.[451] For example, the Russian government could declare that roubles are fully convertible at, say, 3000 to the dollar. Any person who presents one dollar to the Russian government would receive 3000 roubles, and perhaps more importantly, vice versa – the government would be willing to give one dollar in exchange for 3000 roubles. In order to credibly make such a commitment, the Russian government, which can print roubles but not dollars, must ensure that the 'market value' of 3000 roubles is not less than $1; otherwise, there will be a 'run' on the government, as people try to exchange 3000 roubles for the more valuable dollar.

To prevent such a run, then, the government must not allow people to think that 3000 roubles are less valuable than a dollar. By 'committing' to a fixed exchange rate, governments presumably tie their hands not to inflate the domestic currency more quickly than world inflation; otherwise, the run would eventually occur. The fixed exchange rate therefore serves as a 'nominal anchor', i.e., it anchors the domestic price level by restricting the government's ability to profligately print roubles. Indeed, the stabilization of expectations – convincing people that you are committed to a non-inflationary policy – is the main argument for employing a fixed exchange rate during a transition.

Expectations that the fixed exchange rate will hold can perhaps be purchased by a stabilization fund of foreign exchange, which indicates to holders of the domestic currency that the opportunity to obtain foreign currencies at the fixed rate will continue to be honoured. If they adopt such expectations, there will not be a run against the domestic currency, and the stabilization fund remains intact.[452]

Once again, however, commitment arguments in reform are not completely persuasive. It is true that with a fixed exchange rate, government budget deficits that are paid for by printing money quickly come to the attention of the government, by a run against the domestic currency. But this outcome is not so dire that no government would ever choose not to print money. Instead, faced with a run, the government can simply devalue the supposedly 'fixed' exchange rate. A fixed exchange rate can be viewed as providing an incentive to alter the rate when domestic inflation mounts, as opposed to providing a nominal anchor. Stabilization funds do not provide free commitment to an otherwise uncommitted government policy.

A fixed exchange rate is not a necessary component of rouble convertibility. Many market economies (like the United States) employ floating exchange rates, whereby the value of the currency is determined in the market in which it is exchanged with other currencies. As opposed to a fixed exchange rate regime, maintaining a floating exchange rate does not require that the government have substantial foreign currency reserves. (It was the lack of such reserves that probably prompted the move to a floating exchange rate in Russia.)

The government of a transitional economy that implements sound fiscal and monetary policies has little to fear, in terms of inflation, from either fixed or floating exchange rates.[453] Simultaneously, a government that implements inflationary policies will face a rapid depreciation of its currency in a floating-rate regime, or a run against domestic currency and eventual devaluation in a fixed exchange rate regime. It is sound monetary policies, and not the exchange rate regime, that are important for improving a transitional economy's price stability.

Nevertheless, short-term balance-of-payments support has become a part of the received aid wisdom.[454] To the extent that Russia meets the usual requirements for such support, Western aid in the form of a rouble stabilization fund and balance-of-payments support may be a desirable policy. This is not a pressing issue, however. While full rouble convertibility would undoubtedly be beneficial, the most advantageous trade (such as oil exports and food imports) is generally already taking place. Furthermore, market-oriented reforms can proceed and generate large improvements in Russia, even without rouble convertibility.

## WESTERN AID

And, as we hear you do reform yourselves,
We will, according to your strength and qualities,
Give you advancement.

William Shakespeare, *King Henry IV*, Part II

On 1 April 1992, Western leaders announced a $24 billion aid package to the states of the former Soviet Union.[455] While this programme has been amended and augmented since, major components of planned Western aid remain balance-of-payments support and a rouble stabilization fund. Once again, the pre-reform situation is a crucial determinant of the potential impact of Western aid.

Consider first the balance-of-payments support, which is equivalent to giving the former Soviet states Western goods. What form the goods take, whether food or clothing or medical supplies, is largely irrelevant. Such direct aid is fungible, in the sense that aid received in the form of food, for instance, frees internal Russian resources for other purposes.

The pre-existing debt owed by the former USSR to the West greatly alters the impact of Western aid. The states of the former Soviet Union owe some $60–85 billion to the West – a debt that they are having difficulty servicing. Indeed, the repayment of principal due on this debt was postponed in December 1991.[456] The situation is further complicated by the disappearance of the entity – the USSR – that was the original borrower.

The existence of this potentially unrecoverable debt implies that Western aid to Russia may largely be returned to the West in increased debt repayment.[457] Aid effectively transfers funds from the IMF, World Bank, or Western governments to Western banks, simply passing through Russia.[458]

As opposed to balance-of-payments support, the rouble stabilization fund is designed to work in an indirect fashion. If a rouble stabilization fund achieves its purpose, it will not actually be used – with a stable rouble, the extra foreign exchange comprising the stabilization fund will remain in place, since there will be no run against the rouble. Such forms of indirect assistance are therefore conceptually different from direct aid. As noted in the previous section, however, a rouble stabilization fund is neither necessary nor sufficient for achieving rouble convertibility, which itself will bring limited benefits to Russia in the short-term.

The current instability in the rouble, however, results in Russian aid to the West, of a sort. Because of high inflation and the possibility of another currency confiscation, many people in Russia hold foreign currency, chiefly dollars and deutschemarks, instead of roubles. But how do Russians originally acquire the foreign currency? They must sell something to the West, that is paid for, say, in dollars. Instead of using the dollars to buy US goods, however, the dollars circulate (or are hoarded) in Russia. The US has therefore acquired Russian goods, and, until the dollars actually return to the United States, has not had to provide any goods in exchange. In essence, the use of dollars in Russia represents an interest-free loan from Russia to the United States. The US does not have to repay the loan until the Russians finally divest themselves of their dollars by purchasing US goods. In the meantime, the widespread use of foreign currency in Russia is a form of Russian aid to the West.

The existence of widespread formal and informal market activity in Russia, as described in the previous chapters, does not imply that the Russian economy is in good shape, or that Western aid to Russia and other states of the former USSR is inappropriate. While there are many countries that are poorer than Russia, aid to the Russian economy could have a sustained impact. Systemic change such as Russia is undergoing holds out the possibility, not just for temporary improvements in living standards, but for movement to a higher growth path that will raise living standards in the future. Aid that helps to ensure successful systemic change will benefit both current and future generations of Russians. There is little possibility of creating a long-term dependence on aid, as can occur with assistance to developing countries, nor will other nations be enticed to embrace socialism as a means of qualifying for Western aid. For these reasons and because of the strategic importance of the former USSR, the Russian claim to Western aid is strong.[459] Also, because of the pre-existing debt, aid can be a useful measure to promote market reforms, without actually imposing significant net costs. But not all forms of aid are equally useful, and some may be detrimental.

Government involvement in economic production and distribution in the former Soviet Union remains extensive, despite many years of partial reforms and widespread private activity. An anecdote from post-coup, independent Lithuania illustrates this point. A police officer confiscated the goods of a seller at a flea market. Her crime was speculation. She had purchased some chocolates in Moscow and was selling them for a higher price in Vilnius.[460] The economic reform most needed in the former Soviet Union is for the government to allow the private sector to bloom, while clamping down on coercive private impediments to business: organized crime.

Economists differentiate between private goods, everyday items such as apples, where one person's consumption of an apple effectively rules out another person's consumption of the same apple, and public goods like national defence, where one citizen's 'consumption' does not interfere with another citizen's consumption. There is little reason for the government to be in the business of producing private goods, because private actors in free markets generally do a good job in ensuring good social outcomes. Public goods, however, involve an externality, and hence their provision can potentially be improved by government intervention. The pre-reform Soviet government dominated the production of both public and private goods. In reforming Russia, state provision of private goods such as food and consumer goods should diminish – the private sector is much better placed to efficiently produce the right private goods. State provision of some public goods, however, should continue.[461]

Western aid to the former Soviet Union should therefore be aimed at promoting private provision of private goods, and continued (or improved) state provision of public goods. Aid that enables continued state control of the economy is counterproductive, whether the aid is directed at the national, regional, or local level. Aid provided at the national level that allows, for example, Lithuania to continue to harass chocolate 'speculators' is obviously misplaced.

Private economic activity in Russia can be promoted either by directly helping private economic agents, or by helping the state provide the public goods – the legal system, the banking infrastructure, etc. – that indirectly promote private activity. Aid to private economic agents is difficult to implement, however, in an official aid programme. This type of 'aid' is probably best left to private economic agents in the West, in the form of undertaking profitable ventures within Russia and possibly with Russian partners.

Official Western aid should therefore focus on helping the Russian state sector provide public goods that promote private market activity. The Russian government's economic policy forms one such public good. Conditioning aid on the removal of price controls on gasoline, for example, would be an example of subsidizing the provision of a public good. The danger of unconditional aid, and to a degree conditional aid, bears re-iterating – aid directed at the state sector could inadvertently foster continued state interference in economic affairs best left to private actors.

Technical assistance for improving public goods such as the legal system or communications infrastructure is obviously important, though not always straightforward. Technical assistance in the economics realm may differ substantially depending on who provides the assistance. Transformations from socialism remain sufficiently complex that disagreements persist among Western economists. In other areas, say, in setting up accounting procedures or other elements of market infrastructure, 'appropriate technology' is an issue. With per-capita income approximately one-third of the US level, Russia may want to rely less extensively on computerization of accounting procedures than the US does, for instance.

One state-provided public good that will require significant revamping has already been mentioned – the implicit welfare system must be replaced with an explicit system, and a similar transformation must take place in the realm of tax collection. It has been argued in previous chapters that the costs of these systems need not rise during reform. Nevertheless, technical assistance will be valuable in both of these areas, is relatively inexpensive, and is, in fact, being provided.

Another public good that has been suffering with the collapse of the state sector is in the area of training and research. Western aid can be quite useful here. First, there are some fields, particularly the social sciences, where traditional Soviet training is clearly irrelevant. Few qualified teachers exist. While individuals are proving to be quite industrious in teaching themselves, Western aid in the form of textbooks and graduate student fellowships could help restore these fields much more quickly. Even in areas such as mathematics and the natural sciences where Russian research remains world-class, talented researchers have been enticed into private market, non-research activity, because of the financial incentives there and because of the diminished resources of the Academy of Sciences. While such labour movements are not entirely undesirable, grants to particularly talented researchers could return them to productive research.[462] Russian research fields are also suffering from an inability to attract young entrants, again because of improved alternatives. Fellowships provided by Western foundations, or possibly by Western governments, could support talented young graduate students.

Military conversion, as noted earlier, is not promising from an economic point of view. Western aid aimed at improving Russian living standards should not be directed at such types of physical conversion. Nevertheless, individual defence enterprises that are seeking to convert to consumer goods production, and that are working for their own account, may be good candidates for Western technical assistance, and possibly for private co-operation with Western companies.

One important 'aid' component is a reduction in Western trade barriers. This would involve both opening Western markets to goods from Russia (and other former socialist countries), and in reducing some of the trade controls that have existed because of Western security concerns. Unlike other forms of Western aid, reducing such trade barriers generally has the desirable property of making both Russia and the West better off in a direct way, since the existing trade restrictions tend to be welfare-reducing. Unfortunately, this suggests that the likelihood that trade barriers will be reduced for Russian exports is relatively small. (Alternatively, Western export restrictions to the former Soviet Union based on security considerations are already being dismantled.[463]) Domestic producers in the West have managed to secure protection from imports to the detriment of Western consumers. It is unlikely that their claims to protection will be eroded by the interests of emerging Russian exporters.

Aid may have other purposes than promoting the marketization of the Russian economy. Assistance for centralized Russian military conversion, a policy proposed by Senator Sam Nunn and others, may make sense from the perspective of Western security interests.[464] Money and technical assistance for the dismantling of nuclear weapons, and for the continued employment of Russian nuclear scientists, could be similarly motivated. Assistance in the environmental sphere, such as help in improving the safety of nuclear reactors, can also flow directly from Western self-interest.

Finally, an implicit sub-text of this chapter warrants explicit re-telling. The ultimate success or failure of Russian market-oriented reform is in the hands of the Russians. While Western aid can be useful, most of the gains from Russian reform can be secured without any help from foreign governments.

## GRADUAL REFORM, CHINESE STYLE

Beginning with agricultural reform in 1978, the Chinese have gradually moved towards an increased use of markets. Following agriculture, China has extended its liberalization, first to foreign trade, and then to industry.[465] By all reports, the gradual approach to economic reform in China has been a huge, virtually unprecedented success, with impressive growth in agriculture, industry, and services, and an overall growth rate averaging 8.8 per cent per year between 1978 and 1992.[466] China is therefore exhibit A for the gradualist side in the debate between those who favour gradual transitions from socialism and those who prefer a more rapid introduction of legal markets.

The question then arises, is the Chinese success story of more general applicability? Does China indicate that a gradual transition from socialism, one sector at a time, is preferable to a relatively rapid, broad-based transition? A first step in answering this question requires an examination of the possibility of maintaining a market-based sector (e.g., agriculture), within the larger framework of a centrally-planned economy. This question was addressed by Western economist Gregory Grossman in 1963, and his framework of analysis remains serviceable.[467]

Grossman identifies three potential reasons for failure of an attempt to marketize one sector within a command economy. First, planned sectors may depend on the output of the market sector, and if the availability of that output is unpredictable, the planned portion of the economy may be harmed. Agriculture, therefore, may be particularly well-suited for marketization, since the production of industrial goods and other consumer goods does not generally require direct inputs from the agricultural sector. Simultaneously, the greater the extent to which the unplanned sector requires inputs from the planned sector, the lower the benefits of liberalization are likely to be, since the market sector's growth will be constrained by the availability of planned inputs. Second, according to Grossman, the result of production in the market sector may not accord with the government's values. Increased income differentiation in the market sector, for example, could result in a re-imposition of planning by authorities not accustomed to large, visible discrepancies in living standards. Third, the market sector may not fully utilize its resources. Unemployment, for instance, could again create pressure for more extensive planning.

As noted, these considerations suggest that marketizing the agriculture sector within a planned economy is relatively likely to succeed, if the planning regime can tolerate the distributional impacts both within the agricultural sector and between the agricultural and planned sectors. If the agricultural sector is large relative to the size of the overall economy – in China, 71 per cent of the labour force was involved in agriculture in 1978 – the economic benefits from such a marketization can be significant. In Russia, with only 14 per cent of the work force in agriculture at the beginning of perestroika, the gains are likely to be substantially smaller.[468] Furthermore, Russian farms average 40 times the size of Chinese farms, and Russian agriculture is much more highly industrialized than Chinese agriculture.[469]

The Grossman-style links, therefore, between the planned sector (agricultural machinery) and the unplanned sector (agriculture) are greater in Russia, again suggesting that an agriculture-first market reform is less likely to succeed in Russia than in China.

A successful reform in a single sector such as agriculture is only the beginning, however. Problems will arise as the agricultural sector prospers. The greater productivity brought about by the marketization of agriculture will eventually tend to create new resources and perhaps free other resources employed in the agricultural sector. What new activities will these freed resources undertake? If the only option is for them to enter into the planned sector, then the productivity gains in agriculture would, in all likelihood, not spread to the rest of the economy, which will still be marked by all the usual shortcomings of central planning. The economic boom arising from the liberalization of agriculture will be a useful, but one-time, affair. The agricultural reforms in China led precisely to such a one-time jump in productivity, though the ensuing liberalizations in other sectors allowed growth to spread.[470]

A second method of separating out a market sector in an otherwise planned economy – and a method also pursued in China – is to make the division along geographical lines, by declaring certain areas 'special economic zones'. Within these zones, as with the 'empowerment zones' established in American cities, economic conditions are then liberalized relative to other areas. The Grossman criteria apply as well to this type of partial reform. The importance of links between the controlled and liberalized areas, in particular, are once again quite important. Consider, for example, what might happen if price controls are lifted in a special economic zone, but not in other parts of the country. Typically, nominal prices will then be higher in that zone relative to the planning areas. Firms in the planning areas, to the extent possible, will then prefer to sell their goods in the free zones; i.e., the free zones will tend to draw resources away from the unplanned zones. This argument applies to labour as well. Wages are likely to be higher in the free market sector, so workers will tend to migrate to these zones. Non-market regions will then either have to tighten controls – by forbidding 'exports' of food to the special economic zone, for instance – or by freeing their own prices. In Russia, local controls on the movement of goods became the response of many localities to the situation that arose following central price liberalization but locally-imposed price controls.[471]

Related to the issue of gradual vs rapid transition is the extent to which economic liberalization should be conducted in a centralized or a decentralized manner. The centralized variant of reform involves the mandating of reforms, more-or-less uniformly, from the political centre. The official privatization plan in Russia is an example of such a reform. Decentralized reforms, alternatively, would let localities choose their own rates of transition. The Chinese agricultural reforms were largely of the decentralized variety – in many instances, they were spontaneous, not official reforms – with the central government stepping in only to prevent local officials from squelching the reforms.[472]

Centralized reforms have the advantage that they can perhaps overcome the intransigence of local officials. The related disadvantage, however, is that local resistance might be sufficient to scuttle the reform efforts – and perhaps rightly so, if the central reform plan was not sufficiently sensitive to local conditions. Decentralized reforms, as noted before with respect to regionally gradual reforms, would seem to work best if they create a reinforcing momentum for reform: one region liberalizes quickly, and other regions, noting the flow of resources into the liberal region, respond with liberalizations of their own. Decentralized reforms are less likely to work, however, if the response to a flow of resources out of one region is the strengthening of controls to prevent such a flow.

Decentralized reforms, then, like gradual reforms, are most likely to succeed under two sets of circumstances: either there are few links between the liberalized region and other regions, or, if there are extensive links, they are such as to promote a virtuous cycle of reform. 'Agriculture first' reforms in Russia are not promising on either of these counts, given the important links between the agricultural machinery (and fertilizer) industries and the agricultural sector, and the frequency of locally-imposed price and trade restrictions. The decentralization of more broad-based reforms is also problematic in Russia. Here, the difficulty is that the most pressing reform that remains is to reduce subsidies to state-owned enterprises. Every locality, however, has an incentive to press for centrally-directed subsidies to its own industries. The virtuous cycle of reform may therefore have a hard time getting underway.

## CONCLUSIONS

So many reforms, so little time. The Russian economy is sufficiently distant from a normal market economy that there is scarcely any aspect of the economy that does not require significant change, or that could not benefit from Western assistance. Nevertheless, some reforms have higher priority than others. The most important reforms are those that I have identified with a sufficient reform package: free prices, free enterprise, and explicit systems of taxation and social welfare. The gradual introduction of these reforms, in the Russian context, seems to hold many pitfalls relative to rapid implementation. Other desirable reforms, such as rouble convertibility, military conversion, or, as noted in a previous chapter, large-scale privatization, are of decidedly secondary importance. Indeed, if these subordinate reforms are implemented prior to the more basic measures, they will almost surely fail, and may well worsen the economic situation. Western aid will also tend to have a limited impact unless the basic reform measures are in place. But once the basic reforms are implemented, significant Western aid is probably unwarranted. The main role for Western aid, therefore, is to help promote and cement the fundamental reform measures – measures which Russia should take irrespective of foreign assistance. After Russia implements the basic reforms, Western participation in the Russian economy can be as a partner, not a patron, like standard economic links among market economies.

# Conclusions

In the relations of a weak Government and a rebellious people there comes a time when every act of the authorities exasperates the masses, and every refusal to act excites their contempt . . .'

John Reed, *Ten Days that Shook the World*, 1919[473]

It's a very serious risk to do nothing. It is a very serious risk to do anything unpopular. It is even a very serious risk to do something popular because everyone understands that really popular measures will lead you nowhere.

Yegor Gaidar, 1991[474]

[T]o catch or destroy five rats and ten mice . . .
Part of the 'plan' proposed to Soviet children to further the first 5-year plan, from *New Russia's Primer. The Story of the Five-Year Plan*[475]

China's economic reformer, Deng Xiaoping, is noted for his claim that 'It doesn't matter whether the cat is black or white, as long as it catches mice.' Presumably his point is that as long as an economic system delivers the goods, labels such as 'socialist' or 'capitalist' are irrelevant. The traditional Soviet system was, in many ways, not a planned system at all. Similarly, the market economy that is now growing in Russia, from extensive and largely subterranean pre-existing roots, remains far removed from any notion of what a normal market economy might look like. The difficult task that remains is for the Russian government to nurture the market economy that already exists, by providing the conditions under which the private behaviour of individuals will by and large mesh with the social good – mice will then be caught.

The analysis presented in this book has argued that a useful way to think about Russian reform is as a movement from implicit to explicit versions of pre-existing economic phenomena. A partial list of some of the phenomena that are undergoing such a conversion would include: inflation; unemployment; monopoly power; economic crime; private property rights; taxation; and the social safety net. Many of these economic phenomena more or less automatically revert from implicit to explicit form during any effective transition to a market economy. Since free prices are a sine qua non of a market economy, inflation, for example, of necessity will become largely open in a market-oriented reform. Alternatively, some of the formerly repressed economic phenomena, such as tax and social welfare policy, become open only as the Russian government consciously creates new, explicit systems that accomplish these functions.

The two pillars that underlie the conducive conditions for 'growing' a market economy are free prices, and good incentives to respond to the free prices. The major obstacles to overcome in building these pillars can be characterized as partial reform measures, particularly in the form of keeping some important prices fixed (generally at levels well below the market rate), continuing to subsidize unsuccessful firms or confiscating surpluses from successful firms, providing undue legal restrictions on private enterprise, or failing to provide workable explicit versions of the tax and social welfare systems. A lack of stability in the legal environment also militates against the establishment of a well-functioning market economy. Furthermore, in gauging the effects of reform, traditional indicators of economic perform-ance must be carefully assessed, as such statistics will begin to measure different things when economic phenomena move from repressed to open form. With a reasonably comprehensive market-oriented reform, most of the costs that appear to accompany reform will simply represent more open versions of costs that were being paid surreptitiously under the old system.

None of this is to suggest that the transition from socialism to capitalism is child's play, or to appropriate a phrase of Lenin's, could be accomplished by any kitchen maid. If such a transition were simple and painless, it probably would have taken place in Russia many years ago. But as the quotations that open this section intimate, systemic reform is hard to accomplish.

The difficulty of transition means that countries tend to postpone reform until the pre-reform conditions get nearly intolerable, to the point where those who are clearly better off with the status quo become small in number and influence. But the initiation of reform is, of course, only the beginning; there will be those who are harmed by reforms, as well as others, perhaps responding to the inappropriate statistical measures of the effects of reform, who will succumb to what the historian Edward Gibbon called 'the propensity of mankind to exalt the past and to depreciate the present'.[476] The legacy of the old system in Russia is such that despite a near decade of bad economic news and many voices of despair accompanying reform, there appears to be little interest in turning back.[477] The danger is not so much from a conscious decision to re-impose central planning as it is from the temptation to meet every seeming (and in some cases, real) economic 'crisis' with a government control, until a planned economy arrives more-or-less accidentally.

The road of Russian reform is therefore difficult to traverse, and there will be frequent retreats. In the end, it is likely that Russia will arrive at the destination of a normal market economy, if only because other endpoints are either unstable, or, like the previous system, clearly undesirable. But the timetable for the journey involves years, and with bad economic policies, decades. All is not pessimistic, however. Another Chinese saying is that a journey of a thousand miles begins with a single step. The Russian economy has already taken many steps, even giant leaps, in the direction of a market economy, and in a relatively short period of time. It was only at the end of 1991 that the Soviet flag came down from the Kremlin. Russian streets are alive with private market activity, private farms are blossoming, many state-owned enterprises have been 'privatized'. Russians are not sitting silently, anxiously anticipating their journey to the market economy. They are well on their way.

# Notes

Notes denoted by an asterisk have been added since the text was first completed.

1  Hewett (1989a, p. 18).
2  Evidence for the positive contribution that economic reasoning can bring to the reform debate comes, ironically, from Dr. Hewett's own work (Hewett (1988)), among other sources. Kornai (1990) is an outstanding example of the application of basic economic reasoning to Eastern European reform.
3  McCloskey (1985, p. 131).
4  Gogol (1972 [1842], p. 259).
5  Some of the Gorbachev-era reform flip-flops are chronicled in Goldman (1992).
6  Ericson (1991, p. 26).
7  On the controversy regarding Russian living standards, see Rosefielde (1991), Bergson (1991), and the 'Income and Living Standards' chapter below.
8  From Karl Marx's 'Critique of the Gotha Program'. Feurer (1959, p. 117).
9  *Economic Report of the President* (1992, p. 104).
10  In January 1994, the survey used by the Department of Labor to calculate the unemployment rate was revised. The new survey revealed some unemployment that was previously uncounted, so that the reported unemployment rate increased in January 1994, although calculated on a consistent basis, unemployment actually fell from December 1993.

    A sudden 'loss' of 640,000 US jobs in the first quarter of 1991 was discovered, two years later, to be merely a statistical artefact reflecting a change in how the number of jobs was tabulated. See 'Labor Dep't Overstated Jobs Lost in Last Recession', Durham (NC) *Herald-Sun*, 4 June 1993, p. 16.
11  The full poem appears in Hewett (1989b, pp. 104–106).
12  Wolf (1991) chronicles the many years of difficulties with partial reform measures in Hungary and Poland.
13  This effect on the price of sour cream ignores the supply shift noted earlier in the paragraph. With both the supply and demand of sour cream increasing, the net effect on the price is ambiguous.
14  See, e.g., 'Puzzle of Moscow Milk: Prices Soar, Still Scarce', by Celestine Bohlen, *New York Times*, 7 February 1992, p. A8, and National Public Radio, *Morning Edition*, 'Yeltsin Receives Harsh Criticism, Moscow,' 16 January 1992.
15  This description of the evolution of Russian central planning is drawn from Sedik (1991). A hint of this reasoning also appears in Grossman (1963, p.107).
16  Shlapentokh (1989, p. 210, and endnote 4, p. 244).
17  Nove (1986, p. 364f). Ofer (1987, pp. 1770–1775) provides a good overview of

Soviet statistics. Treml (1988, 1992a) discusses the changes in Soviet statistics, and Western interpretations of the statistics, under perestroika.

18   The undocumented change involving the inclusion of used car sales in the automobile sales statistics was uncovered by Vladimir Treml. See *Radio Liberty Research*, RL 177/77, 26 July 1977.

19   See, e.g., Alexeev and Walker (1991, p. 4f).

20   Åslund (1990, pp. 19–20).

21   Vaksberg (1991, p. 115). The Uzbekistan cotton story is also related in Boyes (1990, p. 149f).

22   Vaksberg (1991, pp. 113–114).

23   This passage from Orwell (1983, p. 37) was brought to my attention during a talk at the Hoover Institution by Robert Conquest in 1992.

24   On the Khanin and Selyunin article, see Treml (1988) and Ericson (1990). Belkin (1993) provides a brief history of Khanin's work.

25   That growth rates will be unaffected by a consistent falsification of output levels is known as the 'Law of Equal Cheating'. See, e.g., Nove (1986, p. 374).

26   Khrushchev (1974, p. 131).

27   Goldman (1992, pp. 97–99). On Gorbachev's announcement of the previously hidden budget deficit, see Birman (1990, p. 25).

28   Incidentally, unreliable statistics at the highest levels are indicative of the types of problems that would render even 'ideal' central economic planning ineffective.

29   Hanson (1991, p. 290f).

30   The political purposes of statistics collection were noted by the last chairman of the USSR State Committee for Statistics (Belkin (1993, p. 59)). Of course, statistics can be used for propaganda purposes in market economies, too.

31   See 'Light at the End of the Tunnel?', by Keith Bush, *RFE/RL Research Report*, 14 May 1993, p. 64, and 'The Russian Budget Deficit', by Keith Bush, *RFE/RL Research Report*, 9 October 1992, p. 31.

32   'Leaders Said to Have Exaggerated Runaway Inflation Risk in Russia', by Steven Erlanger, *New York Times*, 3 March 1993, p. A7.

33   Quoted in Bronfenbrenner, Sichel, and Gardner (1984, p. 9).

34   Hewett (1988, p. 160).

35   Richards (1990).

36   Richards (1990, pp. 76–77). See also her discussion of the inability to generalize on pp. 72–73.

37   On the limits to knowledge, and an analogy to archaeology, see, e.g., Nutter (1969, pp. 70-71, 109–11).

38   Susan Richards (1990, p. 73) also notes how a (perhaps reluctant) reliance on the official story by Western Sovietologists failed to convey the realities of daily economic life.

39   Conquest (1991). See also 'The Party in the Dock', by Robert Conquest, *Times Literary Supplement*, 6 November 1992, p. 7, and the letter by émigré socio-logist Vladimir Shlapentokh to the *AAASS Newsletter*, May 1993, pp. 5, 7.

40   Interviews and surveys of émigrés provided much of the systematic informa-tion that has become available concerning informal economic activity during the Soviet era. The Berkeley–Duke Project on the Second Economy in the USSR has produced more than 30 papers based largely on a survey of émigrés. Thousands of Soviet émigrés were also interviewed for the aptly-named 'Soviet Interview Project'. Millar (1987) provides a compendium of research based on this source (see p. 17).

40*  Treml and Alexeer (1993, p. 18n)

41   See, e.g., 'Capitalism or Bust', *Economist*, 8 February 1992, and Wellisz (1991, p. 212).

42  The state price of oil and natural gas remained at 10%–20% of world prices in mid-1993. 'Light at the End of the Tunnel?', by Keith Bush, *RFE/RL Research Report*, 14 May 1993, p. 65.

The 'tropical flowers in Poland' sort of waste can only occur when based on products that are relatively plentiful in a centrally-planned economy; otherwise, for example, the greenhouse owners could not actually procure energy at the low official price.

43  'Free Market Prices For Coal Could Strengthen Russia's Economy, or Blow it Apart', by Sergei Leskov, *Izvestia*, 23 June 1993, p. 1. Condensed text translated in *Current Digest of the Post-Soviet Press*, Vol. XLV, No. 25, 1993.

44  Smith (1991 [1776], p. 400).

45  The notion that the invisible hand applies as long as all affected parties can costlessly contract in advance is known as the 'Coase theorem' in the economics world. The argument appeared in Coase (1960).

Complete information is important in leading to desirable outcomes because without it, bargaining may be inefficient. Farrell (1987) provides an excellent discussion of the relative merits of bargaining versus 'planning' in the presence of incomplete information.

46  Smith (1991 [1776], pp. 400–401).

47  Lange and Taylor (1938) present one approach to equilibrium pricing under socialism. From a systemic perspective, the informational advantages of markets seem substantial, as argued by Hayek (1945). In more limited arenas with incomplete information, however, planning may offer improvements over free markets. Again, see Farrell (1987).

48  Berliner (1976).

49  Khanin (1992, p. 14).

50  Burawoy and Hendley (1992, p. 373), endnote omitted. Rezina's operations in Moscow began in 1915.

51  Ericson (1991, p. 21).

52  Khrushchev (1990, p. 93).

53  Incidentally, the 'wrong goods' problem probably lies at the heart of difficulties in planned sectors, such as the defence industry, of Western economies. See, e.g., Leitzel (1993a).

54  Hayek (1972, pp. 124–125).

55  *The Myth of the Plan* is the title of a fine, balanced book by Peter Rutland (1985), though its focus is on the extent to which the Soviet command economy served political as opposed to economic objectives. An early contribution examining the reality of Soviet planning is Barton (1957).

56  Barton (1957, p. 43).

57  Goldman (1992) provides a description of the quality-control reform, which established State quality-control committees ('Gospriemka').

58  Hewett (1988, p. 184).

59  Birman (1978). Other important contributions that shed light on the actual workings of centrally-planned systems include Grossman (1963), Powell (1977), Zaleski (1980), Ellman (1983), Wilhelm (1985), and Hewett (1988, chapter 4). For a discussion of planning in a Western economy during wartime, see Devons (1950).

60  Powell (1977, p. 65n) reports on the frequency of plan changes, which for a single enterprise could be as often as 30 times a year. See also Hewett (1988, pp. 188–189).

61  Hewett (1988, p. 190).

62  Berliner (1952, p. 358).

63  Wilhelm (1985, p. 127).

64  Grossman (1963, pp. 108-112).
65  Grossman (1963, pp. 108).
66  See, e.g., Kornai (1992, chapters 11 and 12).
67  Powell (1977) discusses some of the informal methods whereby information on shortages was conveyed and balancing actions were taken in the Soviet economy.
68  Storming is described in Berliner (1956), and is further analysed in Alexeev (1991).
69  Smith (1984, pp. 287–288).
70  Schroeder (1979).
71  Belanovskii (1992).
72  A more sophisticated version of this theory would suggest that there is some-thing inherent in central planning – perhaps the relative ease in measuring technical characteristics as opposed to consumer satisfaction – that results in a large share of official economic activity being devoted to defence.
73  Grossman and Treml (1987, p. 285).
74  General Accounting Office (1991, p. 22) cites one expert's estimate of the second economy in 1988 at 25 per cent of GNP. Grossman (1987) suggests that more than one-third of the income of Soviet urban dwellers in the late 1970s was earned in the second economy. Gaddy (1991) discusses the growth of second economy incomes during the 1980s. Income measures of second economy activity are more reliable than GNP measures because of difficulties in measuring GNP (see the 'Incomes and living standards' chapter) and connections between the first and second economy – some goods produced in the official economy and hence already counted in GNP can be double counted if they serve as intermediate inputs in the second economy. State-sector sugar might become an input into second economy alcohol production, for example.
75  Jones and Moskoff (1991, p. 3). Grossman (1977, 1979) are relied upon heavily throughout this section.
76  The term 'second economy' was defined by Grossman (1977) to include any activity that is conducted for private gain, or is undertaken in knowing, non-trivial contravention of the law, or both. The legal collective farm markets thus formed an important component of the Russian second economy. Sales on these markets would generally not fall under the rubric 'black markets', how-ever, since these were legal markets. Shlapentokh (1989) documents a vast array of activities conducted for private gain in the pre-reform USSR.
77  Grossman and Treml (1987, p. 285).
78  On the theft of time from work, which generally occurred with the connivance of management, see Gaddy (1991), Treml (1992b), and Shlapentokh (1989, p. 52).
79  Shlapentokh (1989, p. 192).
80  Grossman (1989, p. 81).
81  Shlapentokh (1989, p. 191).
82  Jones and Moskoff (1991, p. 16).
83  Åslund (1993) notes many of the ways in which the Gaidar reforms of 1992 fell short of a full liberalization. Starodubrovskaya (1994) discusses many of the remaining barriers to the development of free markets (see p. 30).
83*  European Bank for Reconstruction and Development (1994, p. 34)
84  'Byurokraticheskiy rynok. Skrytyye prava i ekonomicheskaya reforma', by Vitaliy Nayshul'. Nezavisimaya gazeta, 26 September 1991, p. 5. Translated by Clifford Gaddy.
85  Jones and Moskoff (1991, p. 58) describe the conflict of interest in the leasing of equipment by medical cooperatives.
86  For various routes to spontaneous privatization, see Johnson and Kroll (1991).

87  Burawoy and Hendley (1992, p. 379). The authors do not refer to the confusing array of cooperatives as constituting a form of spontaneous privatization.

88  Starodubrovskaya (1994, p. 9), and the references cited therein.

89  Starr (1993).

90  Shlapentokh (1989, p. 193) notes that private construction crews were much more productive than the state crews; indeed, in the springtime official state crews were almost deserted because workers migrated around the country as private builders.

90*  Sachs (1993b, p. 153).

91  Gaddy (1993, p.4).

92  Prosterman, Hanstad, and Rolfes (1993, p. 3).

93  Prosterman and Hanstad (1991).

94  Gaddy (1993, p. 12).

95  Shlapentokh (1989, p. 161).

96  Prosterman, Hanstad, and Rolfes (1993, pp. 18-19), and Gaddy (1993, p. 11).

97  'Rural Reform in Russia', by Stephen K. Wegren, *RFE/RL Research Report*, 29 October 1993, pp. 43–53, on p. 48.

98  The extent and instability of government regulation of cooperatives is detailed in Slider (1991). See also Litwack (1991a).

99  Some examples of contradictory laws are provided in *Delovoy Mir*, 18 February 1993, p. 13.

100  Ownership uncertainty with respect to land, in particular, remains a problem in Russia. For a review of reform-era legislation in the agricultural sector, see 'Yeltsin Decree Finally Ends "Second Serfdom" in Russia', by Don Van Atta, *RFE/RL Research Report*, 19 November 1993, pp. 33–39.

101  Shleifer and Vishny (1993, p. 615).

102  de Soto (1989, p. 24) indicates that in Peru, the value of a house with a secure legal title exceeded the value of a house without legal protection by a factor of 9, on average. This source, Hernando de Soto's acclaimed book about the informal sector in Peru, *The Other Path*, details both theoretically and empirically the high costs associated with market activity, formal and informal, in situations where government restraints on private business are pervasive. Much of the discussion in *The Other Path* is directly relevant for the case of Russia.

103  A classic account of the degree to which business in the United States is actually conducted without legal protection is provided in Macauley (1963).

104  Simis (1982).

105  Rutgaizer (1992, p. 31, endnote 26), touches on this aspect of enforcement of laws against economic crimes.

106  See, e.g., Johnson and Kroll (1991), Burawoy and Krotov (1992), and 'From Soviet Minister to Corporate Chief', by G. Bruce Knecht, *New York Times Magazine*, 26 January 1992, pp. 24–28.

107  Johnson and Kroll (1991, p. 293). Kawalec (1992, p. 133) gives some Polish examples of de facto vertical integration.

108  Incidentally, the prospect to supply collateral for loans helps to underscore the importance of privatization of land and housing in a transition to a market economy. This point, for the case of land ownership, is noted by Prosterman and Hanstad (1991).

109  Aven (1991, p. 191n).

110  Johnson and Kroll (1991, p. 294).

111  See the discussion of barter in the chapter on 'Income and Living Standards'.

112  Burawoy and Krotov (1992) offer a description and generally negative assessment of 'parastatal conglomerates'.

113   Hendley (1992, p. 131).
114   For grain output statistics, see 'Agriculture and Food Supply in the Former Soviet Union', by Timothy N. Ash, *RFE/RL Research Report*, 13 November 1992, pp. 39–45.
115   Shlapentokh (1989, p. 92).
116   Individual Russians in particularly dire economic straits may have trouble affording food – or any other goods – and their plight may fuel the alarmist cries of food shortages. (The distribution of economic costs and benefits during reform is discussed in the chapters that follow.) Some of the voices proclaiming the potential for imminent famine have been raised by Russians, not Westerners. While it is understandable that Westerners might overestimate the importance of the state sector, it is unlikely that Russians would similarly misperceive the situation. Russians who are calling for food aid are generally representatives (and beneficiaries) of the state sector. It may be the state-sector crisis, not the overall condition of agriculture, to which they are responding.
117   See, e.g., *Izvestiya*, 9 September 1991. 'Ending Russia's Bread Lines', an op-ed by Leon Aron, *Wall Street Journal*, 18 December 1991, notes that '[l]ast summer the peasants were paid 200 roubles by the state for a ton of wheat delivered as part of the plan quota, and 400 roubles for each ton above the plan. At the same time, on the black (i.e., free) market, a ton of wheat cost 5,500 roubles!'
118   See 'Free Market Ideas Grow on Russian Farms', by Serge Schmemann, *New York Times*, 6 October 1992, pp. A1–A4.
119   'Yeltsin Decree Finally Ends 'Second Serfdom' in Russia', by Don Van Atta, *RFE/RL Research Report*, 19 November 1993, pp. 33–39, at 36. This article serves as a source for the discussion of remaining government interventions in Russian agriculture.
120   'Rural Reform in Russia', by Stephen K. Wegren, *RFE/RL Research Report*, 29 October 1993, pp. 43–53, at 51n.
121   'Byurokraticheskiy rynok. Skrytyye prava i ekonomicheskaya reforma', by Vitaliy Nayshul'. *Nezavisimaya gazeta*, 26 September 1991, p. 5. Translated by Clifford Gaddy.
122   Schelling (1984a, p. 158).
123   Thanks to opportunities for second economy activity, people employed in trade and services were more likely to own such prestige items as colour TVs than workers in other industries who had higher official salaries, but less control over state goods. See Shlapentokh (1989, pp. 79–80) and Rutgaizer (1992, p. 31, endnote 25).
124   Alexeev (1988b).
125   Simis (1982) and Vaksberg (1991) detail Communist Party control of the judiciary. See also Richards (1990, pp. 331–332), on the extent to which people believed that the Party controlled the law.
126   Shlapentokh (1989, p. 204f) notes the frequent use of the term 'mafia'. Simis (1982) and Vaksberg (1991) detail corruption and organized crime in the Soviet Union. The extent to which this system was known and understood is highlighted by former Moscow mayor Gavriil Popov's advocacy of legalizing the established bribes that are received by civil servants. See 'The Criminal Economy', by Mikhail Glukhovsky, *Delovie Lyudi*, No. 26, September 1992, pp. 14–16.
127   Grossman (1977, pp. 32–33).
128   The discussion of the importance of monopoly and illegality to organized crime draws heavily on Schelling (1984a,b).
129   It is more difficult to avoid paying tribute if the would-be extortionists are the police themselves, or if the business can be easily damaged in ways that are difficult to protect against. Schelling (1984b, p. 189) gives the example of

restaurants, where '[n]oises and bad odors and startling events can spoil the clientele, and even physical damage cannot be guarded against'.

130    Rutgaizer (1992, pp. 45–6).

131    Quoted in 'Wolf at the Door', by Maggie Mahar, *Barron's*, 19 October 1992, p. 20.

132    Valery Chernogorodsky, the former head of government anti-monopoly efforts in Russia who was quoted earlier, left his post when the anti-monopoly committee was put under the jurisdiction of the state committee on real estate. 'The real estate committee is itself a state monopoly . . . From the beginning of privatization, all of the corrupt forces gathered around the real-estate committee. . . . The anti-monopoly committee was supposed to be, in all ways, the opponent of everything the real estate committee stood for'. Quoted in 'Wolf at the Door', by Maggie Mahar, *Barron's*, October 19, 1992, p. 20. In a similar vein, the Russian Tax Service, which has been given the responsibility of registering all large bank accounts in order to fight corruption, has a reputation for being particularly corrupt itself. See 'The Russian Civil Service: Corruption and Reform', by Victor Yasmann, *RFE/RL Research Report*, 16 April 1993, p. 21.

133    See, e g., Åslund (1993, p. 21).

134    In the West, it has been suggested that high wages are the prime deterrent against employee theft. See Lipman and McGraw (1988, p. 58).

135    '"We Need Bribes to Survive", Traffic Cop Says', *The Moscow Times*, 12 June 1992, p. 7.

136    Richards (1990, p. 332). Pre-Soviet Russia was also marked by a good deal of corruption. These words appear in one of the last chapters of Gogol's (1972, p. 382) famous uncompleted novel *Dead Souls*: 'The dishonest practice of taking bribes has become a necessity, something that even people who were not born to be dishonest cannot do without'.

137    Reported in Rutgaizer (1992, p. 47).

138    Shlapentokh (1989, pp. 90–91).

139    See the poll results reported in Rutgaizer (1992, pp. 42–44).

140    Vaksberg (1991, p. 251) makes a similar point.

141    The alternative resolution of the joke is 'it would be a good thing'.

142    The departures from price freedom in the 2 January 1992 Gaidar reform were: (1) some 10 basic goods such as gasoline and milk remained under explicit government price control, though the levels of their fixed prices were raised; (2) state retailers were allowed to mark-up goods by only 25 per cent over their wholesale prices; and (3) in some areas, local controls continued to be placed on prices. See Fischer and Frenkel (1992). Åslund (1993) documents the substantial extent to which the January 1992 Russian reforms fell short of complete liberalization, and Sachs (1994, p. 46), lists the major price controls that remained in mid-1993.

143    The quotation is from an editorial in the *New York Times*, 24 January 1991.

144    This analysis is developed in more detail in Alexeev, Gaddy, and Leitzel (1991).

145    Kolkhoz market prices rose by 7.5 per cent in April 1991, less than the inflation rate for any of the preceding three months. A rise of 53 per cent was recorded for January 1992, somewhat higher than the 33.2 per cent and 39.3 per cent increases in the previous two months. See Koen and Phillips (1993, p. 33). In neither case, however, was there a sudden, overnight surge in free market prices. The monetary compensation that accompanied the price reforms was one source, however, of new inflationary pressure.

146    The inflation figures are the Consumer Price Index for all goods and services. Koen and Phillips (1993, p. 33).

147    Taxes are also not neutral with respect to inflation, so the real amount of taxes

that people pay and hence the real amount of government tax revenues are altered by inflation, even if there is no change in economic activity.

148 Another cost of inflation consists of the resources that are used up in physically re-changing prices. Economists refer to these expenses as 'menu costs', since menus have to be redone as prices rise.

149 John R. Hicks made the comment 'The best of all monopoly profits is a quiet life', in Hicks (1935).

150 Strictly speaking, this information-processing cost arises only to the extent that the inflation is unanticipated; any positive rate of inflation, though, makes relative price change calculations dependent on the approximate date at which the shopper last checked the price in question. The actual amount of inflation is harder to anticipate when inflation is high than when it is low because the variance of inflation rates tends to be higher at high levels of inflation than at low levels. See, e.g., Schultze (1992, p. 127).

151 Dornbusch (1993, p. 6).

152 Yakir Plessner, a deputy governor of the Bank of Israel during years of high inflation, provides a nice account of the perceived costs of inflation from that vantage point in a letter to the *Journal of Economic Perspectives*, Spring 1994, pp. 204-206.

153 See the discussion of the 'sacrifice ratio' in Dornbusch and Fischer (1994, pp. 547–548).

154 Aven (1991, p. 198).

155 Cited in Shleifer and Vishny (1991, p. 6). Russian repressed inflation pre-dates perestroika. Shlapentokh (1989, p. 66) cites sociological studies in 1983 indicating that the average Soviet citizen spent 4–5 hours per day in search of consumer goods and services – though presumably not all of this time was spent in queues.

156 Strictly speaking, repressed inflation should refer only to a situation where the fixed state-sector prices are falling further behind free prices, as opposed to just being at a lower level.

157 The increased diversion of goods from the state sector as repressed inflation worsens is modelled in Leitzel (1993b).

158 'Russians Put Anxiety Aside and Try to Eke Out a Living', by Celestine Bohlen, *New York Times*, 1 March 1992, pp. 1, 9.

159 Uncertainty over who will benefit from reform can serve to delay or prevent reforms that would be socially beneficial. Fernandez and Rodrik (1991).

160 Quoted in Nove (1982, p. 313).

161 As previously noted, indexation of savings and other accounts is itself a source of new inflationary pressure.

162 For a brief commentary on the 2 April 1991 price reform, see Dyker (1992, pp. 207–208).

163 On the currency confiscation see Hewett and Gaddy (1992, p. 142n) and Goldman (1992, pp. 196–197).

164 In July 1993 a similar rouble confiscation scheme was implemented, this time under a regime of largely open inflation.

165 Differences in the pattern of accompanying compensation may have altered the types of people harmed by the two price reforms.

166 Burawoy and Hendley (1992, p. 397).

167 The extent to which people in the West look for government intervention when the price of an important good rises is not inconsiderable. Prices rose for such goods as timber and flashlights in the areas of Florida stricken by Hurricane Andrew in the late summer of 1992. Government efforts to combat 'price gouging' included threats of criminal prosecution against those who sold at prices that were 'too high'. See 'Price Gouging is Widely Cited in Storm Region', by Joseph B.

Treaster, *New York Times*, 30 August 1992, and 'Lessons From a Hurricane: It Pays Not to Gouge', by Steve Lohr, *New York Times*, 22 September 1992.

168  The government fears were well-founded. Increases in meat prices ignited a civil revolt in the southern Russian city of Novocherkassk in 1962. Khrushchev had the uprising forcibly suppressed by the army, and 22 lives were lost in the struggle. See 'Soviet Archives Provide Missing Pieces of History's Puzzles', by Serge Schmemann, *New York Times*, 8 February 1993, p. A6.

169  Åslund (1990, p. 24).

170  'Yeltsin Contemplates Prices, Stress, and His Plans to Retire', *New York Times*, 28 May 1992, p. A8.

171  'Supply shocks' like the Arab oil embargo may also lead to generally higher prices, though in the absence of an accommodating monetary policy, such an effect is not certain, nor could general price increases continue for long. Ball (1993) provides a nice discussion of the causes of inflation.

172  Another method whereby a government can gain control over resources is through voluntary donations, including receipts of foreign aid.

173  All three of the methods that the government can employ to garner resources from the private sector are limited. If taxes become extremely high, people will reduce their amount of taxable activity. Likewise, individuals will eventually become reluctant to buy government bonds as the government becomes further and further indebted, relative to its capacity to repay. Finally, if the government prints too much money, individuals will refuse to accept the rapidly-inflating currency in exchange for goods.

174  Money creation in itself does not necessarily imply inflation. First, productivity may be going up, so the supply of goods can be increasing as fast or faster than the nominal demand. Second, people could choose to hold more currency. It has been argued, for example (Sachs and Woo (1994, p. 128)), that increased money demand in China during transition has allowed the Chinese government to essentially print money without overly severe inflationary consequences. Government interest rate policy affecting the return on monetary assets held in savings accounts can thereby influence inflation through its effect on monetary demand.

175  Émigré economist Igor Birman (1990, p. 27) notes that his research indicates that Soviet government budgets have been in deficit since the Second World War.

176  Together, investment and defence comprised roughly half of Soviet GNP; in the US, these components form about one-quarter of GNP. On Soviet investment in GNP, see Pitzer and Baukol (1991, p.5); on the defence share of GNP, see Rowen and Wolf (1990). Statistics for the US in 1991 can be found in the *Economic Report of the President* (1992).

177  *Izvestiya*, 8 and 24 January 1989, p. 1, as quoted in Birman (1990, pp. 25, 40).

178  There were government bonds in the former Soviet Union, but sales of such bonds were economically inconsequential, though useful for citizens to launder second economy earnings (Malyshev (1907)). The first Russian government bond issue of the post-Soviet era took place in May 1993, but planned bond sales remain very small relative to the size of the Russian state budget deficit. See *RFE/RL News Brief*, 18 May 1993. Foreign aid could also have been employed to finance the budget deficit in a non-inflationary manner, but through the first quarter of 1993 foreign financing was basically used to supply subsidies for imports, and not used to finance the domestic budget deficit (Fischer (1994, p. 16)).

179  On the budget deficit, see Birman (1990), McKinnon (1990b), IMF (1992a, p. 67), and 'The Russian State Budget', by Erik Whitlock, *RFE/RL Research Report*, 23 April 1993, pp. 32–36.

180  Desai (1992, p.51).
181  Hewett and Gaddy (1992, pp. 83–88).
182  McKinnon (1990b).
183  A value-added tax was part of the reform package adopted in January 1992. See IMF (1992b, pp. 89–91, 101–115), and 'The Russian State Budget', by Erik Whitlock, *RFE/RL Research Report*, 23 April 1993, pp. 32–36. Enforcement of the value-added tax was weak in the initial months, with only one-half of the levied tax actually collected during the first quarter of 1992. 'The Russian Budget Deficit', by Keith Bush, *RFE/RL Research Report*, 9 October 1992, p. 32.
184  'The Russian State Budget', by Erik Whitlock, *RFE/RL Research Report*, 23 April 1993, p. 34.
185  On 4 February 1993, Boris Yeltsin rebuked his Economics Minister, Andrey Nacheyev, for not putting a single enterprise through bankruptcy. A new law on bankruptcy took effect on 1 March 1993. See *Current Digest of the Post-Soviet Press*, 3 March 1993, and 21 April 1993.
186  Sargent (1982).
187  Lutz (1949) describes the 1948 German reform, and also details the economic conditions that are almost eerily reminiscent of the reforming Russian economy.
188  Nove (1982, pp. 90–92).
189  It is widely feared that privatization will result in high monopoly prices, however. This perceived difficulty is discussed in the chapter on monopoly.
     One method to link the currency reform with privatization is as follows. Announce that in a certain amount of time, three months, say, old roubles will be exchanged for new roubles. In the meantime, old currency will be accepted as means of payment for shares of state enterprises sold at auction. People who are nervous about the purchasing power of the new currency will then have a strong incentive to purchase the enterprise shares. Simultaneously, the sale of state-owned firms will both increase current government revenue and remove future government financial obligations. Clifford Gaddy and I proposed a similar currency reform–privatization scheme in 'A Plan to Cool the Hot Rouble', *Journal of Commerce*, 11 May 1990. Official privatization with vouchers is sufficiently underway now (see the chapter on privatization) that the reform described here is no longer relevant for Russia.
190  The IMF programme is not guaranteed to provide a credible disinflationary policy, since the conditions of such agreements can sometimes be broken by the government, without a reduction in aid. Foreign aid itself, however, provides another non-inflationary channel for a government to finance its budget deficit.
191  Wellisz (1991, p. 213).
192  Rodrik (1989) examines the importance of clearly signalling a break with past regimes in reducing the costs of reform.
193  See, for example, the letter by Edgar W. Malkin in the *New York Times* on 8 September 1993, p. A22.
194  There would still be a 'peak-load' problem. The demand for parking is quite variable, with demand high during certain hours of the day (or on special occasions) and relatively lower at other hours. Since prices of parking spaces cannot be continuously adjusted at reasonable cost, there would still be times when it would be difficult to find a parking space. This point was brought to my attention by Dani Rodrik.
195  A check on Nexis in July 1993 yielded 451 newspaper and magazine articles after 1991 that included the words 'rouble' and 'worthless' within 5 words of each other, with 194 of the citations occurring after the 2 January 1992 price liberalization.
196  Grossman (1977, p. 30n).

197  Shlapentokh (1989, p. 212).
198  See, e.g., 'Time and Patience are Running in Short Supply in Moscow', by Francis X. Clines, *New York Times*, 15 January 1992, p. A9.
199  Jones and Moskoff (1991, p. 91).
200  Alexeev (1988a).
201  On the rouble shortage, see, e.g., 'Economic Furor is Growing over Changes by Yeltsin', by Celestine Bohlen, *New York Times*, 3 June 1992, p. A3. In Western reports of the difficulties in the Russian economy, it is not uncommon to find a detail or two that indicate that the situation is not completely dire. In this article on the rouble shortage, for example, then First Deputy Prime Minister Gaidar is reported to be ordering government transportation agencies '. . . to accept credit to cover ticket costs as Russians set out for summer vacations'.
202  Quoted in Smith (1990, p. 185).
203  Quoted in Wren (1990, p. 181).
204  See, for example, Institute of Sociology (1992), cited in the comments of Vladimir Mau following Lipton and Sachs (1992, p. 267).
205  See, e.g., Azariadis (1975).
206  See, e.g., Harrison (1986).
207  Hewett (1988, p. 42) suggests that Soviet unemployment rates in the mid-1980s were under 2%. Porket (1989) puts the figure at closer to 3%, and cites the concurrence of Shmelev (1987). Gregory and Collier (1988, p. 616), relying on interview data collected from émigrés, estimate a lower bound for unemployment in the late 1970s to be 1.2–1.3%.
208  Lane (1986, p. 9).
209  Anti-parasite laws were superseded by the 'Law on the Employment of the Population', which also officially recognized unemployment. The law took effect on 1 July 1991 (Heleniak (1991, pp. 16–17)).
210  Bergson (1991, p. 42).
211  About 85 per cent of able-bodied adult Soviet females worked (Moskoff (1984, p. xii)). The over-representation of women in low-paying occupations and in lower category jobs, familiar in the West, was also a feature of the Soviet labour market. See Nove (1986, p. 220f).
212  Gaddy (1991).
213  Moskoff (1984, p. 34).
214  Over 20 per cent of Soviet pensioners held official, full-time jobs (Marnie (1992, p. 156)).
215  Nove (1986, chapter 8) provides a good account of the traditional Soviet labour sector.
216  In 1976, 68.1 per cent of newly hired industrial workers were employed from the factory gate. Bergson (1984, p. 1080).
217  Anti-parasite laws were not strictly enforced in recent years. See Millar (1990, p. 236).
218  The wage component forms only 60-66 per cent of official monetary compensation, with the remainder being made up of bonuses and other additional payments (Spulber (1991, p. 99)). A Pravda article in 1987, cited by Matthews (1989, p. 10), suggested that wages then formed only 50 per cent of official monetary compensation.
219  Nove (1986, pp. 205–210), offers a thorough examination of evasion of wage controls. In their study of Rezina, Burawoy and Hendley (1992, pp. 375–376) note that the management of one Rezina plant (RTI-3) believed that in order to retain one category of worker, 'they should be paid 1000 roubles per month, which would violate limitations on the wage fund. But as the director of RTI-3 told us with a wink and a nod, there are ways around those restrictions'.

220 See Gaddy (1991) for an empirical examination of informal non-wage compensation.

221 Treml (1992b, p. 37).

222 Gaddy (1991) demonstrates the inverse relationship between official wages and informal compensation.

223 See Holmstrom and Milgrom (1991) for a theoretical analysis of 'multi-task principal agent problems' that leads to these sort of conclusions under Soviet conditions.

224 On labour hoarding, see Nove (1986, p. 224).

225 On soft budget constraints, see Kornai (1980).

226 Hanson (1986, p. 86) argues that full employment is maintained primarily via the systemic incentives, as opposed to the law or direct planning guidelines.

227 Spulber (1991, p. 95) notes that planned labour demands exceeded labour supplies by 2 to 2.5 million workers annually, throughout the 1970s. See also Pietsch (1986, p. 181).

228 Porket (1989, p. 119), endnote omitted.

229 Kotkin (1991, p. 17).

230 In the late 1960s the Soviets originated an experiment whereby enterprises could shed redundant labour, and use part of the savings as incentive pay for the remaining workers. (Enterprises were also supposed to help the displaced workers find new jobs.) Named the Shchekino experiment after the Chemical Combine where it was first implemented, the reform extended to enterprises covering perhaps ten per cent of the industrial labour force by 1980. The Shchekino experiment was generally considered a success in reducing redundant labour and raising labour productivity, though nearly half of the displaced workers were transferred to other jobs within the same enterprise. See, e.g., Dyker (1992, pp. 53–54, 69–71).

231 Kotkin (1991, p. 17) makes this observation with respect to the Magnitogorsk steel mill.

232 An early Gorbachev-era reform aimed at increasing the differential in official pay among job classifications. See Atkinson and Micklewright (1992, p. 89), and the sources mentioned there.

233 Millar (1990, p. 220) notes some of the barriers to the free movement of labour into urban areas. Marrying a resident of large cities was one route out of the provinces, creating an informal market in marriages of mobility.

234 Burawoy and Krotov (1992, p. 22n) note average waits of 12 years (at Polar Furniture) and 20 years (at other local enterprises) for apartments.

235 Grossman (1979) provides a list of legal private economic activities.

236 On turnover rates, which have been falling (from approximately 20 per cent) for twenty years, see Marnie (1992, p. 163, endnote 2), Heleniak (1991, p. 4)), Lane (1987, p. 68), and the comparative bar graph in IMF *et al.* (1991, vol. 2, p. 217). Complaints about high turnover rates were frequent in the USSR and in other socialist countries (Vodopivec (1991, p. 139)).

237 Absenteeism in the USSR, about 20 days per worker per year in industry, was twice the American rate (see Moskoff (1984, p. x), and Porket (1989, p. 118)).

238 This point is made with respect to absenteeism in China in Jefferson and Rawski (1991, p. 8).

239 Akerlof, *et al.* (1991, p. 2), estimated that only eight per cent of Eastern German employees were employed in firms that were solvent post-reform. In Eastern Europe (Poland, Hungary, and Czechoslovakia), Jackman, *et al.* (1992, p. 31) suggested that as many as 50 per cent of workers were in jobs that would not have come into existence without the previous central planning.

240 Most of the open unemployment that arose early in the transition process in

Poland, Hungary, and Czechoslovakia was due to reduced hirings, as opposed to layoffs. See Jackman, *et al.* (1992, p. 16).

241   Jackman, *et al.* (1992, p. 13) provide unemployment statistics for Poland, Hungary, and Czechoslovakia. The Russian labour force consisted of approximately 71 million people in 1993 (OECD (1994, p. 80)).

242   The 25 per cent overstaffing estimate for the former USSR is roughly consistent with Eastern European estimates. Svejnar (1991, pp. 128–129) notes that a generous estimate of Eastern European overstaffing is 30 per cent of employment. The International Labour Organization estimate appeared in a press release dated 30 March 1992. The unemployment figure was an estimate for 1992. Actual measured unemployment in the former Soviet Union in 1992 remained substantially below this figure.

243   The Russian labour force fell by approximately 3 million people between 1991 and 1993 (OECD (1994, p. 80)).

244   Tobin (1957, p. 599).

245   A dramatic fall in absenteeism following the German currency reform of 1948 is chronicled in Lutz (1949, p. 133).

246   The rapid growth of the private sector in Eastern Europe is discussed in Svejnar (1991, pp. 130–131). See also Johnson (1992, p. 34).

247   European Bank for Reconstruction and Development (1994, p. 34).

248   Johnson and Kroll (1991).

249   Kotkin (1991, p. 133).

250   See Braithwaite (1991) and Sheila Marnie, 'The Social Safety Net in Russia', *RFE/RL Research Report*, 23 April 1993.

251   Dornbusch (1991) makes a similar point with respect to Eastern Germany.

251*  Sachs (1994, p. 43). The figure of labour costs as a share of total costs is suggested as applying to firms in the military-industrial complex.

252   *RFE/RL Daily Report*, 4 November 1993.

253   Porket (1989, p. 28), footnote omitted.

254   Harrison (1986, p.81).

255   Economists call this the 'Theory of the Second Best'. In the presence of economic distortions, government policies that further 'interfere' with the workings of the market economy may be socially desirable.

256   Akerlof, *et al.* (1991, p. 42).

257   For a good discussion of the possible causes and consequences of fixed wages, see Hall and Taylor (1993, pp.473–502).

258   See, e.g., McKinnon (1990a), who argues that many socialist firms will be illiquid when faced with foreign competition, even if they are solvent in the long run after they adapt their production techniques. Imperfect competition arguments for low employment equilibria are becoming increasing popular in Western macroeconomics. See, e.g., Pagano (1990).

259   Burawoy and Krotov (1992, p. 33).

259*  Rostowski (1994, p. 73) notes an insensitivity of reform to credit unavailability in Poland, and suggests that credit may be unimportant in a transitional economy because the emergence of so many highly profitable opportunities implies that self-financing is available.

260   Åslund (1994, p. 63) Ascertaining real interest rates is not straightforward because an estimate of future inflation is required.

260*  Rostowski (1994, p. 73) notes how credit was allocated to the wrong firms during the Polish transition.

261   Ickes and Ryterman (1992, p. 331).

262   In early June of 1992, the chairman of Russia's Central Bank offered his resignation rather than submit to Parliament's demand that the Central Bank

loan money to 'commercial' banks at 50 per cent annual interest. At the time, the fixed rate in use by the Central Bank was 80 per cent, though in the high inflation environment, even this was probably too low. 'Russian Backlash is Forcing a Delay in Approval of Aid', by Louis Uchitelle with Steven Erlanger, *New York Times*, 7 June 1992, pp. 1 and 4.

Soft loans to state-owned enterprises in 1992 totalled approximately 20 per cent of Russian gross domestic output (Sachs and Woo (1994, p. 108)).

263 See, e.g., Ickes and Ryterman (1992, pp. 359–360). An enterprise may also be willing to extend credit that is unlikely to be repaid if by doing so it can secure an ownership claim during privatization.

264 This paragraph is based on 'Russian Credit Markets Remain Distorted', by Sergei Aukutsenek and Elena Belyanova, *RFE/RL Research Report*, 22 January 1993, pp. 37-40.

265 'Russian Credit Markets Remain Distorted', by Sergei Aukutsenek and Elena Belyanova, *RFE/RL Research Report*, 22 January 1993, p. 39.

266 'The Soviet Miners Strike', by Clifford Gaddy, *The Brookings Review*, Vol. 9, No. 3, Summer 1991, p. 54.

267 Jones and Moskoff (1991, pp. 25–26), for example, provide some figures for the pay of workers in cooperatives. Koen and Phillips (1993, p. 20), note a wage differential of more than one-third between state and private-sector employees.

268 In Poland, taxes on wage increases in state-sector enterprises were also applied to private firms (Johnson (1992, p. 27)). Wage controls in the state sector are themselves not unambiguously desirable, since they may prevent firms that are successfully reforming from hiring new workers, or even make it more difficult to shed lower-quality labour.

269 Machiavelli (1947 [1532], p. 15).

270 Wage rates in market economies may involve 'rent sharing', where workers in successful industries are better paid than their counterparts in less successful industries. Recent empirical evidence on industry effects on wages appears in Holmlund and Zetterberg (1991). They find that workers in strong industries in the US are better paid than their counterparts in other industries, while industry effects are smaller in Germany and even smaller in Nordic countries.

271 On the perceived unfairness of negative movements away from the status quo, see Isaac, Mathieu, and Zajac (1991).

272 The referendum of 25 April 1993, which resulted in majorities both for Yeltsin and his reform programme – despite the overwhelmingly negative reports on the state of the Russian economy – suggests that such concerns may be overblown.

273 On some 'mafia' millionaires in pre-reform Russia, see Vaksberg (1991).

274 Treml (1992b, p. 20).

275 The training of an average doctor in Russia was also much inferior to the training of an average US doctor.

276 The over-supply of technically-trained people in Russia is nicely illustrated by the comments of an American Peace Corps volunteer working in Saratov, Russia: 'You know in America we say, "It doesn't take a rocket scientist". Well, I'd never met one. Now I've met hundreds, and a lot of them are driving taxis'. 'Volunteers From U.S. in Business in Russia', by Steven Erlanger, *New York Times*, 6 April 1993, p. A6.

277 Lutz (1949) notes how traders were the main early beneficiaries of the German monetary reform of 1948.

278 Hanson (1991, p. 308) notes survey evidence indicating that attitudes towards free markets by younger workers are more favourable than the attitudes of older workers.

279  'A Renewal of Public Confidence in the Russian Economy?', by Mark Rhodes, *RFE/RL Research Report*, 3 September 1993, pp. 59–61.
280  The statistics are drawn from *Economic Report of the President* (1992, p. 346).
281  See, e.g., Aven (1991, p. 184).
282  Perhaps co-incidentally, by mid-1992, official real wage statistics had re-achieved the 1987 levels (Koen and Phillips (1993, p. 16)).
283  'Good for Some, Tough for Others', by Nicholas Denton, *Financial Times*, 30 October 1991.
284  Sachs (1993, p. 73).
285  Alford and Feige (1989) call this the 'observer-subject-policymaker' feedback.
286  OECD (1994, p. 80).
287  Rose (1994, pp. 13–14).
288  Marx and Engels (1964 [1848], p. 82).
289  The survey is cited in Starodubrovskaya (1994, p.9).
290  Pinto, Belka, and Krajewski (1993) details the extent of favourable changes in state-owned enterprises in Poland prior to privatization.
290*  Boeva and Dolgopiatova (1994, p, 116)
291  This position echoes that of Weitzman (1991).
292  Grossman (1989, p. 81).
293  Barzel (1989, p. 107).
294  While informal compensation responded to market forces, the bonuses that were supposed to provide incentives for fulfilling the plan were in practice used to iron out horizontal inequities both within and among enterprises. And the plans were regularly revised, in part to reflect the actual output. See, e.g., Hewett (1988, pp. 188–189, 208–210), and Burawoy and Krotov (1992).
295  See, e.g., Dyker (1992, p. 49).
296  Lazear (1991). Housing and energy prices are two examples where internal Soviet prices and world prices differed considerably. It should be kept in mind, however, that prices played different roles under Soviet central planning than they do in market economies.
297  Grossman (1977, p. 31).
298  Grossman (1977, p. 40).
299  See, e.g., Barzel (1989, p. 5).
300  The continuation of subsidies is perfectly sensible as long as continuing price controls, combined with the unknown value of inter-enterprise loans, distort the meaning of profits.
301  See Sutela (1993), and 'You're Privatized. Now What?', by David Brooks, *Wall Street Journal*, 23 April 1993, p. A14.
302  Small enterprises (those with less than 200 employees and a book value of assets as of 1 January 1992, of less than 1 million roubles) must be sold at open or sealed-bid auctions. Medium sized firms and structural subdivisions of larger enterprises (those with 200-1000 employees and a book value between 10 and 50 million roubles) can be privatized into a joint-stock company if their labour collective so chooses.
       A good review of the privatization options is provided in *Izvestia*, 28 September 1992, p. 4. (Translated in *Current Digest of the Post-Soviet Press*, Vol. 44, no. 40, November 4, 1992, pp. 7–9.)
303  Sutela (1993). In many privatizations the percentage of shares auctioned off for vouchers was less than 29 per cent, however.
304  Stiglitz (1991) makes this point. To partly offset the perceived disadvantage of voucher-holders who are not employees of large privatizing enterprises, the Russian government is considering the use of vouchers in the privatization of land.

305   See Weitzman (1991) for an alternative view.
306   Weitzman (1991).
307   Sutela (1993).
308   IMF *et al.* (1990, p. 26) and IMF *et al.* (1991, vol. 2, p. 40). Also see Kahn and Peck (1991, pp. 63–67).
309   See, e.g., Uno (1991, p. 152).
310   More precisely, from output prices that exceed marginal costs.
311   This is a paraphrase of a comment by Indiana University economics professor Michael Alexeev.
312   The US figure is for industries at the SIC 4-digit level (Kahn and Peck (1991, p. 65)).
313   Hewett (1988, pp. 170–176). See also Kroll (1991, p. 146n).
314   Hewett (1988, p. 171).
315   Kroll (1991, p. 147).
316   Newberry and Kattuman (1992, pp. 315, 334).
317   This point was brought to my attention in a meeting (June 1991) with Russian anti-monopoly expert V. Tsapelik.
318   IMF *et al.* (1991, pp. 28–31).
319   Actions for breach of contract could be brought against a supplier, but this was not a very potent weapon. See, e.g., Kroll (1987).
320   Of course there were black markets, and the collective farm markets provided competition in the retail market for food.
321   Such wasteful lobbying efforts fall under the general rubric of 'rent seeking'. See Tirole (1988, Chapter 1) for a good discussion of distortions due to monopoly.
322   Enterprise prices were generally set on a 'planned branch average cost plus profit' basis. See Bornstein (1987).
323   Monopoly producers may not have as strong a bargaining position as may at first appear because they may be teamed with monopsonistic customers. The oil extraction industry, by and large, delivers its output only to the oil processing industry. This example was used by Yegor Gaidar in a Moscow meeting, June 1991.
324   Hewett (1988, p. 173).
325   A second concern with according anti-monopoly legislation a low priority in the reforming Russian economy is that even if the resulting competition lowers the social costs of monopoly, there may be undesirable distributional impacts. It is virtually impossible to detail these impacts, however, and any other course is also potentially subject to undesirable effects with respect to the income and wealth distributions. See the following chapter for more discussion of the importance of distributional problems during reform.
326   Tirole (1991, p. 230).
327   This point was brought to my attention by Professor Barry Ickes of Penn State.
328   In a private meeting in Moscow, June 1991.
329   Koen and Phillips (1993, p. 10) note that by mid-1992, 23 areas in Russia had enacted such trade barriers.
330   The 11 August 1992 government resolution was 'On the State Regulation of Prices and Rates for Goods and Services Produced and Rendered by Monopolist Enterprises in 1992–1993'. See Capelik (1994, pp. 22–23).
331   Samuelson (1970, p. 106).
332   Quoted in 'Chaos Looms Over the Soviets, Gates Says', by Elaine Sciolino, *New York Times*, p. A8, 11 December 1991.
333   Goldman (1992, p. 35).
334   'The Yeltsin Revolution', by Martin Malia, *The New Republic*, 10 February 1992, p. 25.

335  'Shock Therapy in Russia: Failure or Partial Success?', by Michael Ellman, RFE/RL Research Report, August 28, 1992, p. 48. The quoted passage is taken from the abstract that precedes the article. Ellman did note some positive developments. The sentence immediately following the quoted passage reads 'Nevertheless, the situation is not entirely black'.

336  'Clinton's Greatest Challenge', by Richard Nixon, *New York Times*, 5 March 1993, p. A17.

337  Litwack (1991b) provides a detailed theoretical model of coordination failure in a centrally-planned environment.

338  Zubova, Kovaleva, and Khakhulina (1992, pp. 94–95).

339  Flakierski (1992) provides some preliminary empirical evidence of the effects of Russian reform on income distribution.

340  Rose (1994, p. 12).

341  The 'gross' in GNP refers to the measure of investment. Every year, new machines are built, but at the same time, old machines wear out. Gross investment counts all the new machines produced, whereas 'net' investment, and hence 'net national product', excludes those new machines which serve to replace the old machines. Net national product, minus sales and excise taxes (and some other minor items) yields an income measure known as 'national income'.

342  The extent of the 'nation' is the basis for the distinction between gross national product and gross domestic product (GDP). GDP includes all income arising within a given geographical area, while GNP includes the worldwide income of a nation's residents. See Kendrick (1972, pp. 33–34). In order to be more in concert with international standards, the United States is beginning to highlight GDP in its economic statistics. *Economic Report of the President* (1992).

343  Another method of calculating the value of all final goods sold is to sum value added at all stages of production.

344  Exports are included in a country's calculation of GNP because they represent goods made in the country, but will not appear as consumption because they are purchased by foreigners. Imports are not produced in the country, but get included in the consumption component of GNP. To avoid counting this consumption as part of a country's product, imports must then be subtracted from GNP.

345  There are many nuances involved in calculating GNP that are omitted from this discussion. For example, investment represents gross private domestic investment (hence 'gross' national product) which includes investments that only offset depreciation. Kendrick (1972) addresses many of these nuances.

346  Dasgupta and Weale (1992, p. 119).

347  From a Robert F. Kennedy address in Detroit, 5 May 1967, as quoted in Ross (1968, p. 351). Sen (1987) explores many non-market facets of the standard of living. The essay by Muellbauer (1987) in Sen (1987) is particularly stimulating.

348  The identification of these issues relies on Eisner (1989).

349  Imputations are made for certain types of non-market output in the USA, such as the rental value of owner-occupied housing.

350  The discussion of investment follows Eisner (1989, p. 5–6) fairly closely.

351  It is possible to avoid some of the problems with government spending and investment by focusing on the consumption component of GNP. Concentrating on consumption, though, is misleading when people are changing the amount of their income that they are willing to invest as opposed to immediately consuming. Economists would say that GNP is 'neutral' with respect to changes in individual decisions to save versus consume, whereas measures of consumption clearly are not neutral in this respect.

352  The separation of quality improvements from price increases is attempted by the compilers of national income statistics in the USA. See *Economic Report of the President* (1992).

353  Two methods of achieving comparable measures of output are to use market exchange rates, or to assess how much it would cost to produce one country's output in another country – the purchasing power parity approach.

354  Because this section looks primarily at historical calculations of Soviet (i.e., Russia plus the other 14 republics) GNP, the old terminology 'Soviet Union' and 'USSR', will generally be employed here.

355  Goskomstat did begin to publish GNP figures in 1988 – see Treml (1988, pp. 80–81, 86–87). Nove (1986, Chapter 12) offers a good introduction to Soviet economic accounting.

356  See, e.g., Birman (1989), Åslund (1990), and Belkin (1991). For discussions of the controversy, see GAO (1991) and Rosefielde (1991).

357  IMF *et al.* (1990, p. 51).

358  Belkin (1991).

359  In calculating growth rates of Soviet GNP, the CIA relies primarily on data expressed in physical units.

360  The CIA methodology is described in Joint Economic Committee (1982).

361  Generally, higher income individuals had access to goods at lower prices. Citing Goskomstat, Aven (1991, p. 184) writes: '. . . in 1984 a family with a monthly income per person of 150 roubles paid an average of 2.96 roubles for a kilo of meat, while a family with an income of less than 50 roubles paid 3.93 roubles'. Housing subsidies also tended to favour wealthier families (Kosareva (1992, p. 40)).

362  Rosefielde (1991).

363  GAO (1991, p. 29).

364  To calculate the geometric mean, the two estimates are multiplied together, and the square root of the result is the final estimate.

365  The CIA does make some correction for waste in agriculture. JEC (1982, pp. 266–269).

366  Belkin (1991, p.19).

367  Rosefielde (1991, p. 598). Forced substitution occurs when shoppers make purchases of items that they would otherwise find undesirable, because the goods that they would prefer to buy are not available in the shops.

368  Rosefielde (1991, p. 609).

369  Feshbach and Friendly (1992).

370  Bergson (1991, p.37), which presents a useful discussion of Soviet living standards, notes the environmental impact on welfare.

371  See Rowen and Wolf (1990).

372  Åslund (1990, p.22–23, and Appendix 1).

373  See, e.g., Belkin (1991, p. 18).

374  Lipton and Sachs (1992, p. 219).

375  Aven (1991, p. 184) and Åslund (1990, p.57–8).

376  Åslund (1990, p. 20).

377  Pitzer and Baukol (1991, p. 59) provide a graph of the investment component of Soviet GNP since 1960.

378  See, e.g., Birman (1989).

379  Belkin (1991, p. 18).

380  The generally low quality of nominally free education and medical care also impacts negatively on Russian living standards.

381  Kosareva (1992, p. 38).

382  Shlapentokh (1989, pp. 82–83).

383  IMF (1992a, p. 60).

384   Alexeev, Gaddy, and Leitzel (1991).
385   OECD (1994, p. 80).
386   Koen and Phillips (1993).
387   Rose (1994, p. 6).
388   Roberts (1993).
389   The relative improvement in the lot of many rural areas and small towns is supported by a good deal of anecdotal evidence. Zubova, Kovaleva, and Khakhulina (1992, p. 87) briefly note this phenomenon.
390   Gaddy (1992, pp. 7–8).
391   Raleigh (1992, p. 604) discusses the Moscow–St.Petersburg focus of the West, and also suggests that the April 1991 coup plotters themselves misunderstood Russian provincial attitudes.
392   Novosibirsk and Nizhny Novgorod (Gorky) are in a near-tie for third, and fifth is Yekaterinberg (Sverdlovsk). Clifford Gaddy first subjected me to this quiz.
393   Cooper (1991b, p. 23–24).
394   Atkinson and Micklewright (1992, pp. 81, 114).
395   Mickiewicz (1992, p. 14).
396   Rodrik (1991) develops the 'political cost-benefit ratio', which measures how many dollars (roubles) must be shuffled in redistribution per dollar of efficiency gain. In the case of trade liberalization, Rodrik demonstrates that this ratio tends to be much lower when liberalization is accompanied by structural reforms.
397   See Atkinson and Micklewright (1992, pp. 87–89) on distributional changes over time in the USSR.
398   See 'Economic Reform and Poverty in Russia', by Shelie Marnie, *RFE/RL Research Report*, 5 February 1993, pp. 31–36.
399   McGee and Feige (1989, p.83).
400   Kosmarskii (1992, p. 27).
401   Jones and Moskoff (1991, p. 125).
402   Zubova *et al.* (1992, p. 85).
403   Zubova *et al.* (1992, p. 87).
404   Shlapentokh (1989, p. 140), reference omitted.
405   Feshbach (1991, p. 49).
406   Peck (1991, p. 3).
407   See, e.g., Smith (1976).
408   Ickes and Ryterman (1992, p. 345n).
409   'Wolf at the Door', by Maggie Mahar, *Barron's*, 19 October 1992, p. 8.
410   Starodubrovskaya (1994, p. 6). This has been confirmed in discussions that I have had with representatives of Russian enterprises.
411   Boeva and Dolgopiatova (1994, p. 116) discuss some motivations for barter, including tax evasion. Goldberg (1993) notes how the transitional arrangements with respect to foreign exchange led to international barter as a means to escape taxation.
412   Smith (1991 [1776], vol. 2, p. 155).
413   Ilin (1931, p. 33). This fascinating book is an English translation of a Soviet book designed to acquaint 12- to 14-year olds with the first 5-Year plan. The 'socialist vice', the over-emphasis on production and intermediate goods, is evident throughout its pages.
414   Wiles (1962, pp. 282–283).
415   The report is cited in 'Half Soviet Potato Crop Wasted', *Financial Times*, 16 October 1991, p. 7.
416   See, e.g., Wiles (1962, chapter 14).
417   The quote and attribution appear in Wiles (1962, p. 283).
418   '. . . statistical results which in a normal market would be signs of much

increased material satisfaction are accepted as such in circumstances where they actually give no increased satisfaction' (Polanyi (1960, p. 96)).

419   Hewett and Gaddy (1992, pp. 8–9), footnotes omitted.
420   Aven (1991, p. 181n). Åslund (1990, p. 22) cites Soviet economist Abel Aganbegyan's claim that the Soviet tractor stock was 4.5 times as large as in the USA.
421   The tractor factory did close for 2 weeks in January of 1993, and again in the late spring of 1994.
422   On early Gorbachev reforms, see Goldman (1992, chapter 4).
423   Treml (1988, p. 71).
424   Goldman (1992, p. 86f).
425   See, e.g., 'Rutskoi Loses Responsibility for Agriculture', by Don Van Atta, *RFE/RL Research Report*, vol. 2, No. 18, April 1993, pp. 11–16. Graham (1993, p. 14) indicates that a regard for technology and a disregard for economics may have predated the Soviet era in Russia.
426   Treml (1992a, p. 130). This sentiment is echoed by two Russian researchers, Faramazian and Borisov (1993, p. 46): 'It is extremely difficult to estimate the real size of our defense complex primarily because of the lack of statistics that are reliable to any degree. The real figures on Soviet military spending have always been a riddle to both foreign and Soviet specialists'.
427   Cooper (1991b, pp. 25–28).
428   See, e.g., Cooper (1992, pp. 281–283).
429   Alexander (1992, pp. 303–304), and Kireyev (1990).
430   See, e.g., Cooper (1991a, pp. 139–140). Hendley (1992) offers a case study of one privatized defence plant.
431   Eighty per cent of the defence industry was scheduled for privatization by the end of 1994. See Keith Bush, 'Aspects of Military Conversion in Russia', RFE/RL Research Report, vol. 3, No. 14, 8 April 1994, pp. 31–34.
432   This quote appears in 'Weapons Industry Faces Pain in New World Order', by David E. Rosenbaum, *The News and Observer*, Raleigh, NC, 4 August 1991, p. 17A. I would like to thank Richard Stubbing for bringing this article to my attention.
433   Crane and Yeh (1991, p. 108) note that by 1989, 60 per cent of the value of defence industry output in China consisted of consumer goods. The extent to which the actual physical conversion of production lines was responsible for the increased civilian goods production in the defence complex is unclear.
434   Aganbegyan, quoted in Åslund (1990, p. 26).
435   RFE/RL Daily Report, 8 June 1994, and 14 June 1994, indicate that there may still be hidden subsidies that cloud the size of the actual defence budget.
436   See, e.g., RFE/RL Daily Report, 21 June 1994.
436*  Åslund (1994, p. 66).
437   Hewett and Gaddy (1992, chapter 1) provides a good overview of the pre-reform Soviet foreign trade situation.
438   Hewett and Gaddy (1992, pp. 10–11).
439   Hewett and Gaddy (1992, pp. 16–17).
440   The value-added tax is applicable to imports, though exports are zero-rated. Following the January 1992 liberalization, some 70 per cent of Russian exports were still subject to export quotas, partly because of the price controls that remained in place for some goods, such as oil. Aven (1994, pp. 84–85).
440*  Aven (1994, p. 90) indicates that current account convertibility has been achieved in Russia.
441   The separation between current and capital account convertibility is not complete. Current account convertibility often provides informal access for capital transactions.

442 Fischer (1991, p. 23).

443 See, e.g., RFE/RL Daily Report, 6 May 1994.

444 See, e.g., IMF *et al.* (1990, p.23).

445 The total amount of foreign investment in Russia at the end of 1993 was estimated at $2.7 billion [RFE/RL Daily Report, 28 June 1994]. In contrast, foreign investment in China for the year 1992 alone was reportedly $11.01 billion (Perkins (1994, p. 32)). Investment can occur even without capital account convertibility through bilateral agreements and joint ventures.

446 Rodrik (1992) estimated the cost to Eastern European countries of the collapse of COMECON. For example, the end of Soviet trade subsidies is estimated to have cost Poland $5 billion in 1989.

447 Dornbusch (1992). The relative importance of the foreign trade regime is probably greater in smaller, more open economies such as those in Eastern Europe.

448 Lazear (1991).

449 Incidentally, such arbitrage is taking place. It is estimated that up to 1/3 of Russian oil exports are conducted informally – oil is significantly underpriced in the domestic Russian economy.

450 Hewett and Gaddy (1992, p. 80).

451 This was the approach taken to zloty convertibility in Poland. See, e.g., Lipton and Sachs (1990, pp. 118–119).

452 The level at which the exchange rate is fixed must also be low enough to prevent massive attempts to exchange roubles for foreign currencies.

453 This is particularly true for the trade of goods, so-called current account transactions. As noted, it might be sensible for the government to impose some controls on asset sales during a transition.

   The use of a fixed exchange rate creates one issue that may not be easily resolved, namely, at what price should the exchange rate be fixed? And a fixed exchange rate, as with fixed prices more generally, tends to lead to resource misallocations, and can also create an impetus for more central controls to deal with balance of payments problems.

454 See, e.g., David (1985).

455 See 'U.S., Allies Set $24 Billion in Aid for Ex-Soviet States', by Ann Devroy, *Washington Post*, 2 April 1992, p. A1.

456 'Moscow Stops Paying Debt Principal', by Terrence Roth and Tim Carrington, *Wall Street Journal*, 5 December 1991.

457 In a letter to the *New York Times* (4/7/92), Jeffrey Sachs notes that Russia received $15.6 billion in aid in 1990–91, and paid $13.1 billion of the $15.5 billion on accumulated interest and debt that was due during that period. Sachs writes, 'Overall, almost no resources came to Russia in 1990–91, after taking account of debt payments'.

458 This applies to the aid that actually reaches Russia. A substantial amount of 'foreign' aid tends to go to Western firms and consultants, sometimes with minimal benefit to the foreign country.

459 There is a fundamental and difficult theoretical question as to why foreign aid is necessary to induce a government to take policies that are in its own long-run best interests (see Diwan and Rodrik (1991)). The practical importance of this question in the Soviet case is limited, however, since the former Soviet Union is already receiving substantial Western aid.

460 See 'Entrepreneur of Necessity Runs Afoul of Old Lithuania', by Steven Engelberg, *New York Times*, 25 September 1991.

461 State provision need not mean state production. The state should provide defence, but defence enterprises could be private.

462  The low exchange rate of the rouble enables valuable Russian research to be purchased for relatively small amounts of hard currency. Ninety thousand dollars is being used to hire 116 Russian fusion scientists for a year. 'U.S. Plans to Hire Russian Scientists in Fusion Research', by William J. Broad, *New York Times*, 6 March 1992, pp. A1, A4.

463  COCOM, the Coordinating Committee for Multilateral Export Control, which oversaw restrictions on exports to the Soviet Union, is being reconfigured to fight exports to countries that support terrorism or that are trying to develop weapons of mass destruction, and Russia is expected to join. See RFE/RL Daily Report, 9 November 1993.

464  'Nunn Urges US Help to Convert Soviet War Power', *Washington Post*, 20 June 1991, p. 8.

465  Perkins (1994, pp. 23–24).

466  Perkins (1994, p. 24). The 8.8 per cent figure is for the average growth rate in GDP.

467  Grossman (1963, pp. 118–121). His framework was also employed in examining the Chinese reforms by Nystrom (1994).

468  The figures on the percentage of the Chinese and Russian labour force in agriculture are taken from Sachs and Woo (1994, pp. 105–106).

469  Prosterman, Hanstad, and Rolfes (1993, p. 15).

470  Perkins (1994, p. 27).

471  Koen and Phillips (1993, pp. 10–11).

472  Perkins (1994, p. 26).

473  Reed (1967 [1919], p. 61).

474  Quoted in 'The High Risk Options for Russia's Economics Chief', by Leyla Boulton, *Financial Times*, 21 November 1991.

475  Ilin (1931, p. 161).

476  Gibbon (1985 [1776–1788], p. 81).

477  The 25 April 1993 referendum was particularly telling in this regard. Of the four questions on the ballot, one concerned support for the president, Boris Yeltsin, and a separate question concerned support for his economic reforms. It was thus possible for Yeltsin supporters to express their dismay with reform while still backing their president. As it turned out, Yeltsin and economic reform both enjoyed majority support.

# Bibliography

Akerlof, G. A., Rose, A. K, Yellen, J. L. and Hessenius, H. (1991) 'East Germany in from the Cold: The Economic Aftermath of Currency Union', *Brookings Papers on Economic Activity* 1: 1–87.

Alexander, A. J. (1992) 'The Conversion of Soviet Defense Industry', in C. Wolf, Jr and S.W. Popper (eds) *Defense and the Soviet Economy: Military Muscle and Economic Weakness*, a RAND Note.

Alexeev, M. (1988a) 'Are Soviet Consumers Forced to Save?', *Comparative Economic Studies* 30: 17–23.

—— (1988b) 'Market vs Rationing: The Case of Soviet Housing', *Review of Economics and Statistics* 70, 3: 414–420.

—— (1991) 'The "Storming" Pattern of Enterprise Behavior in a Centrally-Planned Economy', *Journal of Economic Behavior and Organization* 15: 173–185.

Alexeev, M., Gaddy, C. and Leitzel, J. (1991) 'An Economic Analysis of the Rouble Overhang', *Communist Economies and Economic Transformation* 3: 467–479.

Alexeev, M. and Walker, L. (1991) *Estimating the Size of the Soviet Economy. Summary of a Meeting*. Commission on Behavioral and Social Sciences and Education, National Research Council, Washington, DC: National Academy Press.

Alford, R. R. and Feige, E. L. (1989) 'Information Distortions in Social Systems: the Underground Economy and Other Observer-Subject-Policymaker Feedbacks', in E. L. Feige (ed.) *The Underground Economies*, Cambridge: Cambridge University Press.

Åslund, A. (1990) 'How Small is Soviet National Income?', in H. S. Rowen and C. Wolf, Jr (eds) *The Impoverished Superpower*, San Francisco: Institute for Contemporary Studies.

—— (1993) 'The Gradual Nature of Economic Change in Russia', in A. Åslund and R. Layard, (eds) *Changing the Economic System in Russia*, New York: St. Martin's Press.

—— (1994) 'Russia's Success Story', *Foreign Affairs* 73, Sept.–Oct.: 58–71.

Atkinson, A. B. and Micklewright, J. (1992) *Economic Transformation in Eastern Europe and the Distribution of Income*, Cambridge: Cambridge University Press.

Aven, P. O. (1991) 'Economic Policy and the Reforms of Mikhail Gorbachev: A Short History', in M. Peck and T. Richardson (eds) *What is to be Done?*, New Haven: Yale University Press.

Aven, P. (1994) 'Problems in Foreign Trade Regulation in the Russian Economic Reform', in A. Åslund (ed.) *Economic Transformation in Russia*, New York: St Martin's Press.

Azariadis, C. (1975) 'Implicit Contracts and Underemployment Equilibria', *Journal of Political Economy* 83: 1183–1202.

Ball, L. (1993) 'What Causes Inflation?', *Business Review*, Federal Reserve Bank of Philadelphia, March/April: 3–12.

Barton, P. (1957) 'The Myth of Planning in the U.S.S.R.', *Saturn* 3, Jan.–Feb.: 38–50.

Barzel, Y. (1989) *Economic Analysis of Property Rights*, Cambridge: Cambridge University Press.

Belkin, V. (1991) 'Comparison of Macroeconomic Indicators in Market and Nonmarket Economies', *Matekon* (1990) Fall: 3–23, translated from *Ekonomika i matematicheskie metody* 26: 790–802.

—— (1993) 'On the Reliability of Information', *Russian Social Science Review* 34: 59–72, translated from *Svobodnaia mysl'* (1992) no. 10: 97–104.

Belanovskii, S. A. (1992) 'The Army As It Is', *Studies on Soviet Economic Development* 3: 55–63.

Bergson, A. (1984) 'Income Inequality Under Soviet Socialism', *Journal of Economic Literature* 22, Sept.: 1052–1099.

—— (1991) 'The USSR Before the Fall: How Poor and Why', *Journal of Economic Perspectives* 5, 29–44.

Berliner, J. S. (1952) 'The Informal Organization of the Soviet Firm', *Quarterly Journal of Economics* 66, Aug.: 342–365.

Berliner, J. S. (1956) 'A Problem in Soviet Business Administration', *Administrative Science Quarterly* I, June: 86–101.

—— (1976) *The Innovation Decision in Soviet Industry*, Cambridge, MA: MIT Press.

Birman, I. (1978) 'From the Achieved Level', *Soviet Studies* 30: 153–172.

—— (1989) *Personal Consumption in the USSR and the USA*, London: Macmillan Press Ltd.

—— (1990) 'The Budget Gap, Excess Money, and Reform', *Communist Economies* 2: 25–45.

Boeva, I. and Dolgopiatova, T. (1994) 'State Enterprises During Transition: Forming Strategies for Survival', in A. Åslund (ed.) *Economic Transformation in Russia*, New York: St Martin's Press.

Bornstein, M. (1987) 'Soviet Price Policies', *Soviet Economy* 3: 96–134.

Boyes, R. (1990) *The Hard Road to Market: Gorbachev, the Underworld, and the Free Market*, London: Secker and Warburg.

Braithwaite, J. D. (1991) 'The Social Safety Net in the USSR in the (Sovereign?) Republics', presented at the 23rd AASSS National Conference, Miami, November.

Bronfenbrenner, M. B., Sichel, W. and Gardner, W. (1984) *Macroeconomics*, Boston, MA: Houghton Mifflin.

Burawoy, M. and Hendley, K. (1992) 'Between Perestroika and Privatization: Divided Strategies and Political Crisis in a Soviet Enterprise', *Soviet Studies* 44: 371–402.

Burawoy, M. and Krotov, P. (1992) 'The Soviet Transition From Socialism to Capitalism: Worker Control and Economic Bargaining in the Wood Industry', *American Sociological Review* 57: 16–38.

Capelik [Tsapelik], V. E. (1994) 'Should Monopoly be Regulated in Russia?', *Communist Economies and Economic Transformation* 6: 19–3.

Coase, R. H. (1960) 'The Problem of Social Cost', *Journal of Law and Economics* 3: 1–44.

Conquest, R. (1991) 'Excess Deaths and Camp Numbers: Some Comments', *Soviet Studies* 43: 949–952.

Cooper, J. (1991a) 'Military Cuts and Conversion in the Defense Industry', *Soviet Economy* 7: 121–142.

—— (1991b) *The Soviet Defense Industry. Conversion and Economic Reform*, New York: Council on Foreign Relations Press.

—— (1992) 'The Contradictions of Soviet Defense Industry Civilianization', in C. Wolf, Jr and S.W. Popper (eds) *Defence and the Soviet Economy: Military Muscle and Economic Weakness*, a RAND Note.

Crane, K. and Yeh, K. C. (1991) *Economic Reform and the Military in Poland, Hungary, and China*, Santa Monica: RAND.

Dasgupta, P. and Weale, M. (1992) 'On Measuring the Quality of Life', *World Development* 20: 119–131.

David, W. (1985) *The IMF Policy Paradigm*, New York: Praeger Publishers.

Desai, P. (1992) 'Reforming the Soviet Grain Economy: Performance, Problems, and Solutions', *American Economic Association Papers and Proceedings* 82: 49–54.

de Soto, H. (1989) *The Other Path*, New York: Harper and Row.

Devons, E. (1950) *Planning in Practice*, Cambridge: Cambridge University Press.

Diwan, I. and Rodrik, D. (1991) 'Debt Reduction, Adjustment Lending, and Burden Sharing', mimeo, September.

Dornbusch, R. (1991) 'Comments and Discussion', *Brookings Papers on Economic Activity* 1: 88–92.

—— (1992) 'The Case for Trade Liberalization in Developing Countries', *Journal of Economic Perspectives* 6, Winter: 69–85.

—— (1993) 'Introduction', *Policymaking in the Open Economy*, Oxford: Oxford University Press.

Dornbusch, R. and Fischer, S. (1994) *Macroeconomics*, sixth edition, New York: McGraw-Hill, Inc.

Dyker, D. A. (1992) *Restructuring the Soviet Economy*, London: Routledge.

*Economic Report of the President* (1992) Washington, DC: US Government Printing Office.

Eisner, R. (1989) *The Total Incomes Systems of Accounts*, Chicago: University of Chicago Press.

Ellman, M. (1983) 'Changing Views on Central Economic Planning: 1958–1983', *ACES Bulletin* Spring: 11–34.

Ericson, R.E. (1990) 'The Soviet Statistical Debate: Khanin versus TsSU', in H. S. Rowen and C. Wolf, Jr (eds) *The Impoverished Superpower*, San Francisco: Institute for Contemporary Studies.

—— (1991) 'The Classical Soviet-Type Economy: Nature of the System and Implications for Reform', *Journal of Economic Perspectives* 5: 11–27.

European Bank for Reconstruction and Development (1994) 'Transition Report', London.

Faramazian, R., and Borisov, V. (1993) 'Two Approaches to Military Economy and Conversion', *Problems of Economic Transition*, Dec.: 42–57, translated from *Mirovaia ekonomika i mezhdunarodnye otnosheniia* (1993) no. 3: 23–34.

Farrell, J. (1987) 'Information and the Coase Theorem', *Journal of Economic Perspectives* 1: 113–129.

Fernandez, R. and Rodrik, D. (1991) 'Resistance to Reform: Status Quo Bias in the Presence of Individual–Specific Uncertainty', *American Economic Review* 81, December: 1146–1155.

Feshbach, M. (1991) 'Untold Story: The Enormity of Soviet Union's Health Disaster', *Cosmos* 1: 44–49.

Feshbach, M. and Friendly, A., Jr, (1992) *Ecocide in the USSR*, New York: Basic Books.

Feurer, L. S. (ed.) (1959) *Marx and Engels Basic Writings on Politics and Philosophy*, Garden City, NY: Doubleday and Co., Inc.

Fischer, S. (1991) 'Issues in International Economic Integration', Working Paper no. 579, MIT Department of Economics, April.

—— (1994) 'Prospects for Russian Stabilization in the Summer of 1993', in A. Åslund (ed.) *Economic Transformation in Russia* New York: St Martin's Press.

Fischer, S. and Frenkel, J. (1992) 'Macroeconomic Issues of Soviet Reform', *American Economic Review Papers and Proceedings* 82, May: 37–42.

Flakierski, H. (1992) 'Changes in Income Inequality in the USSR', in A. Åslund (ed.)

*Market Socialism or the Restoration of Capitalism?*, Cambridge: Cambridge University Press.

Gaddy, C. G. (1991) 'The Labor Market and the Second Economy in the Soviet Union', Berkeley–Duke Occasional Papers on the Second Economy in the USSR, 24, Jan.

—— (1992) 'Inflation, Living Standards, and Russian Reality', mimeo.

—— (1993) 'Economic Reform and Individual Choice in Russia', paper prepared for the Aspen Strategy Group, The Aspen Institute, Aspen, CO, August 8–13.

General Accounting Office (GAO) (1991) 'Soviet Economy. Assessment of How Well the CIA Has Estimated the Size of the Soviet Economy', Washington, DC, September.

Gibbon, E. (1985 [1776]) *The Decline and Fall of the Roman Empire*, London: Penguin Books.

Gogol, N. (1972 [1842]) *Dead Souls*, Middlesex: Penguin Books.

Goldberg, L. S. (1993) 'Foreign Exchange Markets in Russia', *IMF Staff Papers* 40, Dec.: 852–864.

Goldman, M. I. (1983) *USSR in Crisis*, New York: Norton.

—— (1992 [1991]) *What Went Wrong With Perestroika*, New York: Norton.

Graham, L. R. (1993) *The Ghost of the Executed Engineer*, Cambridge, MA: Harvard University Press.

Gregory, P. R. and Collier, I. L. (1988) 'Unemployment in the Soviet Union: Evidence from the Soviet Interview Project', *American Economic Review* 78, Sept.: 613–632.

Grossman, G. (1963) 'Notes for a Theory of the Command Economy', *Soviet Studies* 15: 101–123.

—— (1977) 'The Second Economy of the USSR', *Problems of Communism*, Sept.–Oct., 25–40.

—— (1979) 'Notes on the Illegal Private Economy and Corruption', in *Soviet Economy in a Time of Change*, Joint Economic Committee, US Congress, Washington DC: US Government Printing Office.

—— (1987) 'Roots of Gorbachev's Problems: Private Income and Outlay in the Late 1970s', in *Gorbachev's Economic Plans*, Joint Economic Committee, US Congress, Washington, DC: US Government Printing Office, vol. 1.

—— (1989) 'The Second Economy: Boon or Bane for the Reform of the First Economy', in S. Gomulka, Y. Ha and C. Kim (eds) *Economic Reforms in the Socialist World*, Armonk, NY: M. E. Sharpe.

Grossman, G. and Treml, V.G. (1987) 'Measuring Hidden Personal Incomes in the USSR', in S. Alessandrini and B. Dallago (eds) *The Unofficial Economy*, Aldershot, England: Gower Publishing Company Limited.

Hall, R. E. and Taylor, J. B. (1993) *Macroeconomics*, fourth edition. New York: Norton.

Hanson, P. (1986) 'The Serendipitous Soviet Achievement of Full Employment: Labour Shortage and Labour Hoarding in the Soviet Economy', in D. Lane (ed.) *Labour and Employment in the USSR*, Sussex: Wheatsheaf Books Ltd.

—— (1991) 'Soviet Economic Reform: Perestroika or "Catastroika"?', *World Policy Journal* 8, Spring: 289–318.

Harrison, M. (1986) 'Lessons of Soviet Planning for Full Employment', in D. Lane (ed.) *Labour and Employment in the USSR*, Sussex: Wheatsheaf Books Ltd.

Hayek, F. A. (1945) 'The Use of Knowledge in Society', *American Economic Review* 35: 519–530.

—— (1972 [1944]) *The Road to Serfdom*, Chicago: University of Chicago Press.

Heleniak, T. (1991) 'Unemployment in the USSR: A Growing Problem for Market Transition', presented at the 23rd AAASS National Conference, Miami, November.

Hendley, K. (1992) 'Legal Development and Privatization in Russia: A Case Study', *Soviet Economy* 8: 130–157.

Hewett, E. A. (1988) *Reforming the Soviet Economy: Equality versus Efficiency*, Washington, DC: The Brookings Institution.

—— (1989a) 'Economic Reform in the USSR, Eastern Europe, and China: The Politics of Economics', *American Economic Review Papers and Proceedings* 79, May: 16–20.

—— (1989b) 'Editorial Perspective', *Soviet Economy* 5: 104–106.

Hewett, E. A. and Gaddy, C. G. (1992) *Open for Business. Russia's Return to the Global Economy*, Washington, DC: Brookings Institution.

Hicks, J.R. (1935) 'Annual Survey of Economic Theory: The Theory of Monopoly', *Econometrica* 3: 1–20.

Holmlund, B. and Zetterberg, J. (1991) 'Insider Effects in Wage Determination. Evidence from Five Countries', *European Economic Review* 35: 1009–1034.

Holmstrom, B. and Milgrom, P. (1991) 'Multitask Principal–Agent Analyses: Incentive Contracts, Asset Ownership, and Job Design', *Journal of Law, Economics, and Organization* 7: 24–52.

Ickes, B. W. and Ryterman, R. (1992) 'The Interenterprise Arrears Crisis in Russia', *Post-Soviet Affairs* 8: 331–361.

Ilin, M. (1931) *New Russia's Primer*, Boston, MA: Houghton Mifflin Company.

Institute of Sociology (1992) 'Mirror of Opinions: The Result of a Sociological Poll of the Population of Russia', Moscow: Russian Academy of Sciences.

International Monetary Fund (1992a) 'Economic Review. The Economy of the Former U.S.S.R. in 1991', Washington, DC: IMF, April.

—— (1992b) 'Economic Review. Russian Federation', Washington, DC: IMF, April.

IMF, International Bank for Reconstruction and Development, Organization for Economic Co-operation and Development, European Bank for Reconstruction and Development (1991) *A Study of the Soviet Economy*, vols. 1,2, and 3, Feb.

IMF, IBRD, OECD, EBRD (1990) 'The Economy of the USSR. Summary and Recommendations', Dec.

Isaac, R. M., Mathieu, D. and Zajac, E.E (1991) 'Institutional Framing and Perceptions of Fairness', mimeo.

Jackman, R., Layard, R. and Scott, A. (1992) 'Unemployment in Eastern Europe', presented at the NBER Conference on Transition in Eastern Europe, Cambridge, MA, February.

Jefferson, G. H. and Rawski, T. G. (1991) 'Unemployment, Underemployment, and Employment Policy in China's Cities', Working Paper, Department of Economics, University of Pittsburgh, Sept.

Johnson, S. (1992) 'Private Business in Eastern Europe', presented at the NBER Conference on Transition in Eastern Europe, Cambridge, MA, February.

Johnson, S. and Kroll, H. (1991) 'Managerial Strategies for Spontaneous Privatization', *Soviet Economy* 7: 281–316.

Joint Economic Committee (JEC) (1982) *USSR: Measures of Economic Growth and Development, 1950–1980*, Washington, DC: US Government Printing Office.

Jones, A. and Moskoff, W. (1991) *Ko-ops*, Bloomington: Indiana University Press.

Kahn, A. E. and Peck, M. J. (1991) 'Price Deregulation, Corporatization, and Competition', in M.J. Peck and T. J. Richardson (eds) *What is to be Done?*, New Haven: Yale University Press.

Kawalec, S. (1992) 'The Dictatorial Supplier', in J. R. Wedel (ed.) *The Unplanned Society*, New York: Columbia University Press.

Kendrick, J. W. (1972) *Economic Accounts and Their Uses*, New York: McGraw-Hill.

Khanin, G. (1992) 'The Soviet Economy–From Crisis to Catastrophe', in A. Åslund (ed.) *The Post Soviet-Economy*, London: Pinter Publishers.

Khrushchev, N. (1974) *Khrushchev Remembers. The Last Testament*, translated and edited by Strobe Talbott, Boston, MA: Little, Brown and Company.

—— (1990) *Khrushchev Remembers. The Glasnost Tapes*, translated and edited by J. L. Schecter with V. V. Luchkov, Boston, MA: Little, Brown and Company.

Kireyev, A. P. (1990) 'Conversion in the Soviet Dimension', *International Affairs*, May.

Koen, V. and Phillips, S. (1993) 'Price Liberalization in Russia', IMF Occasional Paper 104, June.

Kornai, J. (1980) *The Economics of Shortage*, Amsterdam: North-Holland.

—— (1990) *The Road to a Free Economy*, New York: Norton.

—— (1992) *The Socialist System*, Princeton: Princeton University Press.

Kosareva, N. B. (1992) 'The Housing Market and Social Guarantees', *Studies on Soviet Economic Development* 3, Feb.: 38–46.

Kosmarskii, V. (1992) 'Public Attitudes to the Transition', in A. Åslund (ed.) *The Post-Soviet Economy*, London: Pinter Publishers.

Kotkin, S. (1991) *Steeltown, USSR*, Berkeley: University of California Press.

Kroll, H. (1987) 'Breach of Contract in the Soviet Economy', *Journal of Legal Studies* 16: 119–148.

—— (1991) 'Monopoly and Transition to the Market', *Soviet Economy* 7: 143–174.

Lane, D. (1986) 'Marxist-Leninism: An Ideology for Full Employment in Socialist States?', in D. Lane (ed.) *Labour and Employment in the USSR*, Sussex: Wheatsheaf Books Ltd.

—— (1987) *Soviet Labour and the Ethic of Communism*, Boulder, CO: Westview Press.

Lange, O. and Taylor, F. M. (1938) *On the Economic Theory of Socialism*, Minneapolis: University of Minnesota Press.

Lazear, E. P. (1991) 'Prices and Wages in Transition Economies', Hoover Institution Working Paper E-91-13, Nov.

Leitzel, J. (1993a) 'The Choice of What to Procure', in J. Leitzel and J. Tirole (eds) *Incentives in Procurement Contracting*, Boulder, CO: Westview Press.

—— (1993b) 'Goods Diversion and Repressed Inflation', in 'Essays on Second Economy Markets', Berkeley–Duke Occasional Papers on the Second Economy in the USSR, 37, Dec.

Lipman, M. and McGraw, W. R. (1988) 'Employee Theft: A $40 Billion Industry', *Annals of the American Academy of Political and Social Science* 498, July: 51–59.

Lipton, D. and Sachs, J. (1990) 'Creating a Market Economy in Eastern Europe: The Case of Poland', *Brookings Papers on Economic Activity*, 75–147.

—— and —— (1992) 'Prospects for Russia's Economic Reforms', *Brookings Papers on Economic Activity*, 213–283.

Litwack, J. (1991a) 'Discretionary Behaviour and Soviet Economic Reform', *Soviet Studies* 43, March: 255–279.

—— (1991b) 'Hierarchical Coordination Failure and Soviet Economic Decline', mimeo, Stanford University, Nov.

Lutz, F. A. (1949) 'The German Currency Reform and the Revival of the German Economy', *Economica*, May 1949.

Macauley, S. (1963) 'Non-Contractual Relations in Business: A Preliminary Study', *American Sociological Review* 28: 55–67.

McCloskey, D. (1985) *The Rhetoric of Economics*, Madison: University of Wisconsin Press.

McGee, R. T. and Feige, E. L. (1989) 'Policy Illusion, Macroeconomic Instability, and the Unrecorded Economy', in E. L. Feige (ed.) *The Underground Economies*, Cambridge: Cambridge University Press.

Machiavelli, N. (1947 [1532]) *The Prince*, T. G. Bergin (ed.) Northbrook, IL: AHM Publishing Corporation.

McKinnon, R. I. (1990a) 'Liberalizing Foreign Trade in a Socialist Economy: The Problem of Negative Value Added', Mimeo, Stanford University, Oct.

—— (1990b) 'Stabilising the Rouble', *Communist Economies* 2: 131–142.

Malyshev, N. (1987) 'Laundering of Money in the USSR through the Purchase of Winning Bonds and Lottery Tickets', in 'Studies on the Soviet Second Economy', Berkeley–Duke Occasional Papers on the Second Economy in the USSR, 11, Dec.

Marnie, S. (1992) 'Employment and the Reallocation of Labour in the USSR', in A. Åslund (ed.) *Market Socialism or the Restoration of Capitalism?*, Cambridge: Cambridge University Press.

Marx, K. and Engels, F. (1964 [1848]) *The Communist Manifesto*, New York: Washington Square Press.

Matthews, M. (1989) *Patterns of Deprivation in the Soviet Union Under Brezhnev and Gorbachev*, Stanford: Hoover Institution Press.

Mickiewicz, E. (1992) 'Findings of Four Major Surveys in the Former Soviet Union', mimeo.

Millar, J. R. 1987) (ed.) *Politics, Work, and Daily Life in the USSR*, Cambridge: Cambridge University Press.

—— (1990) 'The Soviet Household Sector: The View from the Bottom', in J. R. Millar (ed.) *The Soviet Economic Experiment*, Urbana: University of Illinois Press.

Moskoff, W. (1984) *Labour and Leisure in the Soviet Union*, New York: St. Martin's Press.

Muellbauer, J. (1987) 'Professor Sen on the Standard of Living', in A. Sen (ed.) *The Standard of Living*, Cambridge: Cambridge University Press.

Newberry, D. M. and Kattuman, P. (1992) 'Market Concentration and Competition in Eastern Europe', *The World Economy* 15: 315–334.

Nove, A. (1982) *An Economic History of the USSR*, New York: Pelican.

—— (1986) *The Soviet Economic System*, Third Edition, Boston: Allen and Unwin.

Nutter, G. W. (1969) *The Strange World of Ivan Ivanov*, New York: World Publishing Company.

Nystrom, E. J. (1994) 'Can a Hybrid Economy Survive? The Chinese Experience and Its Lessons for Soviet Central Asia', mimeo, Duke University.

OECD [Organization for Economic Co-operation and Development] (1994) 'Short-Term Economic Indicators. Transition Economies', 2/1994.

Ofer, G. (1987) 'Soviet Economic Growth: 1928–1985', *Journal of Economic Literature* 25: 1767–1833.

Orwell, G. (1983 [1949]) *1984*, New York: The New American Library.

Pagano, M. (1990) 'Imperfect Competition, Underemployment Equilibria and Fiscal Policy', *The Economic Journal* 100: 440–463.

Peck, M. J. (1991) 'Introduction.' in M. J. Peck and T. J. Richardson (eds) *What is to be Done?*, New Haven: Yale University Press.

Perkins, D. (1994) 'Completing China's Move to the Market', *Journal of Economic Perspectives* 8, Spring: 23–46.

Pietsch, A. (1986) 'Shortage of Labour and Motivation Problems of Soviet Workers', in D. Lane (ed.) *Labour and Employment in the USSR*, Sussex: Wheatsheaf Books Ltd.

Pinto, B., Belka, M. and Krajewski, S. (1993) 'Transforming State Enterprises in Poland: Microeconomic Evidence on Adjustment', World Bank Policy Research Working Paper.

Pitzer, J. S. and Baukol, A.P (1991) 'Recent GNP and Productivity Trends', *Soviet Economy* 7: 46–82.

Polanyi, M. (1960) 'Towards a Theory of Conspicuous Production', *Soviet Survey*, Number 34, pp. 90–99.

Porket, J. L. (1989) *Work, Employment and Unemployment in the Soviet Union*, New York: St. Martin's Press.

Powell, R. P. (1977) 'Plan Execution and the Workability of Soviet Planning', *Journal of Comparative Economics* 1: 51–76.

Prosterman, R. L. and Hanstad, T. (1991) 'Trip Report Updating Our Monograph on "The Prospects for Individual Peasant Farming in the USSR",' mimeo, Rural Development Institute, Oct.

Prosterman, R. L., Hanstad, T. and Rolfes, L. J., Jr (1993) 'Agrarian Reform in Russia', RDI Monographs on Foreign Aid and Development 11, May.

Raleigh, D. J. (1992) 'Beyond Moscow and St. Petersburg: Some Reflections on the August Revolution, Provincial Russia, and Novostroika', *South Atlantic Quarterly* 91, Summer: 603–619.

Reed, J. (1967 [1919]) *Ten Days That Shook the World*, New York: New American Library.

Richards, S. (1990) *Epics of Everyday Life*, New York: Penguin Books.

Roberts, B. (1993) 'The Initial Welfare Consequences of Price Liberalization and Stabilization in Russia', mimeo, University of Miami.

Rodrik, D. (1989) 'Promises, Promises: Credible Policy Reform Via Signalling', *Economic Journal* 99, Sept.: 756–772.

—— (1991) 'The Economic Opening of Developing Countries Why So Late? Why Now? Will It Last?', mimeo, Hoover Institution, Nov.

—— (1992) 'Making Sense of the Soviet Trade Shock in Eastern Europe: A Framework and Some Estimates', mimeo, January.

Rose, R. (1994) 'Getting By Without Government: Everyday Life in a Stressful Society', Studies in Public Policy Number 227, Centre for the Study of Public Policy, University of Strathclyde, Glasgow.

Rosefielde, S. (1991) 'The Illusion of Material Progress: The Analytics of Soviet Economic Growth Revisited', *Soviet Studies* 43: 597–611.

Ross, D. (1968) *Robert F. Kennedy: Apostle of Change*, New York: Trident Press.

Rostowski, J. (1994) 'Dilemmas of Monetary and Financial Policy in Post-Stabilization Russia', in A. Åslund (ed.) *Economic Transformation in Russia*, New York: St Martin's Press.

Rowen, H. S. and Wolf, C., Jr (eds) (1990) *The Impoverished Superpower*, San Francisco: Institute for Contemporary Studies.

Rutgaizer, V. M. (1992) 'The Shadow Economy in the USSR', Berkeley–Duke Occasional Papers on the Second Economy in the USSR, No. 34, Feb.

Rutland, P. (1985) *The Myth of the Plan*, La Salle, IL: Open Court.

Sachs, J. (1993a) *Poland's Jump to the Market Economy*, Cambridge, MA: MIT Press.

—— (1993b) 'Western Financial Assistance and Russia's Reforms', in S. Islam and M. Mandelbaum (eds) *Making Markets. Economic Transformation in Eastern Europe and the Post-Soviet States*, New York: Council on Foreign Relations Press.

—— (1994) 'Prospects for Monetary Stabilization in Russia', in A. Åslund (ed.) *Economic Transformation in Russia*, New York: St Martin's Press.

Sachs, J. and Woo, W. T. (1994) 'Reform in China and Russia', *Economic Policy* 18, April: 101–145.

Samuelson, P. A. (1970) *Economics*, eighth edition, New York: McGraw-Hill.

Sargent, T. J. (1982) 'The Ends of Four Big Inflations', in R. E. Hall (ed.) *Inflation: Causes and Effects*, Chicago: University of Chicago Press.

Schelling, T. C. (1984a) 'Economics and Criminal Enterprise', in T. C. Schelling, *Choice and Consequence*, Cambridge, MA: Harvard University Press.

—— (1984b) 'What Is the Business of Organized Crime?', in T.C. Schelling, *Choice and Consequence*, Cambridge, MA: Harvard University Press.

Schroeder, G. E. (1979) 'The Soviet Economy on a Treadmill of "Reforms"', *Soviet Economy in a Time of Change*, Washington, DC: Joint Economic Committee, US Congress: 65–88.

Schultze, C. L. (1992) *Memos to the President*, Washington, DC: The Brookings Institution.

Sedik, D. J. (1991) 'Price Policy and the Demise of the New Economic Policy in the USSR, 1923–29', Paper presented at the Western Economic Association International Meetings, Seattle, July.

Sen, A. (1987) *The Standard of Living*, Cambridge: Cambridge University Press.

Shlapentokh, V. (1989) *Public and Private Life of the Soviet People*, New York: Oxford University Press.

Shleifer, A. and Vishny, R. W. (1991) 'Reversing the Soviet Economic Collapse', mimeo.

—— and —— (1993) 'Corruption', *Quarterly Journal of Economics* 108, 3: 599–617.

Shmelev, N. (1987) 'Avansi i dolgi', *Novy Mir* 6, June: 148–149.

Simis, K. (1982) *USSR: The Corrupt Society*, New York: Simon and Schuster.

Slider, D. (1991) 'Embattled Entrepreneurs: Soviet Cooperatives in an Unreformed Economy', *Soviet Studies* 43: 797–821.

Smith, A. (1991 [1776]) *The Wealth of Nations*, New York: Knopf, Everyman's Library.

Smith, H. (1984 [1976]) *The Russians*, New York: Ballantine Books.

—— (1990) *The New Russians*, New York: Random House.

Spulber, N. (1991) *Restructuring the Soviet Economy*, Ann Arbor: University of Michigan Press.

Starodubrovskaya, I. (1994) 'The Nature of Monopoly and Barriers to Entry in Russia', *Communist Economies and Economic Transformation* 6: 3–18.

Starr, S. F. (1993) 'Year One of Capitalism in Russia', Hudson Briefing Paper, No. 150, Hudson Institute, March.

Stiglitz, J. E. (1991) 'Theoretical Aspects of Privatization: Applications to Eastern Europe', Institute for Policy Reform, September.

Sutela, P. (1993) 'Insider Privatization in Russia: Speculations on Systemic Change', Paper presented at American Association for the Advancement of Slavic Studies, Honolulu, November.

Svejnar, J. (1991) 'Microeconomic Issues in the Transition to a Market Economy', *Journal of Economic Perspectives* 5, Fall: 123–138.

Tirole, J. (1988) *The Theory of Industrial Organization*, Cambridge, MA: MIT Press.

—— (1991) 'Privatization in Eastern Europe: Incentives and the Economics of Transition', *NBER Macroeconomics Annual 1991*, 221–267.

Tobin, J. (1957) 'Comment', in *The Measurement and Behaviour of Unemployment*, Princeton: Princeton University Press.

Treml, V. G. (1988) 'Perestroyka and Soviet Statistics', *Soviet Economy* 4: 65–94.

—— (1992a) 'Soviet Statistics Under Gorbachev: A Western Perspective', in C. Wolf, Jr and S. Popper (eds) *Defense and the Soviet Economy: Military Muscle and Economic Weakness*, a RAND Note.

—— (1992b) 'A Study of Labor Inputs into the Second Economy of the USSR', Berkeley–Duke Occasional Papers on the Second Economy in the USSR, Number 33, Jan.

Treml, V. G. and Alexeev, M.V. (1993) 'The Second Economy and the Destabilizing Effect of its Growth on the State Economy in the Soviet Union: 1965–1989', Berkeley-Duke Occasional Papers on the Second Economy in the USSR, No. 36, December.

Uno, K. (1991) 'Privatization and the Creation of a Commercial Banking System', in M. J. Peck and T. J. Richardson (eds) *What is to be Done?*, New Haven: Yale University Press.

Vaksberg, A. (1991) *The Soviet Mafia*, New York: St Martin's Press.

Vodopivec, M. (1991) 'The Labor Market and the Transition of Socialist Economies', *Comparative Economic Studies* 33: 123–158.

Weitzman, M. L. (1991) 'How Not to Privatize', *Revista di Politica Economica* 12, Dec.: 249–269.

Wellisz, S. (1991) 'Poland Under "Solidarity" Rule', *Journal of Economic Perspectives* 5: 211–217.

Wiles, P. J. D. (1962) *The Political Economy of Communism*, Cambridge, MA: Harvard University Press.

Wilhelm, J. H. (1985) 'The Soviet Union has an Administered, Not a Planned, Economy', *Soviet Studies* 37, Jan.: 118–130.

Wolf, T. A. (1991) 'The Lessons of Limited Market-Oriented Reform', *Journal of Economic Perspectives* 5, Fall: 45–58.

Wren, C. (1990) *The End of the Line*, New York: Simon and Schuster.

Zaleski, E. (1980) *Stalinist Planning for Economic Growth, 1933–1952*, Chapel Hill: University of North Carolina Press.

Zubova, L., Kovaleva, N. and Khakhulina, L. (1992) 'Poverty in the USSR', *Problems of Economics*, Feb: 85–98, translation of (1991) 'Bednost' v SSSR: tochka zreniia naseleniia', *Voprosy Ekonomiki* 6: 60–67.

# Index